The Penitents' Treasury

T0364150

The Penitents' Treasury

Indulgences in Latin Christendom, 1175–1375

Robert W. Shaffern

University of Scranton Press
Scranton and London

© 2007 University of Scranton Press
All rights reserved.

Library of Congress Cataloging-in-Publication Data

Shaffern, Robert W., 1963–
The penitents' treasury: indulgences in Latin Christendom, 1175–1375 / by
Robert W. Shaffern.
p. cm.
Includes bibliographical references.
ISBN 978-1-58966-139-4 ((hardcover)) – ISBN 978-1-58966-136-3 ((pbk.))
1. Indulgences. 2. Penance. 3. Church history—Middle Ages, 600–1500.
4. Confession—Catholic Church—History. 5. Absolution—Catholic Church.
I. Title.
BX2281.3.S485 2007
265'.660902—dc22

2007022978

Distribution:
University of Scranton Press
Chicago Distribution Center
11030 S. Langley
Chicago, IL 60628

PRINTED IN THE UNITED STATES OF AMERICA

Table of Contents

Acknowledgments

A great debt of gratitude is owed to the librarians whose cooperation made this book possible. The reproduction staffs at the Bodleian Library at Oxford, the British Library in London, the Bibliothèque Nationale in Paris, the Biblioteca communale in Todi, the Staatsbibliothek in Munich, the Stadtbibliothek in Bruges, the Universitätsbibliothek in Erlangen, and the Hill Monastic Manuscript Library in Collegeville, Minnesota, all graciously supplied the manuscript sources cited in this study. The rare books departments of the following also well served my needs: Cornell University, the Newberry Library in Chicago, and the Institute for Medieval Canon Law, which at the time was housed in Boalt Hall at the University of California, Berkeley. Thanks are also due to the circulation and reference departments at the Hesburgh Library at the University of Notre Dame, the Glenn G. Bartle Library at Binghamton University, and the Weinberg Memorial Library at the University of Scranton. The service of the interlibrary loan department at the Weinberg was likewise indispensable.

In addition, the encouragement of colleagues and teachers must also be recognized. More than a decade ago, John H. Van Engen suggested that a book-length study of indulgences was in order. David d'Avray, R. N. Swanson, and Alastair Minnis contributed further support and recommendations. Timothy M. Thibodeau's friendship and scholarly guidance have been a great blessing for more than twenty years. My colleagues in the History Department at the University of Scranton have been nothing other than gracious and eager to be of any assistance whatsoever. I am, of course, grateful to Jeff Gainey, director of the University of Scranton Press for endorsing and publishing my study.

Finally, I am grateful to our children, Thomas, Monica, Christina, and Caroline, who patiently tolerated their father's preoccupations with the Middle Ages. The love and support of my wife Elizabeth was more important than words can express. This book is dedicated to her.

Abbreviations

AS	*Acta sanctorum. Ed.* Jean Bolland, et al. 68 vols. Paris: Palmé, 1863–.
CCSL	*Corpus Christianorum. Series Latina*
CHR	*Catholic Historical Review*
CIC	Aemilianus Friedberg, ed., *Corpus iuris canonici.* 2 vols. Leipzig: Bernhard Tauchnitz, 1879–1181.
De quan. indul.	John of Dambach, *De quantitate indulgenciarum.* Basel, Universitätsbibliothek C V 18.
De vir. indul.	John of Dambach, *De virtute indulgenciarum.* Heiligenkreuz (Austria) Stiftsbibliothek MS 208.
EETS	Early English Text Society
Geschichte	Nikolaus Paulus, *Geschichte des Ablasses im Mittelalter.* 3 vols. Darmstadt: Primus Verlag, 2000.
Hödl	Ludwig Hödl. *Die Geschichte der Scholastischen Literatur und der Theologie der Schüsselgewalt.* Beiträge zur Geschichte der Philosophie und Theologie des Mittelalters 38. Münster: Aschendorffsche Verlagsbuchhandlung, 1960.
Mansi	Giovan Domenico Mansi, ed. *Sacrorum conciliorum nova et amplissima collection.* 54 vols. Graz: Akademische Druck u. Verlagsanstalt, 1960.
MGH	*Monumenta Germaniae Historica*
McNeill and Gamer	John T. McNeill and Helena M. Gamer, eds. and trans. *Medieval Handbooks of Penance.* New York: Columbia University Press, 1990.
MOPH	*Monumenta Ordinis Praedicatorum Historica*
MS	*Mediaeval Studies*
PL	*Patrologia cursus completus. Series Latina. Ed.* Jacques-Paul Migne. 221 vols. Paris: Garnier, 1844–64.
RHC	*Recueil des historiens de croisades: Historiens occidentaux.* 5 vols. Paris: Académie des Inscriptions et Belle Lettres, 1844–95.
SC	*Summa confessorum.* John of Freiburg. Augsburg: Gunther Zainer, 1476.

Social Factor	Nikolaus Paulus. *Indulgences as a Social Factor in the Middle Ages.* Trans. J. Elliot Ross. New York: Devin-Adair, 1922.
Tanner and Alberigo	Norman Tanner and Guiseppe Alberigo, eds. and trans. *Decrees of the Ecumenical Councils.* 2 vols. Washington, D.C.: Sheed & Ward, 1990.
UB Basel	*Urkundenbuch der Stadt Basel.* Ed. R. Wackenagel and R. Thommen. 2 vols. Basel: C. Detloggs Buchhandlung, 1890–93.
ZKT	*Zeitschrift für katholische Theologie*

Chapter 1

Indulgences and the Persistent Historiography of Confessional Polemics

Even the hastiest reader of the textbooks on medieval religion would learn that indulgences loomed large in the Latin Christian church from the eleventh century until the Reformation. Simply put, an indulgence was (and still is, for that matter) a remission of temporal penalty for sin granted by the episcopal authority of the Roman Catholic Church.[1] Medieval Catholics, from all walks of life and with varying degrees of zeal, some enthusiastically, some matter-of-factly, undertook the good works required for obtaining indulgences (often also called remissions, and in English, pardons). Of course, ever since Martin Luther's public break with Catholic Christianity in 1517, indulgences have often symbolized the decadence of later medieval Catholicism. Not only evangelical, but also Catholic, Christians—whether of Luther's or of later generations—agreed that indulgences had been responsible for much mischief in the church. Even the Council of Trent (1545–1563) admitted that some abuses in the church might be attributed to the granting of remissions. Yet, the council denied the Protestant claim that pardons had no power, because "the power of granting indulgences was given by Christ to the church."[2] The Catholic Church of the Counter-Reformation granted pardons for the same reasons and pious works as the medieval church. Although Vatican II's call for ecumenism in the mid-1960s hinted at a retreat from indulgences, which after all occasioned the split with Protestant Christians, remissions were never repudiated; in fact, Pope Paul VI published a new handbook of indulgences, and as the third millenium approached, Pope John Paul II, in the manner of his medieval predecessors, declared a Holy Year, or Jubilee for the year 2000, during which visitors to Rome could obtain a plenary indulgence, or full cancellation of their debt of sin. Many Catholics and others, as suspicious about the efficacy of indulgences as Luther had been, found John Paul II's offer of the Jubilee indulgence a curious, if not laughable, return to the church's corrupt, medieval past.[3] For many twentieth-century Protestant and Catholic Christians, as for their sixteenth-century ancestors, indulgences suggested embarassment and abuse.

Recent scholarly work on indulgences, however, recommends different and more nuanced interpretations. These researches, which still number far too few, challenge seriously the suppositions and exegesis of the sources upon which the traditional view of pardons rests. New interpretations argue that, instead of a great blemish on the complexion of the medieval Church, indulgences served both as modest incentives to good work and as measures of understanding of the basic teachings of the traditional Christian faith, among which were the power and benefits conferred by the sacraments and the concern for self and neighbor. Instead of widespread confusion about the efficacy of indulgences, the bishops and laity of the Middle Ages generally understood and abided by the canons and teachings on the dispensation and reception of indulgences.

A POWERFUL HISTORIOGRAPHICAL CONSTRUCT

Although indulgences originated during the eleventh-century church reform and had antecedents in Carolingian and Ottonian liturgies (c. AD 750–1000), historians of the Protestant Reformation (after 1517), rather than medievalists, have been much more inclined to examine their historical importance. Consequently, indulgences have generally been studied as a contributing factor to the Reformation. Scholars have, ever since the posting of the Ninety-Five Theses (in 1517), been preoccupied with Luther's denunciation of pardons. That epochal event, in the words of David L. D'Avray, has contributed to "an obtrusive consciousness of the eventual reaction," which has in turn meant that indulgences have been "classified unconsciously under 'abuses'."[4] Indulgences and the corruption that inevitably led to the Reformation have habitually and conceptually been bound together, as by Heiko Oberman, who deemed Johann Wessel (d. 1481) a leading "forerunner" of the Reformation because Wessel denied absolutely the efficacy of indulgences.[5] The seed of corruption that the late medieval Church sowed and cultivated grew into the sixteenth-century crop of evangelical theology.

Indeed, the traditional periodization of the Middle Ages into "Early" (c. 500–1000), "High" (1000–1300), and "Late" (1300–1500), eras has contributed in no small measure to the judgment that abuses like indulgences positively infected late medieval Catholicism. The chronological and conceptual breach between the High and Late Middle Ages implies essential discontinuities in Latin Christian civilization between the thirteenth and later centuries.[6] The period of the High Middle Ages, which climaxed in the thirteenth century, "greatest" of centuries, has long implied a classical, vibrant, and innovative age followed by an era of inevitable decline (about 1300 and later). In the fourteenth century, famine, war, pestilence, and schism dimmed the memory of the peace and prosperity, not to mention the cultural achievements, characteristic of the twelfth and thirteenth centuries. The cultural maelstrom also swept up and damaged the Catholic Church.

Indeed, for some influential historians, Christian culture reflected the transition from the "high" period to the "late" period in two specific ways. First, Johann Huizinga, one of the principal architects of the paradigm of late medieval decline, wrote that in the Late Middle Ages rigidity and formalism replaced the flexibility and conviction of the High Middle Ages: "The spirit of the Middle Ages, still plastic and naive, longs to give concrete shape to every conception. Every thought seeks expression in an image, but in this image it solidifies and becomes rigid. By this tendency to embodiment in visible forms, all holy concepts are constantly exposed to the danger of hardening into mere externalism."[7] In Huizinga's re-creation of late medieval Catholicism, exterior acts were divorced from interior disposition. This divorce resulted in a general spiritual impoverishment and restlessness. André Vauchez echoed Huizinga's presentiments when he argued that in the late medieval period there emerged a "flamboyant piety, which had . . . degenerated into bookkeeping for the beyond."[8]

Traditional historiography, then, assumes a radical distinction between the exterior acts and interior dispositions of medieval Catholics. At the same time, that historiography also assumed that most laity did not know the basic teachings of their church. The masses of Catholic Christians were ignorant of the conditions under which indulgences were believed to remit temporal penalty for sin: "Even if the orthodox view had been universally understood, which it was not, the widespread use of indulgences would still have had the inevitable consequence of transforming the spiritual life of many laymen into a sequence of elaborate rituals."[9] Only a small band of the most spiritually sophisticated men and women successfully resisted the slow deterioration of religious fervor during the Late Middle Ages. "A minority of the population, rejecting this mechanization of religious feeling, stressed the presence of God in the hearts of believers, and the fact that sanctification takes place less through works than by the conformity of man's will to that of Christ in the practice of the Gospel."[10] The penitents who obtained indulgences time and again, in this view, essentially misunderstood the Gospel. True religious devotion excluded the reception of pardons.

Another historiographical tradition connects the increase in the number of remissions granted in the fourteenth and fifteenth centuries with contempt for their efficacy and church authority. For Sir Richard Southern, pardons contributed to a late medieval papal "inflationary spiral." In his words, "The consequences of the unrestricted issue of [bulls of indulgence] were similar to those which face other issues of paper money: the abundance of the notes brought about a decline in the value attached to them."[11] The total number of indulgences available to medieval Catholics increased over the genera-tions, as new indulgences added to the number of those promulgated in the distant past, almost all of which were granted in perpetuity. By the later Middle Ages, the value of indulgences equalled the worth of a mark in early Weimar Germany. A recent study of indulgences in medieval Cologne echoed Southern's metaphor: "In popular piety quantity would be more prized than quality."[12] As used by these scholars, the imagery of money—to be sure, used by medieval Catholics themselves—conflated a grant of pardon with an impersonal, commercial transaction.

Finally, traditional historiography generally agrees that late medieval Catholicism also suffered from a terrifying obsession with death. Once again, Huizinga's musings linger: "No other age has so forcefully and continuously impressed the idea of death on the whole population."[13] Vauchez made similar arguments:

> This century [the thirteenth] of equilibrium and majesty—that of the 'Beau Dieu' of the cathedral of Amiens and the smiling Virgin of Reims—was followed by a more troubled era. It was an age of crises, of the Hundred Years' War and, most signifi-cantly, of the Black Death, which beginning in 1348 mowed down millions of people in a few decades, both in the cities and in the countryside. These events, which made the fourteenth and fifteenth centuries a particularly tormented time, wrought changes in spiritual outlook. The questions of death and the Last Judgment became leading preoccupations of Christians, obsessed by the tragedy of their condition.[14]

Not only might piles of actual corpses be found in fourteenth-century towns and villages—victims of the Black Death—so also might cadaver tombs, most of which were sculpted for high churchmen, with their graphic depic-tions of putrefying and maggot-infested flesh. According to the prevailing historiography, the production of such bizarre images must betray the mel-ancholy dispositions of most late medieval people. Who could blame them, for war, famine, plague, and social tumult more often and more intensely afflicted them than their high medieval ancestors? Hence, the commonplace book of the English reeve Robert Reynes of Acle was full of reminders to gain the indulgences attached to the recitation of the rosary as protection against the day of doom.[15]

Depressed, confused, spiritually adrift, seeking increasingly empty church benefits—such were the majority of Christians in the later Middle

Ages, or at least, so portrays the traditional historiography. While scholars of the current generation have indeed challenged and revised that historiography, nonetheless, the older view, which has a long pedigree dating from the era of Reformation itself, persists, as proven by the scorn which greeted the news of the Jubilee in the year 2000.

INDULGENCES IN THE HISTORIOGRAPHY
OF THE SIXTEENTH CENTURY

Like many other understudied topics in history, the prevailing depiction of indulgences was inherited from late sixteenth-century historiographical traditions. The confessional, polemical historiographies of the Reformation and Counter-Reformation still influence today's points of view. Luther's revolt against the church itself assumed a radical opposition between interiority and exteriority, now often taken for granted in modern Western culture. Even some Tridentine apologists, who wrote a generation after Luther, conceded that too many believers had mindlessly chased after too many indulgences, and that fewer indulgences were better than many.[16] While evangelical theology provided the assumptions, historiographical polemicists such as the Centurians applied them to the history of the Church. The historians of the nineteenth and twentieth centuries—both Catholic and Protestant—often incorporated these paradigms into their own work.

Luther, of course, publicly announced his opposition to indulgences in the famous Ninety-Five Theses of 1517. A number of the objections Luther raised against remissions in the Ninety-Five Theses were centuries old, having already been raised by numerous twelfth- and thirteenth-century scholastic theologians. Of course, Luther employed these objections rather differently than the medieval Schoolmen. For the medieval theologians, criticisms of indulgences served mostly as intellectual straw-men. They often attributed denials of indulgences' efficacy to Waldensians, and so these objections to pardons served the purpose of *elucidating orthodox teaching*, and served as pedagogical tools in the adversarial educational regime of the medieval university. For Luther, however, those same objections played a different rhetorical and pedagogical role, namely, the explication of the doctrine of justification by faith alone.

The great curiosity about this first broadside fired in the religious polemics of the sixteenth century is that scholars have largely ignored Luther's retractions of a number of the Ninety-Five Theses. Luther candidly admitted that a number of opinions he had presented in the Ninety-Five Theses were mistaken. He retracted these errors in the Explanation of the Ninety-Five Theses, written in 1518—a document far less frequently studied, although historically crucial. That Luther retracted certain of the Ninety-Five Theses in no way mitigated his denunciation either of indulgences or of the traditional teaching on justification; however, the retractions mean that the Ninety-Five Theses cannot be taken as eyewitness accounts of the "system" of indulgences in his day, but rather must be understood as the first publicly released argument for evangelical Christianity. Luther's version of justification rejected all traditional theologizing about indulgences, regardless of what statements were retracted in the Ninety-Five Theses. For instance, he had claimed in the Ninety-Five Theses that many Catholics of his day poorly understood the basic teachings about pardons; in particular, the teaching on the treasury of merit eluded them.[17] This view has appeared over and over again in historical and theological literature ever since. However, Luther withdrew this assertion a year later in the Explanation of the Ninety-Five Theses.[18] Again, in the Ninety-Five Theses Luther had stated that unless they were proclaimed *per modum suffragii*, indulgences could not be applied to the dead in Purgatory.[19] He later admitted that papal indulgences for the dead had been thus proclaimed since the fifteenth century.[20] He also objected to those who "teach that contrition is not necessary on the part of those who intend to buy souls out of Purgatory"—although no authority or proclamation of pardon had ever even hinted as much.[21] Despite Luther's retraction of certain of his objections to indulgences, subsequent writers—mostly Protestants and then Catholics responding to them—focused for polemical purposes on the Ninety-Five Theses, without considering the later retractions, most of which made no theological concessions to Catholicism but denounced ignorance and abuses in the reception and distribution of indulgences.

The later Lutheran polemicist, Matthias Flacius Illyricus (1520–1575), skillfully made the Protestant case not by theological argument but through a study of church history. Illyricus led the faction of Lutherans opposed to conciliation with either the Catholics or the Reformed. Along with his associates (called the Centurians), Illyricus gave the Protestants the offensive in polemical church history. With the publication of the *Magdeburg Centuries* (in thirteen volumes from 1559 to 1574), the "intransigent" Lutherans initiated a whole era in the study of church history. This Protestant historiography appropriated two prior scholarly endeavors. First, the Centurians employed the methods of the humanist historians, with their emphasis on discovery, interpretation, and criticism of primary sources. Consequently, for the Catholics "the challenge was particularly grave, for the Centurians, as the editors were called, backed up their version of the events with a large number of ancient documents, some of which they themselves had unearthed during research expeditions around Germany and Denmark."[22] The overall goal of the Centurians was to show through the documentary record that evangelical Christianity was the true heir of the *ecclesia primitiva*— the church of the apostles—which had for generations of church reformers, including the twelfth-century Cistercian Bernard of Clairvaux and the fourteenth-century conciliarist Jean Gerson, provided the programme for church renewal.[23] According to reformers—whether twelfth-century Cistercians, fourteenth-century conciliarists, or sixteenth-century Lutherans— Christendom needed to reestablish and recover the simplicity and faith of the church of the apostles. Of course, competing groups of reformers constructed images of the *ecclesia primitiva* consistent with their *a priori* agendas for reform; as a result, they often quarreled over what version of the *ecclesia primitiva* most faithfully mirrored the church of the apostolic generation. In the twelfth century, for instance, Cistercians forwarded their claim, which their rivals among the traditional Benedictines disputed, to be the true heirs of apostolic observance. In the thirteenth century, the mendicants forwarded their credentials as standard-bearers of the *ecclesia primitiva*, and in the sixteenth, Protestants and Catholics would take up the same dispute, which also surfaced within the Protestant fold.

The Centurians offered no narrative account of indulgences, but rather presented the texts (with introductions) relevant to a given issue in church history. The introductions pointed out that the documents proved that the Catholic Church changed her teaching over the past fifteen centuries, and thus departed from the charism of the *ecclesia primitiva*. The Protestants' championing of the *ecclesia primitiva* required that evangelical scholars depict indulgences as a recent innovation, with absolutely no connection to the church of the apostles. The Centurians thereby hoped to undermine the credibility of indulgences and of the rogues who had created and distributed them, namely, the medieval popes, whose desire to rule the church had prompted them to introduce teachings and practices absent in the Bible: "And because the pope has the plenitude of power over the treasury of the church (that which is not contained in sacred scripture), and other prelates are limited, thence only the pope has the plenitude of power in granting indulgence; the bishops thus according to his concession."[24] In fact, although indulgences were first granted in the eleventh century, they first appear in the thirteenth volume (which concerned the church of the thirteenth century) of the *Centuries*. After summarizing the teachings on indulgences of medieval Schoolmen such as William of Auxerre, Thomas Aquinas, and Giles of Rome, the Centurians warned the reader that the ideas of the high medieval theologians were especially dangerous, for although the strength of Scripture occasionally surfaced in their works, in fact moral and intellectual turpitude perverted their teaching:

> From the scholastic doctors excerpts of teachings must be collected. But we warn the reader, that however we have attempted to select the best ideas from them, because in their writings the spring of Israel has been polluted with much filth—for they spew some uncleanness—that task was not able to be done, yet surely not all the decrees of Scripture were able to have been utterly mutilated. So therefore, the reader may find something prudent in their dung. He may know from pristine rivers that not all clean things are able to be badly impaired; thus may the reader examine the authors, and with judgement he may decide whichever things that he ought to read, of course, according to the norm of the Divine Word. No one should admire the confusion, monstrosity, and other such things in them, because monstrous disputations likewise afflicted theology [then].[25]

As this quote indicates, the Centurians were formidable polemicists, not only because of their documentary discoveries but also because of their scholarly care and cautiousness. In the view of the Centurians, the teaching of the medieval Schoolmen was especially dangerous, not because corruption completely tainted it but because that teaching had *some* of the truth, and because scholastic arguments were *seemingly* supported in Scripture. The Centurians, then, understood and explained Catholic positions much better than had Luther, which made their polemics much more effective.

Other Protestant scholars followed suit. In his *Examination of the Decrees of Trent* (published in four volumes from 1565 to 1573), Martin Chemnitz agreed with the Centurians that medieval papal malefactors had invented indulgences.[26] Pardons had no basis whatsoever in Scripture: "If indulgences are said to be taught and based in sacred Scripture, there stands in the way the fact that the apostolic, primitive, and ancient church, which exercised much greater diligence and piety in treating Scripture, did not see or notice such indulgences in Scripture."[27] According to Chemnitz, Catholic theologians and apologists falsely claimed that indulgences had either patristic or early medieval antecedents: "The satisfactions about which the papalists dispute in the matter of indulgences are far other and different from the canonical satisfactions of the ancient church."[28]

By the end of the sixteenth century, the Centurians and other evangelical students of church history had laid the foundations for the Protestant view of the history of indulgences. Since the Christian Church needed to be reformed according to their portrayal of the *ecclesia primitiva*, Protestant confessional historians scoured the libraries of Europe for documentary proof that evangelical Christianity preserved more faithfully than Catholic Christianity the practice and teaching of the church of the apostles. The

Protestant historians hunted about for manuscripts, and in so doing discovered texts and evidence long forgotten or thought lost. Preoccupied as they were with the search for Christian origins, Protestants applied humanist historical methods to date the first grants of indulgence. They argued that the documentary record—in Scripture primarily—indicated that the early church had granted neither indulgences nor anything resembling them. Rather, the medieval church, whose devotions and doctrines formed a maelstrom of pagan and Pelagian subversions of apostolic purity, granted the first indulgences.

The learning and scholarship of the Centurians demanded a Catholic response. "What finally made Catholics aware of the necessity of adding historical demonstrations to doctrinal formulations, was the publication . . . of the major historical manifesto of the radical Lutherans under the leadership of Matthias Flacius Illyricus."[29] In reply to the charge that evangelicals had rediscovered and restored apostolic purity to the Christian Church, the task of Catholic confessional historians was to prove that the Roman Catholic Church had preserved inviolate the teaching and worship of the *ecclesia primitiva*. The Jesuit master-general Aquaviva insisted that "history is the basis of all Christian doctrine," by which of course he meant Catholic doctrine.[30] In 1571, Pope Pius V assembled a team of intellectuals whom he enjoined to find the Catholic scholar best suited for refuting the Protestant version of church history. They chose the Oratorian Cesare Baronio, better known by the Latin form of his name, Baronius (1518–1607). Baronius was an especially attractive candidate, because he knew the documents preserved in the Vatican Archives, wherein, perhaps, lay the evidence that would overturn the conclusions of the Centurians. Further, he could employ the methods of humanist historiography as well as his opponents. His three principles of historical investigation highlighted the importance of using humanist historical methods to reclaim the *ecclesia primitiva*: "Assert nothing that has not been thoroughly explored; follow the Truth as the first law of history; set down everything in chronological order."[31] The product of Baronius's labors were the *Annales ecclesiastici* in twelve volumes (1598–1607). Whereas the Centurians focused most on the development of doctrine, Baronius investigated the institutional development of the church—the establishment of dioceses and other administrative structures. He tirelessly hunted down the pertinent documents, religious and secular, housed in the Vatican Archives. Baronius's purpose was not to convert the heretic but, rather, to strengthen the belief of those who remained within the Catholic fold, in keeping with the broader program of the Counter-Reformation.

In addition to his work on the *Annales*, Baronius served as a member of the Martyrology commission, which was ordered to sift through editions and manuscripts containing the lives and passions of the martyrs and thereby discover where tradition may have departed from the documentary record. His colleague on that commission was the Jesuit Robert Bellarmine (1542–1621), the most influential and comprehensive theologian of the Counter-Reformation. Bellarmine was convinced (much as Loyola himself had been) that polemical theologizing could be strengthened by the study of church history. For the medieval Schoolmen—whose methods and teachings Bellarmine knew well—the history of the church was indeed important, but in Bellarmine's view their understanding of that history often rested upon uncritically accepted traditions. Furthermore, scholastic theology could have stood well enough on its own, without insights or evidence from history. Like Baronius, Bellarmine was convinced that church history was as necessary as theology in the polemical wars against the Protestants. He wrote the most comprehensive Tridentine discussion of indulgences, which included both scholastic and historical arguments. Bellarmine wrote *De indulgentiis* at the request of Pope Clement VIII (1592–1605). He intended that that lengthy treatise, completed in 1597, be included in the second volume of his famous *Controversies*, but the publisher's haste prevented its publication in that year. A flood of official business postponed its publication in the third volume as well. After its often-delayed publication, however, Bellarmine's *De indulgentiis* became an authoritative discussion not only for Catholic theologians and historians. The treasury of theological, canonistic, and historical sources Bellarmine brought to bear on the issue of pardons impressed even Protestant scholars.

In its exhaustive presentation of historical sources, Bellarmine's method resembled that of Baronius. Like Baronius, Bellarmine paraded and piled up historical documents in support of the theological opinions of the authoritative Schoolmen, the councils, or the decrees of the popes. *De indulgentiis* began with a "necessary" summary of the church's teaching about indulgences.[32] Historical topics and arguments followed the presentation of theological opinions. Bellarmine was certain that correct dating of developments in church history was crucial; nothing was more dangerous than confusing dates, for anachronism heralded error.[33] In a direct assault upon the arguments of the Centurians, Bellarmine attacked the idea that the medieval popes invented indulgences. He situated the dispensation of the first indulgences within the ancient traditions of Christian, Roman, and Hebrew civilizations. According to Bellarmine, pardons had forerunners in Mosaic law, which prescribed jubilee years for the remission of sins.[34] The word *indulgentia*, which the Church appropriated, was coined by Roman emperors and jurisconsults to describe a remission of juridical penalties.[35] Bellarmine further argued that indulgences had antecedents in the *ecclesia primitiva*.[36] The early Church Fathers had taught that good works cancel penalty for sin.[37] Bellarmine went on to explain the teaching of the treasury of merit, and for what works the treasury could be distributed.[38] Contrary to the Centurians, argued Bellarmine, "the treasury of indulgences is not lacking proof in the Holy Scriptures."[39] Indeed, Christ and St. Paul established the church's power to distribute the treasury.[40] The works of Tertullian and Cyprian prove that the early Church applied the treasury of merit to the remission of sins.[41]

Bellarmine marshalled his most sophisticated historical arguments, which targeted those of Martin Chemnitz's *Examination*, in the second book of *De indulgentiis*. The learning demonstrated in Chemnitz's text particularly impressed the Jesuits, and Bellarmine may have felt especially obligated to refute it. Like the Centurians, Chemnitz had argued that no indulgences had been granted before the eleventh century. Bellarmine countered that the texts Chemnitz presented instead proved the contrary: "For we have shown in book one, from Tertullian and Cyprian—the most ancient Fathers—as well as the antique councils like Ancyra and Nicaea, the dispensation of indulgences, and that even the proper name of indulgence dates from the reigns of Gregory I, Leo III, and Sergius II, who all presided over the church before the year 1000."[42] Chemnitz also asserted that although bishops had been granting them since the eleventh century, papal indulgences were unknown before the thirteenth. Bellarmine noted that his argument depended upon the absence of references to indulgences in the works of Anselm, Rupert of Deutz, Bernard of Clairvaux, Peter Lombard, and Gratian. Bellarmine pointed out, quite rightly, that a host of texts showed Chemnitz to be wrong. Pope Alexander III (1159–1181) sent a letter to the Archbishop of Canterbury containing rules for the preaching of indulgences.[43] St. Bernard's treatise *De consideratione* proved that Eugenius III (1145–1153) granted indulgences: "Pope Eugene III, who through general letters granted indulgence to crusaders and contributors to the holy war, began his reign in 1145, and he enlisted St. Bernard to preach those indulgences to the people, so that warriors might join in the crusade. Bernard did as the pope commanded . . . as he modestly wrote at the beginning of the second book of *De consideratione*."[44] Bellarmine strengthened this compelling case with other documents from the reigns of Paschal II (1099–1118) and Urban II (1088–1099).

Whereas all pardons were recent innovations for the Protestant confessional historians, for Bellarmine all indulgences, including those proclaimed for the benefit of the dead in Purgatory, were ancient. Numerous Protestant woodcuts and engravings had mocked these indulgences for the dead, so Bellarmine hastened to their defense in an interesting argument that reveals his strengths and weaknesses as a historian. In keeping with his overall procedure, he began with a theological point, namely, that indulgences for the dead are offered only *per modum suffragii*, that is, pardons for the souls in Purgatory constituted not an act of church jurisdiction but, rather, an especially efficacious form of intercession.[45] He then claimed an antique origin for indulgences for the dead, noting that Augustine had in *De civitate dei* taught that the pious dead were not separated from the church.[46] The living were therefore obligated to extend the benefits of good works to them. Bellarmine believed the first indulgence for the dead had been granted before the year 700 by Paschal I to those who visited churches in Rome.[47] He says that Gabriel Biel (d. 1495), his principal source, mistakenly credited a Paschasius V with this indulgence, since no man of that name ever occupied the chair of St. Peter. However, since Paschal I reigned 817–824, Bellarmine also erred in stating that Paschal I could have granted any indulgence whatsoever before 700. While he did bring a substantial critical acumen to bear on the history of indulgences, at times Bellarmine's command of the subject was faulty.

The ideas and arguments of Matthias Flacius Illyricus, Martin Chemnitz, Baronius, and Bellarmine became the authoritative sources for later writers on the history of indulgences. They also established the issues most often debated between the two confessional camps, among which the most heated was the date of the first pardons. Scholars also debated what indulgences meant for the relationship between piety and authority: did they constitute a deception of ordinary believers, or an inducement to penitence? What did they reveal about the overall moral condition of the later medieval Church? Were indulgences symptomatic of widespread abuse or were the problems related to indulgences—recognized by both sides—an exception in an otherwise sound Catholic Church? Heated polemics aside, the Catholic-Protestant historical debates of the sixteenth century bore much fruit, in that the purposes of both sides prompted the discovery or rediscovery of numerous theological treatises, legal codes, liturgical texts, and church chronicles. The era was also intellectually creative, in that both Protestants and Catholics applied methods first devised to study secular history to the study of church history; consequently they enriched and broadened the tradition of humanist historical scholarship. Catholic scholarship benefitted in particular, for although humanist learning early carried the day among Protestants (there being no evangelical scholastic tradition), until Bellarmine, humanism was suspected of having encouraged the Protestant revolt against the

Catholic Church. His *Controversies* showed that the two scholarly traditions could be harmonized in the defense of the ancestral faith.

The confessional church historians inherited the failings, as well as the virtues, of Renaissance secular historiography. For instance, histories of Florence, such as that of Leonardo Bruni, located the origins of that city-state in the days of the later Roman Republic, on the basis of the most imaginative interpretations of the sources. The purposes of both Protestant and Catholic polemicists generated parallel errors, for both sides either ignored or devised curious interpretations of polemically inconvenient documents. The Centurians ignored the crusading indulgences of the eleventh century, even though they were aware of these documents, because they wanted to argue for as late a date as possible for the first indulgences. In addition, Protestants often badly put the Catholic teachings on indulgences. Catholics were equally culpable. Bellarmine's commitment to demonstrate indulgences' antiquity required that he construct some tortuous interpretations of scriptural and patristic texts. At the same time, he produced evidence that showed that pardons preserved the spirit of patristic penitential customs. For all their considerable contributions to the study of indulgences in the Middle Ages, most of what sixteenth-century church historians did, however, was illuminate what they meant when they recited the Creed.[48] The English Catholic William Allen (d. 1594) typified the enterprise of all Reformation and Counter-Reformation writers when he wrote that "by iuste causes [he] was moved to beleve the trueth of this doctrine of Pardons, before he knewe the meaning of them."[49]

In sum, historians of medieval religious culture in general, and of indulgences in particular, have inherited a number of important questions, assumptions, and paradigms from the pioneering studies of sixteenth-century scholars. First, the dating of the first indulgences much interested Catholic and Protestant polemicists; the former argued for their antiquity and the latter for their modernity. Related historical undertakings investigated any possible antecedents of indulgences in either the antique or early medieval Church. Finally, as reformers, whether Protestant or Catholic, both sides could agree that a spiritual bankruptcy afflicted the later medieval Church "in both head and members." In their own, opposed ways, the polemicists employed history on behalf of polemical theologizing.

INDULGENCES IN THE HISTORIOGRAPHY
OF THE NINETEENTH CENTURY

Another set of developments important to the historiography of indulgences in the Middle Ages took place after the unification of the German Reich in

1871, after which nationalist and liberal preoccupations informed the most important studies of indulgences. German unification encouraged the undertaking of research that examined how indulgences figured into medieval and early modern German politics. For these German historians and theologians, Protestant and Catholic alike, the Reformation's political consequences made indulgences historically interesting, especially since "the indulgence controversy" contributed significantly to the erosion of German imperial authority in the sixteenth century. German Protestant historians agreed that the indulgence controversy of the sixteenth century determined the nature of the Reformation itself: "The great interest in the correct understanding of indulgences' essence, as Luther discovered it, is explained by the momentousness which indulgences had for Luther's development as a reformer, and likewise as of the nature and the justification of the Reformation."[50] And again: "No moment of the history of the Reformation is . . . of greater meaning than the controversy over indulgences."[51] These historians assumed that indulgences played a greater role in the unfolding of German national history than that of any other European people. The controversy over indulgences formed another chapter in the story of German imperial breakdown, which had begun with the Investiture Controversy of the eleventh century. Indeed, German scholar-nationalists often suggested that indulgences were more important because they contributed to the dissolution of the *Reich*, rather than the sundering of unity in Latin Christendom. The historian Adolf Gottlob stated: "Close to the four hundredth anniversary of the first appearance of Luther there is such confusion over the historical interpretation of the occasion for the great division, which has sundered our Fatherland, good for neither Catholic nor Protestant; at the least, that historical interpretation is for us Germans altogether crucial."[52] Influenced by the German tradition of legal and constitutional history, these nationalist scholars had little interest in the religious issues raised by Luther's Ninety-Five Theses.

For their part, German Catholic scholars eagerly worked on studies they hoped would enhance Protestants' understanding of pardons, for since the Reformation Protestant authors had often erred in their portrayals of Catholic ideas. In his lengthy study of medieval handbooks for confessors (*summa confessorum*), the Catholic Johannes Dietterle included transcriptions of the summists' teachings on indulgences, he said, in the hope that Protestant scholars might also find his work useful.[53] Such sentiments not only provided for greater scholarly dialogue but also helped Catholic Germans overcome the cultural and religious suspicions raised by Bismarck's *Kulturkampf*.

The first lengthy history of indulgences in English followed soon upon the researches of the German nationalist historians. Henry C. Lea's *History of Auricular Confession and Indulgences in the Middle Ages*, published in three volumes, was a stridently liberal polemic. He discussed indulgences in only the third volume. Lea relied much on the Centurians, the German nationalists, and Bellarmine's *De indulgentiis*. He agreed with the German nationalists that the Reformation had made indulgences historically significant. While he admired much about medieval Catholicism, he was convinced, like the Centurians, that the medieval church had, over time, departed from the teaching and charism of the *ecclesia primitiva*, such that by the fourteenth and fifteenth centuries Catholicism consisted of a pastiche of superstitious innovations. For Lea, the papal indulgences especially corrupted the medieval church of the fourteenth and fifteenth centuries. In the High Middle Ages, when the faithful rarely felt the heavy hand of the papacy, ordinary believers created an impressive, if mistaken and unscriptural, religious culture and imagination. By the late Middle Ages, however, the papacy's insatiable thirst for money and power impoverished and compromised the church. Grants of pardon for the crusades and the construction of churches dissipated the rigor of the penitential regime inherited from the late antique and early medieval churches. Indulgences offered penitents an easy way out, so they increasingly rejected sincere amendment of life: "We have seen . . . how deplorably lax was the distribution of the treasure [i.e., indulgences] prior to the Reformation."[54] Too many fourteenth- and fifteenth-century Christians starved spiritually because indulgences excused them from honest reflection on their sinfulness. The popes used indulgences to strengthen their standing as Italian princes, rather than as universal shepherds. The mendicant orders, who conspired with the popes, advanced the morbid demoralization of the era by their preaching of the terrors of Purgatory.[55] This irresponsible distribution of indulgences thus fomented hatred of the central religious authority in the years leading up to the Reformation: "There was thus ample reason why there should be a revolt against indulgences and their abuse, and they may fairly be regarded as the occasion of the Reformation, but the cause of a movement so momentous in human development lay deeper and is to be sought in the general hatred of Rome entertained by all classes, clerical and lay."[56] Outside the Papal States, kings, bishops, and princes grumbled that the funds given to preachers of papal indulgences impoverished local economies, governments, and churches.

Still, Lea's was a magnificent, if deeply flawed, work. The scholarship represented in the footnotes is thorough and comprehensive. He incorporated evidence, such as the lives of saints, which previous scholars had usually ignored. His Whiggish inclinations, however, meant he had so much antagonism towards his subject that he often succumbed to apocryphal generalizations. Like other Whigs, Lea believed the medieval Church was a hierarchical monolith, and had a Whig's characteristic paranoia for monarchical government. He assumed many points he needed to prove. His ideological fervor bulldozed scholarly nuance.

Within a few years, however, Lea's work attracted Catholic responses. A. Boudinhon praised Lea for his erudition, but countered with a critique based on Bellarmine's *De indulgentiis* and criticized Lea for ignoring indulgences' antecedents in antique and early medieval penitential practices.[57] He argued that Lea failed to see that indulgences developed out of an early medieval tradition of penitential severity.[58] Boudinhon also corrected Lea's mistaken version of the Catholic theology of repentance, reconciliation, and satisfaction.[59] Other Catholic authors followed Boudinhon's example. A. Lepicier, a French missionary priest who sometimes worked in England, wrote a two-volume study of indulgences, the first multivolume work on the subject by a Catholic.[60] Since its publication, scholars have cited Lepicier's work as an authority. He bluntly confessed his polemical purposes in the introduction to the first volume—he determined to defend Catholicism against "misrepresentation . . . vain shadows and empty dreams."[61] In keeping with Bellarmine's example, he began (the first three chapters of his first volume) with an explanation of the Catholic teaching on sin and penance, and efficacious reception of indulgences.[62] The rest of the work narrated the history of indulgences. Like Boudinhon and Bellarmine, Lepicier argued that pardons had an origin of sorts in the first generation of the church, despite his admission that indulgences have little scriptural support.[63] He agreed with Bellarmine that bishops' commutations of penance in the patristic era were a kind of indulgence, so he seems also to have believed that any reduction of penance amounted to an indulgence.[64] Lepicier admitted that indulgences proliferated especially in the later Middle Ages, but attributed that proliferation to the generosity of the prelates, rather than ambitious popes and greedy friars. The prelates responded generously to numerous requests for grants of pardon from the laity, as well as members of the clergy. Abuses no doubt existed, wrote Lepicier, but the church valiantly fought those abuses, and can hardly be blamed for the failures of human nature.[65] The suggestion that the late medieval escalation in the number of grants of pardon should be attributed to the pleas of ordinary believers, rather than the policies of the popes, was Lepicier's most important contribution to the study of indulgences in the Middle Ages. Once again, in the works of Lea and Lepicier, the confessional historians made valuable additions to the study of indulgences, despite the limitations imposed on their scholarship by their polemical preoccupations.

OLD ROADS BUT NEW DIRECTIONS

A new perspective on the history of indulgences arrived with the work of the Alsatian priest-scholar Nikolaus Paulus. In the 1920s, he published the most comprehensive work to date on indulgences. His magisterial, three-volume *Geschichte des Ablasses im Mittelalter* (*History of Indulgences in the Middle Ages*) revisited a number of old disputes but also introduced a new historiographical approach.[66] In the forward to the first volume, he acknowledged that both Protestant and Catholic historians and theologians had long recognized the importance of indulgences for the origin of the Reformation, but a thorough study of indulgences in their medieval context had not yet been attempted, that is, the history of pardons had always been told "backwards" from the Reformation, but never "forward" from their origins. He, therefore, proposed precisely just such a study, and would start the story of the history of indulgences in the Middle Ages—the era during which they developed—rather than in the sixteenth century or in antiquity.[67]

Paulus's work was the least polemical work on indulgences that had yet been written. To be sure, polemical traditions still influenced his work. He too depended upon and applied some of the sixteenth-century polemical paradigms. Paulus was first and foremost a conscientious Catholic priest whose scholarly work served pastoral purposes. Still, a more rigorously critical reading of the sources breathed a good deal of freshness into his writing. He examined more manuscript evidence than any previous scholar, and he synthesized what was useful in both the Catholic and Protestant polemical traditions. From 1907 to 1923 Paulus had studied the date of the first indulgences,[68] the medieval theologians' and canonists' teachings on indulgences,[69] the validity of some dubious indulgences,[70] and indulgences' social usefulness.[71]

Paulus's study of the first indulgences typified his scholarship. He affirmed, on the basis of Carolingian and Ottonian sources, that the Catholic historiographical tradition correctly asserted that indulgences preserved the spirit of antique and early medieval penitential practices. The Protestant tradition, as far as this question was concerned, was simply mistaken. Paulus agreed with the traditional Protestant position, however, that no indulgences properly so called had been granted before the eleventh century, when episcopal intercessions on behalf of penitents lost their intercessory language and assumed juridical expression. By and large, subsequent scholarship revised his thesis only in its details.[72] After the publication of the *Geschichte*, no serious Catholic historian or theologian even hinted that indulgences appeared earlier than the mid-eleventh century.

Paulus did share Catholics' traditional concern for understanding properly the church's teaching on the efficacy of pardons, and so much of his history catalogued the theologians' and canonists' teachings about indulgences, beginning with the early Schoolmen of the late twelfth century and terminating with the treatises of fifteenth-century intellectuals.[73] Though exhaustive and useful, these chapters amount to little more than a summary of the theologians' and canonists' arguments. Paulus offered little social, devotional, or liturgical contextualization for their arguments. The sections on indulgences for the dead, for instance, or the first grants of indulgence, likewise lack context.[74] Paulus did, however, make two important observations about the learned treatises on indulgences. First, he pointed out that indulgences first appeared in the academic commentaries at the end of the twelfth century. The theology of indulgences, then, postdated the dispensation of the first verifiable indulgences by about one hundred and fifty years. Second, the theologians and canonists reached a consensus about indulgences received by the middle of the thirteenth century. Like many other Catholic intellectuals of the Neo-Thomist revival, Paulus found the most elegant expression of this theology in Thomas Aquinas. In his discussion of the learned commentators, Paulus showed that the texts of the Schoolmen ought to be read as descriptive, rather than prescriptive, sources. They were making comments on established practices and ideas; they were not attempting to hazard new ones.

In the next generation, Bernhard Poschmann built on Paulus's work. He refined some of Paulus's conclusions and more rigorously studied the late antique and early medieval roots of indulgences in his *Der Ablaß im Licht der Bußgeschichte*; he explained those roots more briefly in his *Penance and the Anointing of the Sick*.[75] Poschmann identified the Carolingian intercessory petition as an important antecedent of indulgences. These petitions would be offered by either a bishop or a priest as part of a liturgical observance (not necessarily the Mass). On behalf of the whole church, the petition asked God to cancel the penalty for sin owed by a penitent who, generally because of disability, needed the intercessions of fellow Christians. Poschmann also thought the Carolingian rite of absolution, during which a bishop offered intercession on behalf of a penitent, another forerunner of indulgences. The Carolingians also used the word *absolutio* to name a document, on which were written pleas made in the name of the church for God to remit and reduce a deceased person's penalty for sin. These documents were sometimes placed on the corpse in the grave. Poschmann believed that since they could only be offered by a bishop, and because the term itself referred not only to an intercessory petition but also a document, absolution was the immediate antecedent of the indulgence.[76] Warrior aristocrats, for instance, who had spent a lifetime shedding blood, most often requested absolutions because their sins were serious and numerous, but their time for satisfying the lengthy penances attached to those sins was limited. Without the help of the church, these noble warriors, whose debt of sin was great, had little hope of salvation.[77] By the tenth century, the general absolution had developed, through which a bishop could apply the intercessory powers of the Christian Church to a whole congregation. Like Paulus, Poschmann was convinced that indulgences were first granted in the eleventh century, since the jurisdictional claims found in pardons were absent in absolutions. The last part of Poschmann's book is a survey of the teachings of medieval theologians on the topic of indulgences. Like Paulus, he discerned an initial period of struggling with the theological underpinnings of indulgences, which postdated the first dispensations of indulgences by about a century. The mendicant Schoolmen later systematized the opinions of the earlier theologians.[78]

The work of Paulus and Poschmann, then, made a number of significant contributions to the study of the history of indulgences. For the first time, scholars consciously attempted to construct a medieval context for the importance of indulgences, rather than staging them as a subplot of the Reformation. The studies of both scholars were undertaken with far less polemical intent than were their predecessors'. Indeed, on some issues Paulus well synthesized the best insights of the Catholic and Protestant confessional polemicists. They also introduced a number of new sources; Paulus, in particular, presented findings from manuscripts that had until his time been virtually ignored. The end result was the foundation for new and fruitful examinations of the history of indulgences in the Middle Ages.

CONFESSIONAL PARADIGMS AND VATICAN II

The work of Paulus and Poschmann shows that the hold of confessional historiography had weakened by the advent of the twentieth century. For Catholics, reform movements, which would ultimately usher in Vatican II, diminished Tridentine defensiveness. By the convocation of Vatican II, Protestants had largely lost their interest in scholarly polemics as well. Unfortunately, the work of Paulus and Poschmann enjoyed only a limited influence, for the reason that their best articles and books were never translated into either English or French; their readership was thus restricted to the German-speaking world.

The ecumenism of Vatican II (1962–1965) further undermined the traditional historiography.[79] In the wake of the council, the work of church historians ceased to serve either Catholic or Protestant apologetics; indeed, apologetics virtually disappeared. Vatican II's summons for greater lay participation in worship prompted influential Catholic scholars to study "popular" piety and worship; the traditional historiography's preoccupations with bishops and priests and religious orders yielded to a greater interest in the development of parishes and the laity's practice of religion. While the French Catholic historian Étienne Delaruelle did not write a history of indulgences, he nonetheless made some observations and comments characteristic of the new points of view. Delaruelle explicitly located the proliferation of indulgences not in the venality of friars and prelates, but in the piety of the laity. At the same time, he largely accepted the traditionally negative evaluation of late medieval piety. Delaruelle's chief concern was the damage done to the church during the Great Schism (1378–1417), and so he studied abuses in the church. That he included indulgences among the usual suspects was of course not new, but what was notable was that Delaruelle largely argued the traditional Protestant position, which was that indulgences encouraged mechanistic formalism instead of heartfelt zeal. Since the Reformation, Catholics had also conceded that indulgences were abused, and agreed that the later Middle Ages were spiritually troubled, but none really argued that pardons were in themselves a contributing cause to the spiritual malaise, many scholars believed, characteristic of the later Middle Ages.[80] Of course, the great crisis about which Delaruelle wrote constituted a breakdown of the Catholic Church's central government and authority, during which rival popes used concessions of pardon to win support for themselves and at the same time undermine their counterpart in either Rome or Avignon. No one during the Schism could be sure whose indulgences were valid, since no one could be sure who was the truer pope (in the words of the liturgy, *qui est verius papa*), so confidence in all indulgences was compromised. Any prayer, devotion, or monastery, for example, which had been indulgenced during the Schism was thereby corrupted, such that the Schism damaged not only the authority of the head (pope and curia) but also the piety of the members (parishes and laity), of the church. The rot started at the top and spread to humble, otherwise unsullied parishes.

In a similar vein, the French historians Raymond Foreville and Francis Rapp emphasized the popular roots of the papal Jubilee, the first of which was granted in 1300 by Pope Boniface VIII (1296–1303). The Jubilee was a full remission of sin (plenary indulgence) granted to pilgrims who visited Rome in 1300, a year of heightened millenial expectations. Foreville pointed out that eighty years before this first papal Jubilee, the popular devotion to Thomas Becket, which speedily spread from England to the rest of Christendom, featured similar observances.[81] Rapp believed that Boniface VIII feared that the hordes of pilgrims who had flocked to the Eternal City in 1299 might get violent, if they should get no great benefit from the universal pontiff. Some crowds did demand some form of remission, and so Boniface responded with the Jubilee of 1300, lest rioters destroy the city. This famous indulgence, then, originated with the masses of pilgrims, not the pope.[82]

Other scholars have not only emphasized the roots of indulgences' popularity among the medieval masses, but entertained as well the idea that remissions may in fact have been symptomatic of deeply felt religious impulses rather than of a mechanistic piety. In his survey of the medieval church, Sir Richard Southern ascribed enthusiasm for indulgences as a response to the affective piety characteristic of high and late medieval Catholicism: "it is well to . . . recall the deep personal and emotional springs of the whole development. We have seen how Eugenius III in 1150 took an important step under the influence of a strong emotion, and it would be quite unrealistic to suppose that a similar emotional impulse was absent in the fifteenth century . . . the popes themselves can scarcely have been unmoved by their environment."[83] According to Southern, then, a grant of pardon should be understood as the church authorities' response to and also approbation of devotions and worship that had originated at the parish, diocesan or provincial level. In his fine treatment of late medieval Christianity, Francis Oakley suggested that "for those of appropriately balanced disposition, indulgences could function not as reinforcement to a piety of mechanical formalism but rather as a modest incentive to prayer."[84] In other words, exterior acts should be understood as wedded to, rather than divorced from, interior dispositions.

In that case, indulgences *generally reinforced* the late medieval striving for spiritual introspection and conversion. Richard Kieckhefer, for instance, has suggested that rather than constituting a distinct group among late medieval Catholics, the saints of the fourteenth and fifteenth centuries are hardly distinguishable from their more anonymous contemporaries. He then further speculated that a study of the saints and indulgences promised to shed much light on the question of pardons and interior disposition, for the saints keenly cultivated rigorous, constant examination of interior disposition. Did they also seek out indulgences as eagerly as their fellows?[85]

Still, the traditional historiography has its advocates. Some historians and theologians continued to portray late medieval religion as psychologically damaging and damaged. Late medieval Catholicism failed to reconcile the performance of exterior good works with the torment of interior temptation, and so lost all meaning for the masses of spiritually confused, like Luther, who for the sake of indulgences went on pilgrimage, recited popular devotional prayers, and offered alms to hospitals but found no respite from psychological conflict. Lucien Febvre, for instance, spoke of a "frenzy" of piety in the later fifteenth century. According to him, later medieval Christians anxiously elbowed each other out of the way as they grabbed growing numbers of indulgences in an increasingly desperate search for peace of mind. In contrast, the Protestant message of justification by faith alone restored emotional and mental health and relieved the anguish of sixteenth-century men and women, who in the past had invested far too many emotional and psychical resources in obtaining masses and indulgences in the pathetic hope of cancelling the torments of Purgatory.[86] Bernd Moeller likewise characterized the mass pilgrimages of the fifteenth century as a psychosis. After describing the devotion to relics and pursuit of indulgences in the later fifteenth century, he commented: "These anxious, craning gestures, indicating spiritual destitution and the misery of existence, were of a greater extent and higher intensity than before that time." In Moeller's opinion, the "significance of the indulgence attained in this period by the indulgence sermon—so sub-Christian in its materialism and so misunderstood in its essence—is the most distinctive symptom of this negative state of affairs."[87] Whereas earlier critics had blamed the papacy for the trade in indulgences, Moeller indicted a fundamentally disturbed, barely Christian civilization. The editor of *The Commonplace Book of Robert Reynes of Acle: An Edition of Tanner MS 407* concurred. He described the fifteenth-century devotionalisms as "heavily superstitious."[88] Jean Delumeau also believed medieval Europe to be a pre-Christian civilization, wherein most people tightly grasped an uncertain hope that masses and indulgences would relieve the terrors of punishment in the afterlife.[89] William Bouwsma argued that the anxiety of the later Middle Ages and early modern period deeply informed the cultural development of modern Europe. Whereas the men of the twelfth and thirteenth centuries were "reasonably comfortable about human existence," the period after 1300 was an era of "unusual anxiety."[90] A recent study on public penance in high medieval France concluded that medieval sacramental theologians established an excessively legalistic penitential system, which offered penitents little pastoral sensitivity: "In the end the theologians were the prophets less . . . of private sacramental confession than of the voluntary lay devotions of the later Middle Ages, the books of hours and ascetic self-discipline, and indeed, the flagellant processions and indulgences. The theologians had wanted contrition and ended up with a legalistically applied sacramental penance; so they continued to preach contrition and ended up with the late medieval indulgence trade."[91]

Indeed, when the historian Thomas Tentler defended the psychological benefits of later medieval pastoral care in *Sin and Confession on the Eve of the Reformation*, critics quickly said he had refuted his own thesis. Basically, Tentler argued in his book that sensitivity to the complexities of human motivation and behavior better described the later medieval pastoral manuals (many of which had short treatises on indulgences) than the derogatory psychological categories of neurosis and psychosis. Tentler's detractors pointed out the byzantine degrees of consent and culpability contained in the manuals, one of which alerted "the priest to sixteen degrees of sexual transgression, ranging from unchaste kisses to bestiality." Even "the more lenient works of Sylvester Prierias, Anthony of Florence, and Jean Gerson mitigated such penitential probing only by degree when they instructed the priest to scold only those penitents who confessed to having thought of someone other than their spouse during sexual intercourse. Is such interrogation really designed to cure anxiety?"[92] As in the traditional, confessional historiography, some scholars dismissed the possibility that a late medieval Catholic might be spiritually whole because of Catholicism, of which the dispensation of pardons formed a distinctive part.

BEYOND THE HISTORIOGRAPHY OF CONFESSIONAL POLEMIC

A number of unpolemical studies, however, have been published during the last thirty years. German scholars took the lead here with investigations of individual grants of pardon, on the one hand, and specific controversies about indulgences, on the other. A series of interesting and illuminating monographs have been the result. Two such studies, one for Cologne, the other for Westphalia, have shown that the upsurge and abatement of devotions best explains the waxing and waning of certain indulgences' popularity.[93] A fading enthusiasm for one type of indulgence, and a growing zeal for another, reflect the pietistic ebb and flow of the later Middle Ages, as old devotions yielded adherents to new ones.

Other studies have examined how indulgences were publicized. Many manuscript copies of proclamations of pardons circulated and have survived, but medieval Christians, most of whom could not read, learned about the location and benefits of new indulgences in other ways. Many indulgences have survived not in episcopal or papal documents but, rather, as marginalia copied into devotional texts or carved into the entrances of churches or convents. After the invention of printing, the number of copies of pardons increased exponentially. The printed indulgences, as well as those copied into devotional handbooks by pious laity, present the modern historian with significant problems of authenticity.[94] Handbooks of indulgences available at Christendom's holiest sites also circulated throughout medieval Europe. These printed and manuscript texts, as well as the inscriptions, have preserved important devotional impulses for the student of medieval Catholicism.

Yet another group of studies pointed out that while indulgences sparked controversies even before the Reformation, these medieval quarrels involved issues very different from those of the sixteenth century. One important study, for instance, discovered a fourteenth-century movement to limit the number of indulgences. Some scholars interpreted this movement as proof of the widespread abuse of indulgences, and evidence for an equally widespread sentiment to eliminate that abuse. In the opinion of Karlheinz Frankel, however, this movement had to be understood within the peculiar context of the Great Schism (1379–1417). He argued that the Schism created a confused church government, for neither the Avignonese nor the Roman claimants succeeded in winning over the adherents of the opposing pope. Many throughout Latin Christendom greeted the pardons conceded by either the Roman or Avignonese pope with the contempt then felt for all exercises of papal authority.[95] Similarly, a study of indulgences for the dead, which Protestant polemicists mocked as fraud and Tridentine apologists cautiously defended, also occasioned an argument between thirteenth- and fourteenth-century theologians and canonists. This study showed that the antagonists agreed on the basic understanding of these indulgences and, indeed, held in common many more ideas than they disputed. Notwithstanding, the issues upon which they differed reflected competing, vested interests of churchmen and religious orders.[96] Both studies showed that medieval arguments involving pardons concerned legal and jurisdictional differences rather than theological disputes.

Recent scholarship has also used pardons to understand better the relationship between the devotion of the masses of medieval Catholics and the authority of bishops, cardinals, and popes. Traditional accounts have studied how the popes used indulgences to advance their policies, especially in terms of the crusades; in such works, indulgences originated with the hierarchy—a "top-down" model.[97] In contrast, Walter Principe and David D'Avray have pointed out that the popes granted many indulgences which had little to do with papal political goals. These grants of pardon represent the popes' and bishops' responses to and endorsements of the religious impulses present in medieval Christendom. D'Avray asserted that since the pope's power to remit sin manifested his plenitude of power, so church authority and religious sensibility intersected in a grant of pardon. Consequently, "the idea and practice of indulgences put the papacy in the middle of powerful currents of religious sentiment . . . [the] popes lent their support to other spiritual movements characteristic of the period: the Franciscan revival, female mysticism, and the *devotio moderna*. The link between the institution of the papacy and late medieval religious sentiment is a prominent feature of the age."[98] The popes in fact patronized and encouraged many religious movements that originated independently of their authority or guidance. Their grants of indulgence indicate that the popes were eager to embrace and support new devotionalisms if they could be deemed orthodox.

Principe's monograph echoed D'Avray's findings. His study of twelfth- and thirteenth-century *sententiae* and *summae* showed that the Schoolmen's thoughts about preaching and confessing accompanied their thoughts about the popes' authority to concede remissions.[99] For Alexander of Hales, Bonaventure, Thomas Aquinas, and others, the dispensation of pardons was in no way inconsistent with the quest for interior conversion. Righteous deeds and interior perfection had to accompany one another, for a righteous act testified to the conversion wrought within the soul; conversely, a sinful deed reflected interior corruption. Thus, the rise of papal power, along with the proliferation of indulgences, to say nothing of the prominence of moral theology in the works of the Schoolmen, were all coherent aspects of the spiritual regeneration of high medieval Catholicism.

The past two scholarly generations, then, have substantially revised the historiography of indulgences. Still, most recent studies of medieval religion are not focused on pardons *in themselves*, but only as indulgences are related to other concerns, such as gender, or what has too often come to be called "popular religion." The importance of indulgences in medieval religion, however, means that pardons remain much understudied, and that more issues and texts could be taken under learned consideration. Only a few books and articles (some of which are outstanding, to be sure) have been written, but the dearth of secondary literature in English is especially dramatic. Scholars need to reappraise documents with which they have long been familiar and seek out manuscripts that have yet to be examined thoroughly. Many of the issues scholars have long debated about indulgences also demand revisitation.

Fortunately, new studies can now proceed from solid foundations. Paulus's chronological reorientation of the narrative of indulgences eliminates many of the pitfalls of anachronism. That bishops granted the first indulgences in the middle of the eleventh century, with all the epochal changes of that era for the history of western Christianity, has rarely been appreciated—even by Paulus himself. Along with the first pardons, powerful currents of church reform and new well-springs of spirituality flourished in the eleventh-century church. To borrow a metaphor from Herbert Butterfield, historians ought now to grab the other end of the scholarly stick and stop portraying indulgences as an inexplicable curiosity.

The number and variety of indulgences that medieval peasants, merchants, warriors, churchmen, artisans, scholars, physicians, lawyers, and academics from all over Christendom often made great sacrifices to obtain indicate the confidence men placed in the power of pardons to remit penalty for sin. They conceptualized the power of indulgences in the metaphors drawn from powerful persons. Medieval Christians likened indulgences to the treasuries of rulers. Pardons were withdrawals from an inexhaustible treasury of merit, which the sufferings and merits of Christ and the saints had won for the church. Although scholars have long credited the Middle Ages with rich imagery, the significance and the sources of the metaphor of the treasury have scarcely been appreciated. The image of the treasury encapsulated the relationship between believers, Christ, and Christ's stewards on earth, the bishops. The treasury was perhaps the starkest image of the corporate Christianity of the Middle Ages— an expression of the communion of the saints recalled in the Creed.[100] The image of treasury testifies to the deep penetration of the essential teachings of the Christian faith among the medieval masses, for it originated in no papal, synodal, or conciliar decree. Rather, the religious imagination of the era synthesized the mundane rendering of accounts with the most sublime biblical imagery into an eminently concrete and meaningful depiction of human salvation.[101]

The logic of the metaphor of the treasury summoned up another significant picture in the high medieval religious imagination. What did payments from the treasury of merit "buy?" Thirteenth-century penitents came to see indulgences as promissory notes to be applied against the debt of penalty in Purgatory. Since Purgatory was obviously a place to be avoided, what was it like? Was Purgatory an awful, painful place? Did medieval Christians hold one unified portrayal of Purgatory, or did different depictions coexist? Modern scholars have often asserted that fear of Purgatory terrorized later medieval Christians. Will a reexamination of the documents bear out that interpretation? Another appraisal of the imagery of Purgatory beckons, for the traditional historiography focused on horrifying visions and imaginings.

Aside from the imagery of the treasury and Purgatory, the witness of the great spiritual celebrities of the era constitute another avenue to the site indulgences occupied in the medieval religious imagination. The *vitae* of the saints shed light on the relationship between the search for indulgences and the characteristic emphasis on the cultivation of the interior life. Ordinary Catholics, whose religious fervor was by definition unextraordinary, sought out pardons, but did the spiritual vanguard of the era do likewise? Or did they eschew pardons as a distraction to their quest for interior regeneration? Did the spiritual program of the religious heroes and heroines of the later Middle Ages resemble or differ from their more obscure contemporaries? These are crucial questions, for in the answers lies the connection or inconsistency between pardons, on the one hand, and union with the human Jesus, on the other. If indulgences encouraged formalism, the saints should have denounced them as a pious fraud (after all, they often and courageously criticized church authority). On the other hand, if the saints endorsed them, can remissions continue to be understood as corrupting of medieval spirituality? A third possibility, of course, would be that no explicit endorsement, or rejection, of indulgences may be said to characterize the *vitae*, in which case the traditional view is still compromised.

Finally, the controversies that indulgences raised in the medieval centuries cannot be passed over mutely. A number and a variety of controversies that antedate the Great Schism await the further researches of historians. The nature of these controversies, however, first requires some inspection, since the historical importance of these conflicts would be lost without recognizing the different contexts within which sets of antagonists quarreled. Some arguments involved disputants from all over Latin Christendom, such as the dispute over the validity of indulgences for the dead. Other conflicts were confined to towns or provinces, such as a controversy over pardons south German Dominicans preached around the year 1350. Clearly, some contested issues raised universal concerns, but others only regional interest.

To say anything useful or meaningful about indulgences in the Middle Ages requires chronological and thematic limits. Little was said by medieval writers about indulgences before 1175, so the late twelfth century serves as a convenient starting point. Since most medieval Catholics probably encountered the hierarchy of their church most often in the form of pardons, the onset in 1379 of the Great Schism, which seriously compromised that church authority, recommends itself as an ending point. Within these dates, something of the context and variety of indulgences can be explored, as well as the ideas and controversies that indulgences occasioned for thirteenth- and fourteenth-century Catholic penitents, the aim being to understand better what light a study of indulgences has to shed on Latin Christianity from about 1175 until 1379. The conclusions reached from such an investigation must necessarily be made cautiously, owing to the scholarly work that remains. But all journeys begin with a first step.

NOTES

1. Catholic Church, *Catechism of the Catholic Church* (Vatican City: Libreria Editricia Vaticana, 1994), 370, no. 1471.

2. Tanner and Alberigo, 2:796.

3. Catholic Church, *Enchiridion indulgentiarum* (Vatican City: Typis Polyglottis Vaticanus, 1968). The news of the indulgence for the Jubilee year of 2000 was carried not only by the Catholic press but also by the mainstream print media, for instance, Andrew Sentella, "The Way We Live Now," *New York Times*, March 14, 1999, sec. 6, p. 24; "Pope Declares 2000 Holy Year," *The Daily Telegraph* (Sydney), November 30, 1998, p. 19; along with the sniggering of Stewart Lamont, "When the coin rings, the soul from purgatory springs," *The Herald* (Glasgow, Scotland), December 5, 1998, p. 14.

4. David L. D'Avray, "Papal Authority and Religious Sentiment in the Late Middle Ages," in Diana Wood, ed., *The Church and Sovereignty c. 950–1918*, Studies in Church History Subsidia 9 (Oxford: B. Blackwell, 1991), 395.

5. See the discussion and translated primary texts in Heiko Oberman, *Forerunners of the Reformation* (New York: Holt, Rinehart, & Winston, 1966), 93–119.

6. Michael Goodich, *Violence and Miracle in the Fourteenth Century* (Chicago: University of Chicago Press, 1995) is a good example.

7. Johann Huizinga, *The Autumn of the Middle Ages*, trans. Rodney J. Payton (Chicago: University of Chicago Press, 1996), 174. The popularity of this new translation shows just how attractive this way of thinking about the later Middle Ages remains.

8. André Vauchez, *The Laity in the Middle Ages*, trans. Margery J. Schneider (Notre Dame, IN: University of Notre Dame Press, 1993), 25.

9. Jonathan Sumption, *Pilgrimage* (Totowa, NJ: Rowman & Littlefield, 1975), 144.

10. Vauchez, *Laity*, 25.

11. R. W. Southern, *The Western Church and Society in the Middle Ages* (New York: Penguin, 1970), 141.

12. Christiane Neuhausen, *Das Ablasswesen in der Stadt Köln vom 13. bis zum 16. Jahrhundert* (Cologne: Janus, 1994), 53: "In der Frömmigkeit wurde Quantität höher als Qualität veranschlagt."

13. Huizinga, 156.

14. Vauchez, *Laity*, 13. Cf. Robert E. Lerner, *The Age of Adversity: The Fourteenth Century* (Ithaca, NY: Cornell University Press, 1968), 33.

15. Eamon Duffy, *The Stripping of the Altars: Traditional Religion in England, 1400–1580* (New Haven, CT: Yale University Press, 1992), 72.

16. James Brodrick, *Robert Bellarmine* (London: Burns & Oates, 1961), 148–149.

17. H. J. Grimm, *et al.* ed. and trans., *The Career of the Reformer*, in *Luther's Works* (Philadelphia: Fortress Press, 1955), 31:30. Ninety-Five Theses, no. 56.

18. *Luther's Works*, 31:212. Explanation of the Ninety-Five Theses, no. 58.

19. *Luther's Works*, 31:26. Ninety-Five Theses, no. 26. Indulgences proclaimed *per modum suffragii* differed from other indulgences in that, as the phrase suggests, they were an especially efficacious suffrage of the church applied to those who, although dead, still belonged to the *ecclesia militans*. Indulgences granted to the living were a juridical act on the part of a bishop.

20. *Luther's Works*, 31:162. Explanation of the Ninety-Five Theses, no. 3.

21. *Luther's Works*, 31:28. Ninety-Five Theses, no. 35. That Luther names no specific offenders is noteworthy, since he names intellectual opponents in earlier works such as the Disputation against Scholastic Theology (1515).

22. Eric Cochrane, *Historians and Historiography in the Italian Renaissance* (Chicago: University of Chicago Press, 1981), 458.

23. See Louis B. Pascoe, *Jean Gerson: Principles of Church Reform* (Leiden: E. J. Brill, 1973), and "Jean Gerson: The *ecclesia primitiva* and Reform," *Traditio* 30 (1974), 379–409.

24. Matthias Flacius Illyricus, *Historia ecclesiastica* 13.4 (Basel: I. Oporinum, 1574), 13:391: "Et quia papa plenariam potestatem habet super thesaurum ecclesiae (id quod non extat in sacris litteris), et alii prelati limitatam: ideo solus papa plenariam potestatem habet dandi indulgentiam, episcopi vero secundum eius concessionem."

25. Illyricus, *Historia*, 13.4 (ed. I. Oporinum, 13:26): "Ex scholasticis doctoribus aliquid colligendum est de doctrina. Sed monemus lectorem, nos conatos esse optima ex eis seligere. Verum cum in iis fons Israel sit multo coeno inquinatus, ideo fieri non potuit, quin aliquae sordes etiam influxerint, quia nimirum sententiae omnes non potuere prosus mutilari. Si quid igitur earum sordium prudens lector invenerit, sciat ex lutulentis fluviis non potuisse omnia tam munda proferri: atque autoribus imputet, ac cum iudicio quaelibet censeat esse legenda, videlicet iuxta normam verbi divini. Perplexitatem et monstrositatem, aliaque eius generis nemo miretur, quia monstrosae disputationes eiusmodi theologiam pepererunt."

26. Martin Chemnitz, *Examination of the Council of Trent*, trans. Fred Kramer, vol. 4 (St. Louis: Concordia Publishing House, 1986), 149–150.

27. Chemnitz, 4:156.

28. Chemnitz, 4:189.

29. Cochrane, 457–458.

30. Cochrane, 454.

31. Cochrane, 459.

32. Robert Bellarmine, *De indulgentiis*, preface, in Robert Bellarmine, *Roberti Bellarmini politiani opera omnia*, vol. 7 (Paris: Louis Vivès, 1873), 14.

33. Cochrane, 380.

34. Bellarmine, *De indulgentiis*, 1.1 (*Opera omnia*, 7:16): "Fuit [indulgentia] autem sine ullo dubio jubilaeus Hebraeorum [Lv 25.10] typus et figura Evangelii." Pope Clement VI used the same pericope to justify the Jubilee indulgence for 1300.

35. Bellarmine, *De indulgentiis*, 1.1 (*Opera omnia*, 7:15): "Videtur autem Ecclesia ad hanc rem significandam nomen hoc derivasse ab usu veterum imperatorum, et jureconsultorum. Siquidem illi indulgentiam solemni, proprioque vocabulo appellant remissionem generalem criminum, quam aliquando principes saeculi publicae laetitia causa faciebant."

36. See especially the fund of texts presented by Bellarmine, *De indulgentiis*, 1.3, and 2.18–20 (*Opera omnia*, 7:22–25 and 7:93–99).

37. Bellarmine, *De indulgentiis*, 1.2 (*Opera omnia*, 7:17–22), where a series of texts from Augustine, Cyprian, and John Chrysostom is cited.

38. Bellarmine, *De indulgentiis*, 1.2 (*Opera omnia*, 7:17–18).

39. Bellarmine, *De indulgentiis*, 2.1 (*Opera omnia*, 7:59): "Indulgentiarum thesaurum non carere fundamento scripturarum sanctarum."

40. Bellarmine, *De indulgentiis*, 1.3 (*Opera omnia*, 7:22–23).

41. Bellarmine, *De indulgentiis*, 1.3 (*Opera omnia*, 7:24): "Atque ita vetus etiam Ecclesia ad thesaurum respiciebat cum indulgetias daret." Cf. *De indulgentiis*, 2.18–20 (*Opera omnia*, 7:93–99).

42. Bellarmine, *De indulgentiis*, 2.11 (*Opera omnia*, 7:81): "Ostendimus enim in libro superiore, ex Tertulliano, et Cypriano vetulissimis patribus, necnon ex conciliis antiquissimus, Ancyrano, et Nicaeno, usum indulgentiarum, et proprie sub nomine indulgentiae idem ostendimus ex Gregorio I, Leone I, et Sergio III qui omnes ante annum millesimum ecclesiae praefuerunt."

43. Bellarmine, *De indulgentiis*, 2.17 (*Opera omnia*, 7:91). That letter was included in the Decretals of Gregory IX (X 5.38.4, *Quod autem*).

44. Bellarmine, *De indulgentiis*, 2.17 (*Opera omnia*, 7:91): "Eugenius III Pontifex sedere coepit anno 1145. Is autem per litteras generales concessit indulgentiam accipientibus Crucem, et profiscentibus ad bellum sacrum; et S. Bernardo injunxit, ut eas indulgentias praedicaret populis, eosque ad bellum illud accenderet. Paruit S. Bernardus Pontifici. . . . ut ipse modeste indicat initio libri II. *De consideratione*."

45. Bellarmine, *De indulgentiis*, 1.6 (*Opera omnia*, 7:91): "Defunctis non dicitur dare simpliciter indulgentiam, sed per modum suffragii, quia non ipse, sed deus acceptat compensationem pro defunctis, et eosdem defunctos absolvit." He has also a long consideration of indulgences for the dead in *De indulgentiis*,1.14 (*Opera omnia*, 7:50–56).

46. Bellarmine, *De indulgentiis*, 1.14 (*Opera omnia*, 7:51): "Neque enim (inquit S. Augustinus lib. xx de Civ. Dei c. 9) piorum animae defunctorum ab Ecclesia separantur, quae est regnum Christi." A direct quotation of Augustine's text.

47. Bellarmine, *De indulgentiis*, 1.14 (*Opera omnia*, 7:51): "Praeterea idem probatur ex usu Ecclesiae: constat enim Paschalem Summum Pontificem ante annos 700, concessisse indulgentiam pro defunctis, quae habetur in Ecclesiae S. Praexedis in introitu cappellae S. Zenonis."

48. Marvin R. O'Connell, *The Counter-Reformation, 1559–1610* (New York: Harper & Row, 1974), 359.

49. William Allen, *A Treatise Made in Defense of the Lawful Power and Authoritie of Priesthod to Remitte Sinnes* (Louvain: Apud Ioannem Foulerum, 1567), 251.

50. Eduard Bratke, *Luthers 95 Thesen und ihre dogmenhistorischen Voraussetzungen* (Göttingen: Vandenhoeck & Rupprecht, 1884), 7.

51. A. Wilh. Dieckhoff, *Der Ablaßstreit: Dogmengeschichtliche dargestellt* (Gotha: F. A. Perthes, 1886), v.

52. Adolf Gottlob, *Kreuzablass und Almosenablass: Eine Studie über die Frühzeit des Ablasswesens* (Stuttgart: Ferdinand Enke, 1906), 1.

53. Johannes Dietterle, "Die *Summae confessorum*," *Zeitschrift für Kirchenge-schichte* 24 (1903), 356. Dietterle's study of the *summae* extended to volumes 25 through 27 of the *Zeitschrift*.

54. Henry C. Lea, *A History of Auricular Confession and Indulgences in the Latin Church* (Philadelphia: Lea Brothers, 1896), 3:112–113.

55. Lea, 3:65, 3:234, and 3:296.

56. Lea, 3:403.

57. A. Boudinhon, "Sur l'histoire des indulgences," *Revue d'histoire et de litterature religieuses* 3 (1898), 436–437. H. De Jongh, "Les grandes lignes des indulgences," *La vie diocésaine* 6 (1912), 69–80, is a similar, later monograph with good bibliography in the footnotes.

58. Boudinhon, 448.

59. Boudinhon, 445.

60. A. H. M. Lepicier, *Les indulgences*, 2 vols. (Paris: P. Lethielleux, 1903).

61. Lepicier, 1:ix.

62. Lepicier, 1:67.

63. Lepicier, 1:68.

64. Lepicier, 1:147.

65. Lepicier, vol. 1, chap. 7 and chap. 9.

66. Nikolaus Paulus, *Geschichte des Ablasses im Mittelalter*, 3 vols. (Darmstadt: Primus Verlag, 2000 [reprint of 1922–1923]).

67. *Geschichte*, 1:lxxix–lxxx.

68. Nikolaus Paulus, "Die Ablässe der römischen Kirche vor Innocent III," *Historisches Jahrbuch* 28 (1907), 1–8; "Die ältesten Ablässe für Almosen und Kirchen-besuch," *ZKT* 33 (1909), 1–40; "Die Anfänge des Ablässes," *ZKT* 39 (1915), 193–230; and "Die Bedeutung der älteren Ablässe," *Historische-politische Blätter für das katholische Deutschland* 167 (1921), 15–25.

69. Nikolaus Paulus, "Die Ablaßlehre der Frühscholastik," *ZKT* 34 (1910), 433–472; and "Die Einführung des Kirchenschatzes in die Ablaßtheorie," *Theologie und Glaube* 6 (1914), 284–298.

70. Nikolaus Paulus, "Die Anfänge des sogenannten Ablässes von Schuld und Strafe," *ZKT* 36 (1912), 67–96, 252–279.

71. Nikolaus Paulus, *Indulgences as a Social Factor in the Middle Ages*, trans. J. Elliot Ross (New York: Devin-Adair Co., 1922). The introduction to this book indicates that it was written for a more popular Catholic audience.

72. Such as Bernhard Poschmann, *Der Ablaß im Licht der Bußgeschichte* (Bonn: Peter Hanstein, 1948).

73. *Geschichte*, 1:146–177 discusses the references to indulgences made by the theo-logians and canonists prior to 1250, while *Geschichte*, 1:188–291 (the last third of the first volume) contains the teachings of the theologians and canonists from 1250 to 1350. *Geschichte*, 2:141–158 examines the doctrine of the treasury of merit. *Geschichte*, 3:1–99 contains the teachings of the later medieval theologians and canonists on indulgences.

74. The most ancient indulgences for alms and church visitations are discussed in *Geschichte*, 1:94–133. *Geschichte*, 1:134–144 examines the earliest crusade indulgences. On indulgences for the dead, see *Geschichte*, 2:121–140.

75. Poschmann, *Der Ablaß*, and also his *Penance and the Anointing of the Sick*, trans. Francis Courtney (New York: Herder & Herder, 1951), 210–232. Karl Rahner reviewed the former in *ZKT* 71 (1949), 481–490. See also Francis Courtney, "New Explanations of Indulgences," *Clergy Review* 44 (1959), 464–479, for another examination of Poschmann's latter book.

76. Poschmann, *Der Ablaß*, 43.

77. Poschmann, *Penance*, 211.

78. Poschmann, *Penance*, 219.

79. For the council's decree on ecumenism, see Tanner and Alberigo, 2:908–920.

80. Étienne Delaruelle, *L'église au temps du grand schisme et de la crise conciliare*, vol. 14 in *Histoire de l'église* (Paris: Bloud & Gay, 1962), 812. Some Catholics, both before the Reformation and after, had also suggested that indulgences compromised penitential rigor. Delaruelle's position is notable among Catholic viewpoints for the responsibility he heaped upon indulgences for the impoverishment of medieval devotion.

81. Raymonde Foreville, "L'idée de jubilé chez les théologians et les canonistes (XII–XIIIe s) avant l'institution du jubilé romain (1300)," *Revue d'histoire écclesiastique* 56 (1961), 402.

82. Francis Rapp, "Les pèlerinages dans la vie religieuse de l'occident médiéval aux XIVe et XV siècles," in *Les pèlerinages de l'antiquité biblique et classique à occident médiévale*, ed. Freddy Raphaël, Études d'histoire des religions, vol. 1 (Paris: P. Guenthner, 1973), 138.

83. Southern, 140.

84. Francis Oakley, *The Western Church in the Later Middle Ages* (Ithaca, NY: Cornell University Press, 1979), 123.

85. Richard Kieckhefer, "Holiness and the Culture of Devotion: Remarks on Some Late Medieval Male Saints," in Renate Blumenfeld-Kosinski and Timea Szell, eds., *Images of Sainthood in Medieval Europe* (Ithaca, NY: Cornell University Press, 1991), 290. Robert W. Shaffern, "Indulgences and Saintly Devotionalisms in the Middle Ages," *CHR* 84 (1998), 643–661 was an attempt to consider this question.

86. Lucien Febvre, "The Origins of the French Reformation: A Badly-Put Question?" in P. Burke, ed. and trans., *A New Kind of History* (New York: Harper & Row, 1973), 44–107.

87. Bernd Moeller, "Religious Life in Germany on the Eve of the Reformation," in Gerald Strauss, ed., *Pre-Reformation Germany* (London: Macmillan, 1972), 17–19, and "Piety in Germany around 1500," trans. Joyce Irwin in Steven Ozment, ed., *The Reformation in Medieval Perspective* (Chicago: Quadrangle Books, 1971), 55–56, 63.

88. Louis Cameron, ed., *The Commonplace Book of Robert Reynes of Acle: An Edition of Tanner MS 407* (New York: Garland, 1980), 110–112. Cameron immediately goes on to say that "it is dangerous to apply this term to anything medieval." Then why do so?

89. See Jean Delumeau, *La peur en occident (XIVe–XVIIIe siècles)* (Paris: Hachette Littératures, 1978) and *Sin and Fear: The Emergence of a Western Guilt Culture, 13th–18th Centuries*, trans. Eric Nicholson (New York: St. Martin's Press, 1990).

90. W. J. Bouwsma, "Anxiety and the Formation of Early Modern Culture," in ed. B. Malament, *After the Reformation* (Philadelphia: University of Pennsylvania

Press, 1980), 217–218. Another, very recent contribution to the historical role of fear in late medieval and early modern culture is William G. Naphy and Penny Roberts, eds., *Fear in Early Modern Society* (New York: St. Martin's Press, 1997).

91. Mary C. Mansfield, *The Humiliation of Sinners: Public Penance in Thirteenth-Century France* (Ithaca, NY: Cornell University Press, 1995), 289.

92. Steven Ozment, *The Age of Reform, 1250–1550* (New Haven, CT: Yale University Press, 1980), 218–219. See Thomas N. Tentler, *Sin and Confession on the Eve of the Reformation* (Princeton, NJ: Princeton University Press, 1977), 180–185, for an evaluation of the moral teaching of the pastoral manuals of the late Middle Ages.

93. Joseph Prinz, "Vom mittelalterlichen Ablaßwesen in Westfalen. Ein Beitrag zur Geschichte der Volksfrömmigkeit," *Westfälische Forschungen* 23 (1971), 107–171.

94. Bernhard Schimmelpfennig, "Römische Ablaßfälschungen aus der Mitte des 14. Jahrhunderts," in *Fälschungen im Mittelalter. Internationaler Kongreß der Monumenta Germaniae Historiae, München 16–19. September 1986*, MGH Schriften 33 (Hannover: Hahnsche Buchhandlung, 1998), 5:637–658; Hartmut Boockman, "Ablaßfälschungen im 15. Jahrhundert," in *Fälschungen im Mittelalter*, 5:659–668, and by the same author, "Über Ablaß-'Medien,'" *Geschichte in Wissenschaft und Unterricht* 34 (1983), 709–721.

95. Karlheinz Frankl, "Papstschisma und Frömmigkeit: Die '*ad instar*' Ablässe," *Römische Quartalschrift* 72 (1977), 57–124; 184–247. Neuhausen did much the same in *Das Ablasswesen*, 115–121.

96. Robert W. Shaffern, "Learned Discussions of Indulgences for the Dead in the Middle Ages," *Church History* 61 (1992), 367–381.

97. For an older such study, see Gottlob, *Kreuzablaß und Almosenablaß*, and for a more recent contribution, see Maureen Purcell, *Papal Crusading Policy, 1244–1291* (Leiden: E. J. Brill, 1975).

98. D'Avray, "Papal Authority," 407–408.

99. Walter H. Principe, C.S.B., "The School Theologians' Views of the Papacy, 1150–1250," in Christopher Ryan, ed., *The Religious Roles of the Papacy*, vol. 8 in *Papers in Mediaeval Studies* (Toronto: Pontifical Institute of Medieval Studies, 1989), 65.

100. On corporate Christianity, see Duffy, 131–154, and on the treasury as an expression of the communion of saints, see Ovidio Capitani, "L'indulgenza come espressione teologica della '*communio sanctorum*' e nella formazione della dottrina canonistica," in Alessandro Clementi, ed., *Indulgenza nel medioevo e Perdonanza di Papa Celestino V* (Aquila: Centro celestiano, Sezione storica, 1987), 17–32.

101. Robert W. Shaffern, "Images, Jurisdiction, and the Treasury of Merit," *Journal of Medieval History* 22 (1996), 237–247.

Chapter 2

The Emergence and Variety of Indulgences

Since the Protestant Reformation, the "discovery" of the first indulgences has occupied numerous historians and theologians on both sides of the confessional divide. Some Catholics thought that the early church granted "protoindulgences"—so to speak—while Protestants correctly insisted that no pardons had been granted before the eleventh century. Since they pertain to historical context, however, the first dispensations of indulgences remain an important topic for modern historians. In addition, the extraordinary variety of indulgences in the Middle Ages may also be understood better through a firmer grasp of the first concessions, for later grants of pardon were modelled after and justified on the first remissions. As a new, but not unprecedented, development in eleventh-century Latin Christendom, indulgences grew out of an intersection of new practices and ancient ideas.

Indulgences emerged from the energetic and militant Latin Christianity characteristic of the mid-eleventh century. In the German Empire, aggressive reformers such as Cardinal Humbert of Silva Candida attacked the traditional alliance between church and ruler. The momentum for reform slowly transformed medieval church and society, and resulted in greater church independence from royal or imperial control. The reformers defended the "liberty of the church" (*libertas ecclesiae*) with the arsenal of canon law. With ever greater sophistication, canonists scrutinized and rationalized the rights, privileges, and responsibilities pertinent to every rank of churchman. Burchard, bishop of Worms, had compiled between 1008 and 1012 what came to serve for many years as the definitive collection of Western canon law. The canons, which included scriptural texts, the writings of the Fathers, conciliar decrees, and the letters of the popes, had accumulated over the centuries. In numerous instances, these authorities contradicted each other; consequently they needed to be rationalized. Burchard organized the canons according to subject, so that canonists could see what various authorities had to say about important issues. The arrangements that Burchard imposed on these materials tended to support the claims of church reformers.

At the same time, movements for monastic renewal proliferated. A succession of movements to renew Western monastic observance had already begun in the ninth century. Emperor Louis the Pious (814–843) entrusted his reform agenda to Benedict of Aniane, who replaced all other monastic rules in the Carolingian Empire with the Rule of St. Benedict of Nursia. In the following century, Duke William of Aquitaine stirred up another wave of reform when he founded the monastery of Cluny in 910. In the foundation charter of that famous monastery, which became the spiritual center of Latin Christendom for two centuries, Duke William renounced his overlordship over the monks and placed them directly under the protection of the pope. Cluny became one model for professed religious eager to throw off the burdens of feudal obligations. In the early eleventh century, an eremitical movement flourished. Spiritual giants such as Romuald (c. 950–1027) and Peter Damian (1007–1072) fled into the wildernesses to imitate the Apostles in silent, solitary reflection. The monastic reformers influenced the whole Church, since the monk, unstained by contact with the world and, as such, long revered as the exemplar of the perfect Christian, now served as the model for all priests and bishops. Reforming monks thundered against simony and clerical marriage among diocesan clergy.

By the middle of the eleventh century, emperors and popes took over the leadership of the church reform movements. The pious emperor Henry III (1039–1056) defeated the noble Roman families that had made the papacy a prize for the winners of their feuds. In 1046, he deposed three rival claimants for the chair of St. Peter. Three years later, he elevated his cousin Bruno of Toul to the papacy (Leo IX, 1049–1054). Together, emperor and pope worked to eliminate simony and clerical marriage. In the next generation, of course, reform leaders such as Cardinal Humbert and Pope Gregory VII (1073–1085) added lay investiture to the list of crimes against the church. Gregory and his allies fought a war not only with arms but also with ideas, against Emperor Henry IV (1056–1106). This conflict marked only the first of many great battles between church and crown in the High Middle Ages.

The eleventh-century reformers—whether monastic, papal, or imperial—all shared the conviction that Christendom must be remade through a renewed emphasis, ultimately grounded in the Gospels, on interior devotion to the human Jesus, for a fallen world could be renewed only if the followers of Christ had overcome the consequences of original sin within their own hearts and souls. Only the spiritually regenerated could establish the New

Jerusalem. Thus, the eleventh-century spiritual vanguard insisted upon a sincere desire to imitate Christ (*imitatio Christi*) and live a life of apostolic simplicity (*vita apostolica*). Reformers insisted on a more rigorous formation for those charged with the ministration of the sacraments, upon which depended the salvation of the faithful. No man could truly be accepted as priest or bishop who had purchased, or inherited, or received as a political favor his benefice. Rather, priests and bishops must freely choose to serve the church; only then could they serve as examples of Christian virtue to their charges. A penitential regimen of continual self-examination properly prepared the clergy for their sacramental ministrations. The first dispensation of indulgences took place within this relentlessly self-critical age.

THE TRADITION OF THE PENITENTIAL REGIME

The eleventh-century reformers, of course, claimed that they advocated nothing new, and, in fact, they abhorred innovation. Rather, they wanted to restore the customs, worship, and zeal of the primitive church, and they cited antique precedents in favor of their agenda. Reformers sometimes spoke of rediscovering the rigor of the early penitential regime. Many modern historians, captivated by the powerful rhetoric of the reformers, have overplayed the differences between the medieval and late antique penitential regimes, both of which were much more preoccupied with the cultivation of interior discipline than has generally been appreciated. To be sure, some innovations were introduced in the eleventh century, but those innovations presumed, rather than replaced, most inheritances from the Roman, Carolingian, or Ottonian eras. In the high medieval church, ancient customs coexisted with recent developments and created the patchwork of parallel and overlapping practices characteristic of high medieval Catholicism. Like their late antique predecessors, for instance, thirteenth-century French bishops imposed public penances, although private confessions had long been heard as well.[1] Thus, as Catholic apologists have long, and correctly, maintained, the bishops who granted the first indulgences relied on long-standing traditions of the church.

From the earliest times, serious sinners were reconciled to the Christian church after confession of guilt and completion of the penance then enjoined by the confessor (in antiquity, usually the bishop). The antique church recommended confession and penance only for those who had committed serious sins (renunciation of the faith, for instance, even if compelled by threat of harm from Roman imperial authorities). Church law and custom permitted bishops to impose greater or lesser penances at their discretion. When Pope Leo I (440–461) recommended that penances be based on the disposition of individual penitents, he merely reaffirmed an already ancient practice.[2] Pope Innocent I (401–417) wrote that "it belongs to the priest to pass judgement when there is question of weighing the seriousness of sins, as is natural in one who listens to the penitent's confession and the weeping and tears of the one making amendment."[3] Pope St. Gregory I in *De cura pastorali* taught pastors to mind the differences among those charged to their spiritual care.[4] Truly contrite sinners deserved lenient penances, but a more rigorous judgment should be imposed on the lukewarm. Lesser penances, of course, might mean that enough satisfaction for sin might not be made, in which case the intercessions of the church, and in particular the merits of the martyrs, were believed to make up the "difference" between "how much" penance *should be*, versus what *had been*, imposed.

The penitential manuals of early medieval Ireland and England preserved and enriched the penitential regime of the late Roman imperial Church. How the penitentials were used—perhaps as reference books—remains shrouded in mystery, but that they represent continuity between the penitential regimes of late antiquity and the early Middle Ages is beyond doubt. Essentially, the penitentials consist of lists of sins with the appropriate penances. Like Leo I and Innocent I, they recommend that the severity of the penance reflect the gravity of the sin; they also consider the interior disposition and the legal status of the penitent. Whereas the late antique penitential regime was confined to grave sins, the penitentials also included penances for lesser sins. The penitential of Finnian (written in Ireland between 525 and 550), for instance, recommended a penance of six years for practicing magical deception. For the first three years of the penance, the confessed was to eat only bread and water. During the second three years, he had also to abstain from meat and wine. If, however, the magician "does not mislead anyone but gives [a potion] for the sake of wanton love to some one, he shall do penance for an entire year on an allowance of bread and water."[5] The author of Finnian's penitential, then, deemed thoughtful deception, which came from a wicked mind, a more heinous sin than abetting concupiscence, a weakness of the flesh. The penitential suggested that confessors examine intentions, as well as actions: "If anyone has thought evil and intended to do it, but opportunity has failed him, it is the same sin, but not the same penalty."[6] Most penitentials prescribed harsher penances for sinful clerics, whose souls should have been disciplined by the monastic life, than wayward laymen, whose continual exposure to the temptations of the world inevitably led into sin: "If anyone has started a quarrel and plotted in his heart to strike or kill his neighbor, if [the offender] is a cleric, he shall do penance for half a year with an allowance of bread and water and for a whole year abstain from wine and meats . . . but if he is a layman, he shall do penance for a week, since he is a man of this world and his guilt is lighter in this world and his reward less in the world to come."[7] Less should be expected of the laity than of monks, and mercy more quickly extended to those imperilled by the evils of the world. Finnian's penitential also assumed that penance not only satisfied the penalty of sins already committed but also served as a remedy against sinning again in the future, an idea that passed into medieval penitential theory.[8]

Scholars have often claimed that the penitentials contributed to a mechanistic approach to the imposition of penances, and that the penitentials evince little concern for the interior disposition of penitents. This argument assumes that, upon hearing a confession, the priest would look up the confessed sins in the penitential and pluck out the adjoining penances. The difficulty with these arguments is that no one has yet been able to demonstrate how confessors used penitentials. Furthermore, "it is difficult to know how anyone who had read the penitentials could suggest that they promoted an automatic, mechanical imposition of predetermined penances in disregard of the personal status of the penitent. There is not a shred of evidence to support the claim, and overwhelming evidence to the contrary in the penitentials themselves."[9] For instance, the penitentials recommended that two penitents who had committed the same sin might not deserve the same penance, since one might plainly display greater contrition than the other. Circumstances—health, age, or status, for example—might mitigate penances. Penances for monks, for instance, were more severe than for laymen. The authors of the penitentials, then, had an acute interest in, sympathy for, and understanding of, the various psychological and spiritual conditions of penitents. The writers of the penitentials were convinced that the commission of a premeditated sin involved a greater wickedness than a transgression committed in the heat of passion. After all, the authors of the penitentials were monks whose very lives enjoined constant examination of conscience. The penitentials' authors, then, studied the interior disposition of penitents as vigilantly as had the Fathers of late antiquity. Indeed, the genre of the penitentials might best be understood as a tradition of commentary on the patristic teaching concerning reconciliation and atonement.

The early medieval penitential regime also inherited from the late antique church the belief that without the aid of the universal church, few penitents would be able to satisfy their debt of penalty for sin. The liturgy itself, derived from Scripture, attested to each Christian's need for the prayers of the universal church. According to the Gelasian penitential liturgy (compiled c. 680), which was celebrated on Ash Wednesday, the pope prayed thus while penitents lay prostrate before him: "Let thy mercy, we beseech Thee, O Lord, be of assistance to this thy servant, and with speedy indulgence may all his iniquities be wiped away . . . be propitious, O Lord, to our supplications, nor let Thy merciful clemency be far from this Thy servant."[10] The deacon and pope offered similar prayers on Holy Thursday.[11] The penitential liturgy of the Roman pontifical, also celebrated on Holy Thursday, concluded with the pope's intercession for the absolution of the penitents. The pope sprinkled the contrite with holy water and offered incense over them while offering this prayer: "Through the entreaties and merits of Blessed Mary may the Almighty and Merciful God save and strengthen you in every good work. . . . May the almighty and merciful God grant you pardon (*indulgentiam*), absolution, and remission of all your sins."[12] Finally, the Roman penitential of Halitgar (c. 830), derived in part from Celtic and English sources, called on all the faithful to fast along with those who had accepted fasting as an enjoined penance.[13]

In the Carolingian and Ottonian churches, aid for penitents often took the form of the absolution. The Latin word *absolutio* was used to name a document and a rite, both of which had the same purpose. As document, an absolution was the written pledge of a bishop to invoke the intercession of the Church on a penitent's behalf. As a rite, the absolution was a set of prayers wherein bishops begged that God remit the penalty of the confessed. Bishops usually granted absolutions—whether as document or as rite—during the liturgy; documents could otherwise also be issued within the text of letters. Most absolutions that survive were offered on behalf of the mortally ill, who feared they would die before the completion of their imposed penances, and so be unfit for heaven. In 872, the west Frankish king Charles the Bald (843–877) wrote to Robert, bishop of Le Mans, asking for an absolution for his sins. Charles feared for the state of his soul because he had become seriously ill, but had not yet completed all his imposed penances. Robert returned to the king a letter of absolution in which he begged God to grant Charles, whom the letter says had made his confession, the remission of all his sins.[14] When Hildebold, bishop of Soissons, contracted a grave illness, he requested an absolution from Hincmar, the bishop of Rheims. Hincmar answered him:

> Since you have sent me your presbyter and forwarded again your confessional brief (*breviculum*), asking that I send on to you a letter of absolution (*absolutorias litteras*), I have gladly taken this as evidence of your devotion . . . animated by these divine sentiments, to you, Hildebold, our brother and fellow-priest, who have confessed your sins, by the ecclesiastical power of our apostolic authority, which our Lord Jesus Christ handed on to His disciples and apostles . . . by His grace and omnipotence, in

the power of the Holy Spirit, who is the remission of all sins, may He forgive you all your sins, deliver you from all evil, preserve you in all good, and lead you to life eternal and the fellowship of holy priests.[15]

In Hincmar's letter may be found two features that would later be characteristic of indulgences. First, absolutions benefitted only confessed penitents. Second, Hincmar's grant of absolution originated *with the receiver not the grantor*. The idea of sending an absolution was Hildebold's, not Hincmar, who thus prefaced his absolution: "when I learned that our brother Hodo was going to visit you, *I did not think it necessary to send you a letter*, since his sentiments are the same as mine, and possessing the episcopal ministry, he could personally do for a sick brother what needed to be done."[16] Hincmar, then, had no intention of granting an absolution. Because of his mortal peril, however, Hildebold feared he might die without having satisfied God's anger and justice; he needed the help of fellow Christians, which would enable him to stand confidently before the judgement seat of the Almighty. Hincmar understood Hildebold's very request for an absolution as proof of sorrow for his sins. For Hincmar, the act of asking for an absolution testified to interior regret for sin.

Frail health was but one reason Carolingian penitents desired the intercessions of the church. Like their Celtic forerunners, the penitentials of the Carolingian era recommended long penances. The Burgundian penitential (c. 700–725), for instance, prescribed a penance of five years for involuntary homicide and a penance of seven years for perjury.[17] The St. Hubert penitential (c. 850) called for a penance of five years for taking a goddaughter or god-sister in marriage.[18] The Roman penitential (c. 830) recommended a penance of five years for theft (seven if a cleric), and of seven years for graverobbing; in either case the penitent could eat nothing but bread and water for three years out of the total.[19] These penances suggest a penitential system inclined to severity. Since absolutions mitigated that severity, they may also have encouraged many, who were otherwise disinclined, to make confessions and accept penance.

By the Ottonian period, absolutions took on two types, both of which were issued as documents, not rites. The general absolution was offered to any confessed who would complete a pious work determined by the grantor of the absolution. By and large, earlier absolutions were granted individually (as in the cases of Charles the Bald and Hildebold) to great lay and ecclesiastical lords. Nonetheless, anyone who completed the prescribed work could benefit from a general absolution. Pope Stephen VIII, for instance, in 941 proclaimed an absolution for contributions to the repair of a convent in Buxer.[20]

A second type of absolution was offered on behalf of the dead. The statutes of Lanfranc, a ninth-century Benedictine liturgical text, ordered that
after a deceased monk had been placed in the grave, an absolution should be
read to the brethren; then, the document itself should be placed on the breast
of the deceased. Another such absolution survives in a Benedictine burial
liturgy, offered for a dead brother named Elias: "May the Lord God
Almighty, who gave to his holy apostles the power of binding and loosing,
himself deign to absolve thee, brother Elias, of all thy sins; and in so far as it
is allowed my frailty, mayest thou stand absolved before the countenance of
him who lives and reigns world without end."[21]

In addition to the absolution, the Carolingian church offered yet another
aid to penitents—the redemption (*redemptio*), sometimes also called an
equivalence or commutation. Redemptions, another Carolingian inheritance
from the Irish penitentials, simply transformed long, difficult penances into
shorter, easier ones. Many late Carolingian penitentials contained whole
chapters devoted to redemptions, such as the *Ecclesiastical discipline* of
Regino of Prüm (c. 906):

> ccccli. *Of the equivalent of one day.*—But the equivalent of one day [of penance] is a
> meal for two or three poor men, or one denarius. Some prescribe a whole psalter in
> summer; however, in winter, spring, or autumn, fifty psalms. Some prescribe twelve
> stripes or strokes.
>   *Again, of the commutation of one day.*—Therefore, he who can fulfill what is written
> in the penitential shall give thanks to God. But to him who cannot complete it, we give
> advice through the mercy of God. First, for one day on bread and water let him sing
> fifty psalms kneeling, or seventy, standing in a single place, or give one denarius, or
> feed three poor men. Some say fifty strokes, or fifty psalms, for one day in fall, winter
> or spring, or in spring a hundred strokes or fifty psalms; in summer one psalter or a
> hundred strokes.
>   *Of the commutation of three years.*—He who is not able to do penance as we have
> said above in the first year shall expend in alms twenty-six *solidi*, in the second year,
> twenty, in the third, eighteen; this comes to sixty-four *solidi*.[22]

Redemptions commonly commuted periods of fasting into some other form
of penance, since the lack of food might endanger the health of some penitents. As the *Ecclesiastical discipline* indicates, alms for the poor figured
prominently as substitutes for other penitential works; in later centuries,
indulgences would make a similar commutation. The completion of a
redemption was believed to equal the obligation to complete all imposed
penances.

A conciliar decree testifies to the popularity of redemptions in the late
Carolingian period. In 923, a council met in Rheims, the sole purpose

of which seems to have been the imposition of penances on warriors. The bishops

> decreed this enjoined penance on those who personally took a life during the war between Robert and Charles, namely, that they do penance for three Lents over the course of three years, such that for the first Lent they should be outside the church, and would be reconciled to the Eucharist. Each of the warriors, during each Lent, shall consume only bread, salt, and water on the second, fourth, and sixth days of the week, *unless they shall be redeemed.* Likewise, they shall abstain during the fifteen days before the feast of the nativity of John the Baptist [24 June], and the fifteen days before Christmas, as well as all of Holy Week, *unless they shall be redeemed.* [23]

The bishops assumed that some warriors first would confess that they had killed the enemy, and that some of them then would obtain redemptions to reduce their penances for having shed Christian blood. Soldiers probably desired redemptions more than churchmen or rustics. Mortally wounded warriors, certain to die before completing their penances, would at least have the motivation of fear. Other troops would have desired them because subsequent campaigns or administrative responsibilities made the completion of penances inconvenient. The sick could not fast and recover health. Whatever the reason for obtaining either redemptions or absolutions, the increasing petitions for such aids reveals a growing familiarity with elementary Christian ideas about sin and atonement in the late Carolingian period.

Later Carolingian penitentials contain more redemptions than earlier ones, which suggests an increasing desire over time for a more convenient, indeed reasonable, penitential regime. Other evidence confirms this impression. Several Carolingian councils denounced a general retreat from the severity of the ancient penitential canons; the blame was laid at the feet of confessors who used penitentials, with their lists of redemptions. The Council of Chalons (813) fretted that the manuals had been responsible for the slaying of "souls which should not have died and saved souls alive which should not have lived" (Ez 13.19), because confessors "inflict certain light and strange sentences of penance for grave sins." The bishops complained that although penitentials were anonymous, full of errors, and lacking authority, confessors preferred them to the canons. The bishops wanted confessors to employ the authority of Scripture and the ancient penitential canons, which recommended harsher penances.[24] In 829, the Council of Paris called for the abolition of the penitentials

> since they are opposed to the authority of the [ancient penitential] canons. For many priests, partly by carelessness, partly by ignorance, impose the measure of penance upon those who confess their state of sin at variance with what the canonical laws

decree, making use, forsooth, of certain booklets written in opposition to canonical authority, which they call "penitentials," and on account of this they do not cure the wounds of sinners but rather bathe and stroke them . . . to all of us in common it seemed salutary that each one of the bishops in his diocese diligently seek out these erroneous booklets and, when they are found, give them to the flames, that through them unskilled priests may no longer deceive men.[25]

Such condemnations failed to prevent either the use or the composition of penitentials, which were only superceded by the confessors' manuals of the High Middle Ages. The reason for their longevity as a genre of religious literature must be that the manuals somehow served confessors and penitents reasonably well. While current scholarship offers no firm answers, educated speculation may provide reasonable educated guesses as to their impact. For one, whether they were so used or not, the penitentials offered confessors a reasonably coherent set of guidelines that were sensitive to the spiritual needs of a variety of penitents. For another, their mitigation of early penitential severity made possible the devotion characteristic of the High and Late Middle Ages, which featured the regular undertaking of penitential satisfaction.

By the beginning of the eleventh century, then, the penitential regime that gave birth to indulgences had already been in place for about one hundred and fifty years; certain aspects of that regime were much older than that. Sinners who wished to be reconciled to the Church needed first to confess their sins to a priest, who would then impose a penance, the completion of which was believed to restore fully the penitent to the church and to God. Confessors had long been taught to take penitents' individual needs, such as health and status, into consideration. They also had guidelines, such as the penitential canons and the penitentials, to help them assign the best penances. Since the debt of serious sin was thought great, many penitents believed that without the intercession of the universal Church, they could not hope to complete their penances. That intercession often took the form of absolutions and redemptions. Absolutions petitioned God to render a penitent's debt settled, while redemptions transformed one satisfactory work into another. Commonly, redemptions changed fasting into either prayer or almsgiving.

THE FIRST INDULGENCES
Given the penitential regime of the Carolingian and Ottonian eras, the first indulgences marked an incremental development in the history of penitence in the Western Church, as Thomas Tentler stated: "When we consider the true meaning of indulgences, it becomes clear that far from representing a

radical departure from the older discipline, they manage to preserve that mentality with some success. For indulgences are couched in the language of the penitential canons . . . in other words, indulgences imply that the old discipline was accurate in its estimate of the bill of suffering to be paid for sin."[26] Every inheritance from the Carolingian penitential regimen may be found in each grant of indulgence—confession, imposition of penance, the commutation of penance by competent church authority.

Indeed, the words used to name the first indulgences were borrowed from the earlier regimen. The first indulgences were known as *remissiones, absolutiones,* or *relaxationes,* meaning either a "letting up" of the days, weeks, months, and years of fasting or prayer enjoined on penitents, or a transformation of those penitential exercises into another form.[27] The word *indulgentia,* which only became common at the end of the twelfth century, was borrowed from Roman law, where the word referred to the Christian emperors' customary cancellation of criminals' penalties at Eastertide.[28] Even after *indulgentia* became the preferred name, the older nomenclature coexisted with the new.[29]

Indulgences, however, differed from the Carolingian absolutions and redemptions in one crucial respect. The absolution, whether in the form of a rite or a document, was cast in the language of intercession. The bishop, while expressing confidence that the absolution would be efficacious, nonetheless petitioned God to remit penance. Indulgences, which invoked the authority of the saints (particularly Peter and Paul, as well as the Blessed Mother) and of the martyrs, declared the penance remitted, provided the requirements of confession, contrition, and the performance of some good work were met. In the absolution, the bishop offered a prayer; in an indulgence, the bishop exercised the *jurisdiction* that had been handed down to him from the apostles. Indulgences, then, were an offshoot of the canonistic vine climbing up the eleventh-century Church.[30]

The first indulgences, however, were more than a new legal device; they were part and parcel of new, or renewed, wellsprings of religious devotion. Pilgrimage first became a favorite work of piety and penitence in the fourth century. Many late antique Christians, such as the famous Egeria, travelled great distances to visit the holy places in Palestine, where they prayed at Jesus's tomb and the site of his resurrection. The collapse of the western Roman Empire, the onslaught of the Muslim Arabs, and the collapse of the Carolingian Empire interrupted the parade of Latin Christians to the Holy Land. By the eleventh century, travel had become somewhat safer, and many Christians once again took to the seas and highways to visit holy shrines and make amends for their transgressions—the bellicose Fulk Nerra, count of Anjou (from 987–1040), made the pilgrimage to Jerusalem three times, the last when he was in his mid-sixties, to make satisfaction for a lifetime spent in the shedding of Christian blood. Indeed, in the religious imagination of the West, indulgences never lost their close connection to pilgrimage, which in subsequent centuries served as a favorite metaphor for other indulgenced works of piety—crusade, observance of the Truce of God, bridge-building, church-building, prayer, as well as alms-giving to hospitals and schools.

The first verifiable indulgences were granted in the south of France, for making pilgrimage to churches or abbeys.[31] Reports of these pilgrimage indulgences date from the first half of the eleventh century. Mabillon recorded the following (from 1029, but without documentary corroboration):

> We shall grant absolution from all great and minor sins, thus releasing penitents who shall come to the church of the Psalmody, from their obligation of three days' fasting each week to one day, so that if someone should die before forty days of penance are over, he may be rendered free from all sin that has been confessed to a priest.[32]

Like a redemption, this proclamation reduces three days' fasting to one, and thereby illustrates the dependence of the first indulgences on the earlier penitential regimen. However, it differs from a redemption in key respects. First, there is no guideline for commutations, only the concession of several bishops, who declared on their own authority a reduction of the pilgrims' penance, probably in response to a request from the monks of the monastery to which the church of the Psalmody was attached. Again, this grant also resembles some Carolingian absolutions, but the language is juridical, not intercessory. So, the text, if as authentic as Mabillon thought, preserves an early indulgence—a remission of temporal penalty for sin granted through the episcopal authority of the Catholic Church.

A more reliable source dates from only six years later. In 1035, the four bishops who consecrated the monastery church of San Pedro de Postilla in Spain promulgated what Paulus believed to be the first authentic and verifiable indulgence:

> And I, Wifred, archbishop of the holy see of Narbonne, with the bishop Raimballus, of most holy life, of the holy see of Arles, with seventeen other bishops gathered for council in Narbonne, at the request of the venerable man Wilfred, who is founder of the new church, for the love of God and the honor of St. Peter, first in honor among the Apostles, we grant establishment to the church of St. Peter de Postilla, that any obedient man or woman . . . who shall visit . . . the aforesaid church for the remission of their sins, or who shall make a contribution thereto out of their own property, or shall provide candles, in an amount that the price is able to be estimated of one denarius, by the authority of God and of ourselves, shall be remitted from one serious sin—which is

much feared, and moreover calls for great penance. We also ordain that any of the faithful who persevere in the worship of God during the whole of Lent, and hold a lamp in the church of St. Peter for the whole forty days, or who shall there for some reason so persevere for at least part of each of the days of Lent, and so hold his lamp enough time on each day in Lent, if he has a penance of three days or of two days and certainly of one day, for the love of God and the honor of St. Peter, we absolve from three days, two days, and one day, over the whole of the forty days. If, however, someone does penance for the remission of sins, such that he wishes to go to the church of St. Peter, and then to the said monastery of St. Peter a pilgrim shall take pains to come seven times with candles of his own, he shall benefit so much, just as if he had taken a pilgrimage of great length. Again, anyone who wishes to go there, and merits the grace of God, shall be freed of everything by our affirmation and absolution.[33]

The bishops here exercised their jurisdiction more explicitly than in Mabillon's report, since their authority causes the reduction of the penance. Further, the bishops here called this exercise of their power and authority a constitution (*constitutio*), a legal term borrowed from the Roman emperors, which implied a legally binding proclamation of authority that set aright the affairs of (in this case) the Church, thus serving the chief aim of the eleventh-century church reform.

Pilgrims confronted many dangers, and endured much suffering. The medieval countryside harbored numerous thieves and murderers eager to prey on travelers. For safety's sake, pilgrims journeyed in crowds, as in Chaucer's *Canterbury Tales*. Sickness, especially away from hearth and home, likewise threatened the lives of pilgrims, to say nothing of thirst and hunger. Indeed, suffering made pilgrimage the most efficacious of penitential works, for pilgrims imitated Christ's journey to Calvary itself. The most dangerous of all travel for religious purposes in the Middle Ages were the Crusades. Crusaders expected all the trials that other pilgrims encountered, and more. Their journeys were just as harrowing, and climaxed in mortal combat with the infidel. Many survivors of travel and battle returned home to estates that had been ruined in their absence. Indulgences and the crusade were inextricably linked together; indeed, a war could scarcely be considered a crusade without a grant of remission. The association between full remission of sin (plenary indulgence) and the crusade lasted until the end of the crusading era. Several studies have pointed out that, in itself, warmaking against the infidel was not considered a crusade, but that a grant of full pardon for the campaign was also necessary.[34] To be sure, crusaders enjoyed many privileges, but "of all . . . spiritual privileges, by far the most important by any standard of measurement was the crusade indulgence. Indeed, the granting of this indulgence for any expedition may well be considered to define it as a crusade; expeditions for which it was not given can scarcely be considered crusades at all."[35] In 1063, Pope Alexander II granted the very first crusade indulgence to warriors who fought the Muslims in Spain:

> In paternal charity, we encourage those who resolve to make the journey to Spain, so that what they thought divinely inspired to embark upon, they may care for with the greatest sollicitude; let him confess to his bishop or to his spiritual advisor according to the seriousness of his sins, and the rigor of penance shall be imposed by the confessors, lest the devil be able to level the charge of impenitence. We, therefore, attending with prayer, by the authority of the blessed apostles Peter and Paul, grant them remission of sins and release from penance.[36]

Thirty-two years later, at the Council of Clermont, Pope Urban II offered a full remission to warriors who would fight to recover the Holy Land—the First Crusade, which culminated in the conquest of Jerusalem in 1099: "Whoever will go to the Holy Land in order to liberate the church of Jerusalem solely out of devotion, not for the collection of money or honor, may be absolved from all penance."[37] The following year, Urban extended the same indulgence to Bolognese who joined the expedition, "seeing that they have committed their property and their persons out of love of God and their neighbor."[38]

Some recent scholarship has argued that what Urban conceded to the warriors assembled at Clermont differed fundamentally from later grants of indulgence, and that a good deal of confusion attended Urban's grant of pardon. Jonathan Riley-Smith, for instance, has correctly pointed out that conceptualizations of indulgences did change from the era of the First Crusade to that of Innocent III.[39] However, other scholars have drawn starker distinctions: "what Urban did not offer was the later medieval indulgence." In this view, later indulgences depended upon the teaching of the treasury of merit, from which bishops distributed spiritual benefits to validly confessed penitents. "This developed idea presupposed a clear distinction between the punishment which attached to sin—in this world and in the afterlife prior to entry in into heaven—and the guilt of sin, which could be forgiven through sacramental absolution."[40] Another account claimed that "the distinction between penance and punishment was not fully or clearly grasped by pontiffs, theologians, or canonists in the twelfth and early thirteenth centuries."[41] Still another view holds that the pardon attached to the First Crusade might well be understood in more than one way.[42]

While academic sacramental theologians had not yet elucidated the distinction between guilt (*culpa*) and penalty (*pena*), nor systematized the teaching of the treasury of merit, still the similarities between the grants of Alexander II and Urban II, on the one hand, and those of their successors, on the other, are rather more striking than the differences. Both the earlier and the later popes granted a remission of the penalty that remained after valid confession. In 1096, Pope Urban II's letter to the Bolognese clergy clearly insists upon confession as requisite to the spiritual benefits of the crusade: "By as much as our authority, as of all the archbishops and bishops who are in France, we shall remit all penance for sin, for which shall be made a true and perfect confession, through the mercy of almighty God and the prayers of the Catholic Church, since the crusaders will risk their belongings and their persons for love of God and neighbor."[43] The crusaders must have had a similar understanding of the crusade indulgence, for the chroniclers of the crusades report that the warriors believed that taking up the cross wiped clean their spiritual slate. Robert the Monk and Fulcher of Chartres both wrote that crusaders would receive eternal life for their efforts. During the era of the Second Crusade, Bernard of Clairvaux preached that taking up the cross was "worth the Kingdom of God."[44] Whatever the popes' grants may have been called, there was general understanding that those grants benefitted only those who had confessed, and that they constituted a full cancellation of the debt of sin. Thus did José Goñi Gaztambide, who affirmed the authenticity of Alexander II's bull, assert that that pope "granted a plenary indulgence . . . in the strict sense." In his recent study of the Spanish *Reconquista*, Joseph F. O'Callaghan added that "there seems no significant difference, therefore, between [Alexander's] concession to 'the knights destined to set out for Spain' and later bulls of crusade to the Holy Land."[45]

The crusaders' motivations confound modern ways of thinking. Simply put, like the monastic reformers, the crusaders wanted to imitate Christ. For monks and commoners, the imitation of Christ meant fasting or praying, as it did for the warriors of Latin Christendom. But in addition, these warriors would also wield the sword in defense of fellow Christians, and of the holy sites of Christendom; they would endure patiently all the suffering— hunger, weariness, pain, and death—that war and the enemy would inflict upon them. One account of Urban's sermon at Clermont said that the pope reminded his audience of Christ's words "he that loveth father or mother more than me is not worthy of me. And everyone that hath left house or father or mother or wife or children or lands for my name's sake shall receive an hundredfold and shall possess life everlasting (Mt 10.37 and 19.29)."[46] The anonymous author of the *Gesta francorum* wrote that Urban struck a devotional chord with his contemporaries, for "there was a great stirring throughout the whole region of Gaul, so that if anyone, with a pure heart and mind, seriously wanted to follow God and faithfully wished to bear the cross after him, he could make no delay in speedily taking the road to the Holy Sepulchre."[47] As feudal warriors these men owed the deepest sentiments of love and zeal to counts, dukes, and kings. As crusaders, those sentiments would also be offered to Christ, their brother, who had lost his inheritance, his patrimony, the Holy Land, to the infidel. The lovers of Christ were obliged to recover the land sanctified by His footsteps, even at the risk of their own lives.[48] Crusaders also believed that the Gospel injunction to love neighbor demanded making war upon the infidel, who had murdered and despoiled the Christians of the East.[49] Urban went so far, according to one account of Clermont, to call Eastern Christians, "your own blood-brothers, your companions, your associates (for you are sons of the same Christ and the Church)."[50] The infidel jeopardized the salvation of many Christians, for their impious swords imperilled all pilgrims to Jerusalem. Now, the sword of the crusaders could once again make the way safe and could help secure salvation for themselves and their brother Christians.[51] Like the church reformers of the eleventh century, the crusaders intended to set aright the order of the world, and since they freely accepted great danger, as well as personal despoliation, the pope (as all accounts of Clermont agree) rewarded them with plenary indulgence—a full remission of penalty. One study of the Fifth Crusade has argued that by the beginning of the thirteenth century, the crusades had been fully integrated into the penitential regime of the church.[52] The motivations of the earliest crusaders suggest that the penitential regime and the crusading movement were united at the outset.

Indeed, zeal, rather than conquest or plunder, compelled most warriors to "take up the cross." Like pilgrimage, crusade involved travel to remote, strange, and often dangerous places. Pilgrims and crusaders risked both life and property, for highwaymen terrorized the roads, and native populations understandably feared these foreigners, who might plunder them for supplies. Of course, the crusaders exposed themselves to even greater dangers than other pilgrims. Only a handful of the most powerful crusading lords seized new lands in the East. Most of the crusaders returned to ruined lands and homes, for despite the popes' protection of their property in their absence, enemies back at home often seized or destroyed crusaders' estates. Enemies were not the only threat to the crusaders' patrimonies. Relatives financed the crusaders, sometimes to the point of impoverishment.[53] Even the sincerity of the mercenaries in the crusading ranks should not be doubted, for only as a mercenary could the humblest man-at-arms afford to serve, since the cost to participate in a crusade amounted to about *five times the average annual income* for a knight.[54] Mercenary captains generally paid soldiers out of plunder, which was harder to come by on a crusade. Like the feudal warriors, then, paid soldiers returned from the Holy Land poorer than when they had left. The only benefits most crusaders gained were spiritual.

Some crusaders themselves testified to their desire for conversion and the satisfaction of God's justice. Tancred (1075/76–1112), the south Italian Norman, often wrestled with remorse for having shed Christian blood in war. The benefits of the crusade indulgence itself contributed to his conversion from feudal warrior to knight of Christ:

> Frequently [Tancred] burned with anxiety because the warfare he engaged in as a knight seemed to be contrary to the Lord's commands . . . but after the judgment of Pope Urban granted him remission of all their sins to all Christians going out to fight the gentiles, then at last, as if previously asleep, his vigour was aroused, his powers grew, his eyes opened, his courage was born. For before . . . his mind was divided, uncertain whether to follow in the footsteps of the Gospel or the world.[55]

A knight by the name of Nivelo likewise suffered guilt for having killed, beaten, and plundered Christians during feudal wars:

> I, Nivelo, raised in a nobility of birth which produces in many people an ignobility of mind, for the redemption of my soul and in exchange for a great sum of money given for this, renounce for ever in favour of St. Peter the oppressive behaviour resulting from a certain bad custom, handed on to me not by ancient right but from the time of my father, a man of little weight who first harassed the poor with this oppression . . . in order to obtain the pardon for my crimes which God can give me, I am going on pilgrimage [i.e. crusade] to Jerusalem which until now has been enslaved with her sons. . . .[56]

The sermons of later preachers of crusade also betray the essentially religious aims of crusaders. With the emergence of a liturgy wherein warriors took up the cross (thus becoming *crucesignati*) both figuratively and literally—by having a cross sewn onto their tunics—crusaders imitated Christ and participated in his suffering and death for love of fellow Christians. Around 1212, James of Vitry preached that the crusade stood as an *outward* sign of the *inward* acceptance of the cross, that is, the very willingness to fight in crusade was proof that the warrior's interior disposition had fundamentally altered.[57] Indeed, the religious motivations of the later crusaders may well have been stronger than their predecessors. Because of the rapidly escalating costs of war, the crusades became increasingly ruinous. Furthermore, by the Fifth Crusade (1213), Christendom's military record against Islam afforded little reason to be optimistic about any chances for success, and so only the quixotic displayed crusading fervor. Besides the most pious, such as France's King Louis IX (in 1248–1254 and again in 1270), few Westerners took up the cross to recover the Holy Land in the thirteenth century, although enthusiasm—and turnout—for the much more successful *Reconquista* in Spain remained strong.

Bishops indulgenced works related to the crusading movement as well. Though the Truce of God predated the crusading movement—French bishops first called upon the nobility to spare churches and peasants before the turn of the eleventh century—many believed that the fight against the Muslims would fail without peace among the Christian barons. The Truce generally prohibited war between Christians during Advent and Lent. Like crusaders, warriors who observed the Truce came to take vows in a liturgy, during which the warriors venerated holy relics. The Truce, however, only prohibited warring upon Christians. Warriors could still attack infidels. Hence, in an effort to aid the Spanish *Reconquista*, the provincial synod of Rheims in 1092 proclaimed an indulgence remitting one serious sin to nobles who refrained from attacking other Christian aristocrats.[58] Bishops sponsored the Truce through indulgences into the twelfth century. In 1105, a council of clergy and laity resolved that the Truce would be observed in the neighborhood of Constance. In the presence of the papal legate, the city's bishop, Gebhard III, granted an indulgence of two years to nobles who kept the peace.[59] A twelfth-century legatine indulgence even offered a plenary remission to those warriors who died while defending the Truce in battle![60]

In Paulus's words, "the development of indulgences reached its culmination in the pontificate of Innocent III (1198–1216)."[61] Before Innocent's pontificate, peasants and town-dwellers had few opportunities to receive a plenary indulgence. Through two innovations, Innocent established precedents making such indulgences commonly available to peasants and town-dwellers. Traditionally, historians have argued that the cost of warfare prompted Innocent to extend the crusade indulgence for the first time to non-combatants. The launching of a crusade was difficult to get underway because the rapidly escalating costs of warmaking rendered the costs of crusade prohibitive for all but the wealthiest warriors. More recently, however, Jessalynn Bird has asserted that "Innocent's policies were not primarily motivated by finance, but by the fusion of crusade and reform which he shared with the Paris circle [of Peter the Chanter]."[62] Bird is certainly correct here, but Innocent did worry about the costs of crusades. Thus, he proclaimed at the Fourth Lateran Council (1215) that the confessed and contrite who contributed money to the campaign would receive the same indulgence as those who took part in the fighting, the first time that non-combatants were offered a principal benefit of *crucesignati*.[63]

Innocent's second innovation was to offer crusade indulgences to those who fought heretics instead of Muslims. During most of the twelfth century, the Albigensian heretics of southern France had been particularly resistant to missionary efforts to restore them to communion with the Catholic Church. Several generations of peaceful missioners, which included such spiritual giants as Sts. Bernard of Clairvaux and Dominic, failed to return them to orthodox Christianity. Although exasperated with the heretics, Innocent took no forceful measures against them until the papal legate Peter of Castelnau was murdered in 1207 in southern France. Innocent's suspicions and rage fell immediately upon the heretics. His patience exhausted, Innocent rallied the nobles of Christendom for a crusade against the southern French heretics. He offered the same crusade indulgence to the warriors of this campaign as he had offered for the conquest of the Holy Land. The Albigensian War marked the first time that a crusade indulgence was granted for a campaign against dissident Christians.

Medieval and modern critics have questioned the wisdom of Innocent's innovations. Warriors in the Middle East grumbled against the pope for granting the crusade indulgence to the conquerors of the Albigensians. The defenders of the Holy Land told the pope that his actions discouraged knights from fighting in the East. They believed that because of Innocent, potential comrades against the infidel would now stay at home.[64] In contrast, the crusade preacher James of Vitry justified Innocent's extension of the crusade indulgence in a sermon *ad crucesignatos*. He defended the pope's liberality by invoking the parable of the vineyard in the Gospel of Matthew [Mt 20.1–16]. The owner of the vineyard paid all his workers the same amount, regardless of how long they worked. The workers did not merit their pay, which the landlord granted them out of his generosity. In the same way, the pope offered the crusade indulgence to undeserving non-combatants. The pope, like the God whom he serves, is generous and cannot be questioned in his generosity.[65]

Innocent's successors followed suit. Henceforth, crusade indulgences helped raise numerous armies against the enemies of the orthodox Church, whether Christian or infidel. Pope Gregory IX (1227–1241) helped re-establish the lordship of the archbishop of Bremen over the Stedinger peasants of the northwestern German Empire by means of a crusade indulgence. The Stedinger descended from Saxon and Frisian peasants. They gained much personal freedom during the first quarter of the thirteenth century because of exhaustive conflicts between the Danes, Welfs, and Hohenstaufen. While civil war preoccupied their nominal overlords, the count of Oldenburg and the archbishop of Bremen, the Stedinger industriously drained vast swamplands, which they then plowed and harvested. From the 1220s, the Stedinger cultivated these lands free of any tithes or rents.

After political stability returned, the count of Oldenburg ceded his lordship over the newly cultivated lands, but the archbishop, anxious to restore the health of the archiepiscopal finances, determined to collect tithes. When the peasants refused, the archbishop ordered his armies to attack them. The numerous and angry Stedinger defeated the archbishop's armies. After this embarassment, the archbishop declared the Stedinger heretics and asked Pope Gregory IX to grant indulgences to warriors who would attack them. Gregory reluctantly agreed to a partial indulgence for participation in this campaign. When the second offensive also stalled, Gregory elevated his grant to the status of a full crusade indulgence. The second attack defeated and subdued the Stedinger. In this case, the pope and archbishop used a crusade indulgence not for the defeat of infidels or heretics but to preserve what they understood as peace and right order in Christendom, meaning the restoration of the archbishop's temporal, as well as spiritual, authority over his subjects.[66]

Similar crusade indulgences continued to be granted throughout the thirteenth and fourteenth centuries. Innocent IV (1243–1254) elevated his struggle with Emperor Frederick II (1215–1250) to a crusade, with the attendant indulgences. Innocent pursued the same policy against Frederick's son Conrad.[67] Pope John XXII (1316–1334) offered partial indulgence to priests who would introduce into their celebrations of the Mass two collects invoking the wrath of God on his enemy, Emperor Louis of Bavaria (1314–1347).[68] The popes used indulgences as instruments of policy towards other monarchs as well. Thomas Aquinas off-handedly used the example of a papal indulgence offered to those who would pray for the pope's ally, the king of France.[69]

Historians have sometimes said that the system of indulgences owed everything to the crusading movement. This overstatement contains more than a fragment of the truth. A militant Catholic Church indulgenced numerous peaceful endeavors as contributing to the defense of the faith. For instance, during the thirteenth century, a number of prelates gave indulgences for university study. The justification for these pardons said that universities educated servants of the church and apologists for the faith. Scholars waged intellectual war in defense of the faith, just as the crusaders attacked the troops and fortifications of Christendom's heretical and infidel enemies. In 1229, the cardinal legate Romanus granted a plenary indulgence to all students and professors who attended the new University of Toulouse.[70] Romanus's justification for the plenary indulgence equated study with taking up the cross. In 1262, Pope Urban IV issued a partial indulgence to the benefactors of poor students in the newly founded Sorbonne of

Paris.[71] In 1244, several bishops joined Innocent IV in granting indulgences to a Cistercian school for poor boys in Paris.[72]

Indeed, the close connection among indulgences, crusades, and pilgrimages endured until the end of the Middle Ages and beyond. Throughout the course of the twelfth and thirteenth centuries, bishops and popes conceded innumerable new indulgences for making pilgrimages to equally innumerable churches, convents, hospitals, and monasteries all over Christendom and *in partibus infidelibus*. Most of these indulgences were obtained by those who lived within a few miles; most shrines and saints had only a local following. Others, like the journey to Canterbury in England, familiar even today to students of English literature, or to that of Compostela in Spain, had an international appeal.

Perhaps the most famous pilgrimage indulgences of the last two medieval centuries were the Roman Jubilees. In February 1300, Pope Boniface VIII (1295–1303) proclaimed the first Jubilee, which offered a plenary remission for making the pilgrimage to Rome:

> A trustworthy tradition of ancient times holds that great remissions and indulgences of sins were given to visitors of the honored basilica of the prince of the apostles at Rome. . . . We, entrusted by the mercy of almighty God, and by the merits and authority of his previously mentioned apostles [i.e., Peter and Paul], with the advice of our brothers and with the plenitude of apostolic power, to all persons during the present year 1300, from the passed feast of the nativity of our Lord Jesus Christ through the year following . . . who shall truly repent and confess . . . grant and have granted not only great and plentiful, but rather the most complete remission of all their sins.[73]

According to one account, the vast throng of pilgrims impressed Boniface into proclaiming this new indulgence.[74] Hence, like most other indulgences, the Jubilee may well be said to have originated among the pious faithful, who flocked to the Eternal City because the advent of a new century intensified apocalyptic expectations. For their part, pilgrims apparently spread rumors that the pope would soon offer them a plenary pardon. To receive the indulgence, Boniface required that residents of Rome pray for thirty consecutive days in the basilicas of the city; foreigners had to pray for fifteen days.[75] As news of the Jubilee spread throughout Latin Christendom, even greater numbers of penitents left hearth and home to journey to Rome. Dante himself testified to the crowds that congested the streets of the Eternal City:

> Just so the Romans, because of the great throng in the year of the Jubilee, divide the bridge in order that the crowds may pass along, So that all face the castle as they go on one side toward St. Peter's, while on the other, all move along facing toward Mount Giordano.[76]

The penitential fervor which prompted the Jubilee held sway in the fourteenth century as well. Pope Clement VI (1342–1352), who seems to have positively revelled in the concession of church benefits, proclaimed another Jubilee for 1350, even though Boniface had declared that Jubilees be held once every hundred years.[77] Clement reasoned that a Jubilee offered once a century benefitted only a few penitents. Like many other fourteenth-century church leaders, Clement desired that many more pilgrims avail themselves of this plenary indulgence.[78] Furthermore, Clement claimed biblical precedent in his favor. According to Mosaic law, a full remission of sin was to be proclaimed to the children of Israel every fifty years.[79] Nevertheless, the Jubilee of 1350 attracted smaller crowds than that of 1300. A Jubilee was proclaimed for 1390, but the Great Schism (1379–1417) tempered penitents' enthusiasm. Particularly petty and bitter disputes between the rival popes broke out over this Jubilee. Each claimant forbade his loyalists from receiving the indulgences proclaimed by his rival, whether the remissions were Jubilees or others, even though another round of heightened penitential and apocalyptic enthusiasm greeted the turn of another Christian century. Under Nicholas V (1447–1455), however, a Jubilee was celebrated in 1450 that attracted another great legion of pilgrims.[80] By the mid-fifteenth century, the fading memories of the Great Schism helped restore the confidence of penitents in papal indulgences.

Towards the end of the thirteenth century, the collective indulgence became the most common form of pilgrimage indulgences. While the testimony of Raymond of Peñafort suggests that such indulgences were known by the 1230s, the eschatological expectations that surged at the end of that century contributed to a very notable proliferation of them. Briefly, collective indulgences were visitation pardons granted by more than one prelate to a single place for the same occasion or, more often, occasions. The following collective remission, granted in 1299 to the monastery of St. Clare at Ghent, was typical:

> To all the sons of Holy Mother Church to whom these presents shall come, we, by the divine grace bishops, Brother Giles the Patriarch of Grado, Lando of Naples, Brother Bartholomew of Montecorvino Pugliano, Thomas of Sauveterre, Nicholas of Semur, Landulphus of Bressanone, Brother James of Chalcedon, Brother Maurus of Amelia, Nicholas of Caorle, Thomas of Charonea, Stephen of Oppido, and Nicholas of Tubula, offer greetings in eternal God. Holy Mother Church, out of a concern for the salvation of souls, is accustomed to invite the devotion of the faithful through certain spiritual rewards, namely, remissions and indulgences, in order to give the honor of worthy servant to God and to the holy places, so that the more frequently and devoutly Christian people assemble there to seek the grace of the Savior through common prayers, so much the more quickly they will deserve to receive forgiveness

of their sins and the eternal glory of the heavenly kingdom. Wishing, therefore, that the monastery of the order of St. Clare, in the neighborhood of Ghent in the diocese of Cambrai, may be venerated by the appropriate honors, visitation, and the pious faithful of Christ, we, to all truly penitent and confessed, by the mercy of God our Savior, and by the grace of His sweet Mother, and also by the authority of the trusted apostles Peter and Paul, mercifully remit in God forty days of enjoined penance, provided the will of the diocesan agrees and consents to this, for visitors of the said monastery on the following feast-days, namely, Christmas, Easter, the Ascension of our Lord Jesus Christ, Pentecost, the four feast-days of the glorious Virgin Mary, of St. John the Baptist and St. John the Evangelist, of St. Michael the Archangel, of Sts. Peter and Paul and all the other apostles, of St. Laurence, Vincent, and Stephen the martyr, of St. Martin, and of Pope St. Nicholas, of the Sts. Catherine, Margaret, Lucy, Cecilia, Agnes, and of the virgin St. Clare, of St. Mary Magdalene, of All Saints, and for the anniversary of the dedication of the said monastery, and to those who shall visit for the eight days immediately following the aforesaid feast days because of devotion and in a spirit of humility. We also extend remission to those who shall provide aid for the monastery's building materials, structural needs, candles, ornaments, or its other necessities, and to laborers who during emergencies donate, offer, or obtain whatever of their skills to the monastery, for the particular needs of the monastery. To which end, we shall confidently present this signed document to be confirmed with our seals. Dated at Anagni, in the year of our Lord 1299, in the fifth year of the pontificate of Lord Pope Boniface VIII.[81]

These proclamations of indulgence, then, named the bishops who were participating in the concession of pardon, the church or monastery where the indulgence was available, and the days when the remission was offered. Grants of collective indulgence decreased after 1300, although they continued until the end of the Middle Ages.

Despite the fascination of the chroniclers and poets with the great crowds of pilgrims to Rome, Canterbury, Compostela, and Jerusalem, most medieval pilgrimages consisted of short journeys to local shrines and churches, most of which long antedated Boniface VIII's Roman Jubilee.[82] Some of these pilgrimages were attached to the regular cycles of the liturgy. In particular, "Pentecost week was often the occasion for the annual pilgrimage of country parishioners to their mother cathedral, a journey that the bishops and their synods attempted to encourage by linking it to promises of indulgences."[83] Such pilgrimages, which often amounted to long processions, made a treasured, convenient, and safe pilgrimage, and offered the laity more participation in the annual rhythms of the liturgy. While such journeys lacked the hardships of long-distance travel, the myriad indulgenced pilgrimages known but to the inhabitants of a shire or county served as a common metaphor for the Christian life—the journey of the *viator* from earthly life to Beatific Vision.

INDULGENCES AND PIOUS BUILDING

Pilgrimages were not the only pious works that testified to the great wave of religious enthusiasm characteristic of the High and Late Middle Ages. Hundreds of small rural and urban churches were built during the twelfth century, as towns grew dramatically and as country parishes consolidated all over Latin Christendom. Indulgences came to be offered for the building of churches, as well as a whole host of pious works of engineering and architecture. Medieval bishops and popes proclaimed countless indulgences to penitents who contributed in some way to the building of churches, monasteries, convents, bridges, roads, dams, fortifications, and hospitals. While modern sensibilities might find a grant of pardon for the building of a church understandable enough, remissions for roads and fortifications might be thought rather more curious. For the Christians of the High Middle Ages, however, whatever served the material, political, military, and spiritual welfare of the Christian community was also sacred, and could therefore be encouraged through grants of pardon.

Numerous churches in western Europe—from the great cathedrals to humble parishes—were built and maintained with the aid of indulgences. Bishops indulgenced money or labor contributions to the construction of churches beginning in the twelfth century, and so indulgences likewise aided the maturation of the parish system. In the tradition of St. Benedict, the medieval Church taught that manual labor was a good work. Hence, in the thirteenth century, Bishop Heinrich of Strasbourg granted indulgences to workmen for hauling stone to church construction sites.[84] In 1283, laborers on a parish church in Hagenau were rewarded with pardons.[85] The Pomerian chronicle, though compiled by a sixteenth-century Protestant, admits that indulgences could be crucial in the reconstruction of a damaged church. In 1384, for instance, a church and tower in Stralsund had collapsed. Prohibitive costs prevented the citizens of the town from making repairs immediately. The bishop of Schwerin then granted an indulgence of forty days to anyone who would help clear the site of stones. People came from miles around with their wagons to haul away the wreckage of the old church. The chronicler believed that the indulgence thus saved the townspeople one hundred gulden, not to mention a good deal of time.[86] Many of these pardons stipulated that after a church had been completed and consecrated, indulgences would still be available to visitors on the anniversary of the consecration of the church building. In this way, funds for the maintenance of a church could be raised, as pilgrims customarily gave alms.

Remissions benefitted houses of religious women even more generously. The strict enclaustralization of nuns meant that religious women depended almost solely on donations for the construction and maintenance of build-ings. Unlike monks, who cultivated fields, tended flocks and dressed vines, nuns did no labor and therefore produced no wealth. Indulgences encouraged donations to the construction of convents and nunneries. The order of the Magdalenes, founded during the reign of Gregory IX (1227–1241) built a convent in Cologne with the help of grants of pardon.[87] Grants of remission also helped popularize important devotionalisms that originated in houses of women religious, such as the famous celebration of Corpus Christi.

Among the indulgences granted for "secular" constructions, those for bridge- and road-building were probably the most widespread. The preacher Berthold of Regensburg included contributions to bridge-building in a standard list of pious works, including almsgiving, the endowment of masses and chapels, the foundation of hospitals, feeding the hungry, giving drink to the thirsty, and clothing the naked.[88] According to Guibert of Nogent (d. 1124), monks often maintained nearby roads. They, in turn, solicited the help of local laity:

> In our own time, I saw an elderly monk there who had been a knight, a plain man, it was believed, who had been appointed by his abbot to a certain small house of the monastery in the Vexin, because he was a native of the region. With the consent of his prior, he proposed to repair the foundation of the public road, which was in very bad shape. He carried out this work with the help of the gifts of the faithful.[89]

For Christians of the High Middle Ages, the symbolic meaning of bridges equalled their practical usefulness. The Latin for bishop, *pontifex*, derived from the word for a bridge, *pons*, thus highlighting the bishop's mediatorial and sacramental ministrations. Bridges themselves symbolized the span from earthly to eternal life, as well as the bond of faith that embraced neighbors and foreigners. In practical terms, a bridge made travel safer, improved commerce, and thus contributed to the prosperity of the people who lived in its vicinity. Consequently, medieval Christians deemed a donation of money or labor to the building of a bridge or road a work of charity toward pilgrims, merchants, and anyone else who used them. Monks and nuns were especially enjoined to pray for bridgebuilders because bridges enabled more penitents to visit their convents and hospitals. The benefactors of a bridge deserved indulgences because they advanced the welfare of Christendom.

In his treatise on the sacraments, an anonymous thirteenth-century theolo-gian of Metz explicitly defended indulgences for bridge- and road-building. He argued that since bridges and roads served pilgrims and travellers, dona-tions to the construction of bridges and roads constituted a kind of almsgiving:

> If pardon is granted for building bridges, or for extending, levelling, or making other improvements in roads, it ought to be known that it is permitted to whomsoever of the

grantors to encourage works to complete the tasks of his lord; likewise is it permitted to the prelates of the churches to grant indulgences to laborers on a task of this sort, which the prelates shall, by considering the result of the work, deem to be to the benefit of that church, because improvement of roads and bridges serve pilgrims and those travelling the road for other pious purposes, for almsgiving is indeed even a literal obedience of the precept of God, *make straight a path and clear it of stones.*[90]

He also thought that the repair of a highways removed near occasions of sin. When roads are in poor repair, and travel dangerous, travellers curse and blaspheme the damage done to their property and persons by ramshackle roads, and so imperil the salvation of their souls:

Travellers on broken paths and dangerous and difficult roads are put upon. They hack through the woods and are vexed and their carts are turned over, and wine spills all over and they beat their horse and men become angry. These travellers grumble and curse all those who ought to have repaired the road, and the blasphemers sin mortally by most shamefully swearing against God and the saints.[91]

A bridge or road in good repair helped travellers avoid the deadly sin of anger!

Only a generation after Guibert wrote his anecdote, a decretal of Pope Alexander III (1159–1181) reveals that by the middle of the twelfth century, bishops were granting donors indulgences for the construction of bridges. In this decretal, Alexander responded to an inquiry from the archbishop of Canterbury, who had asked the pope whether Christians could receive indulgences granted for the construction of churches or bridges, even if they were not subject to the bishop who had proclaimed those remissions.[92] By the second half of the twelfth century, indulgences for bridge-building were common. In southern France, confraternities (often interested in procuring indulgences for their members) devoted to the building of bridges were founded.[93] In the neighborhood of the port of Pisa, the brothers of a local hospital began building a bridge. They asked Pope Lucius III to favor their work with an indulgence. In 1185, Lucius extended an indulgence of thirty days to benefactors of the project. Three years later, Clement III (1187–1191) renewed the indulgence, as did Celestine III (1191–1198) and Innocent III later.[94] Innocent III also granted remission for the construction of a bridge in the neighborhood of Lyons.[95] In 1236, Bishop Rudiger of Passau granted an indulgence of fifteen days for contributions to a bridge over the Traun River in the town of Wels.[96] Pope Innocent IV (1243–1254) not only granted an indulgence of one year and forty days to the benefactors of a bridge near Lyons, but also took the local bridge confraternity under his protection and, in 1254, asked the bishops to permit preachers of the indulgence to collect alms and preach word of the indulgence.[97] Through grants of indulgence, prelates of the church sponsored the construction of bridges until the Reformation.

Towards the end of the thirteenth century, prelates also offered indulgences for other public works, like dams, embankments, and fortifications. For the prelates, the obvious contribution made to the common good by such structures justified the remissions. In 1328, Pope John XXII aided the rebuilding of an embankment belonging to a monastery in Stavoren, in the diocese of Utrecht.[98] In 1302, Boniface VIII helped the builders of a breakwater in Naples with a grant of one hundred days of indulgence.[99] At the frontiers of Christendom, bishops granted indulgences to encourage the building of fortifications (since these too guaranteed the safety of the Christian commonwealth) and to foster colonization (which contributed to the spread of the Christian religion). Accordingly, Honorius III patronized the construction of a fort built by the Templars in 1222.[100] His successors Gregory IX and Innocent IV conceded similar pardons.[101] To protect Christians from Muslim aggression, Clement V (1294) granted remissions for the construction of fortifications in Cyprus.[102] In 1253, Innocent IV authorized an indulgence to Christian settlers of Corsica; their settlement, with its fortifications, served as a bulwark against Islam in the southwest Mediterranean.[103]

Of all the buildings devoted to public welfare, none profitted as much from indulgences as did hospitals. Hospitals particularly benefitted from itinerant preachers of indulgence (*quaestores*, in Latin; pardoners, in English). The pastoral manual *Summa predicantium* (compiled before 1353) said, "we see that messengers come round to the churches, from diverse hospitals, and preach that they have many weak and impotent inmates, and display large indulgences."[104] A decree of Lateran IV (1215) assumed that pardoners would raise money for hospitals. The formula for episcopal credentials included in that council's decree on preachers of indulgences concluded thus:

> Since the resources of a hospital may not suffice for the support of the brethren and the needy who flock to it, we admonish and exhort all of you in the Lord, and enjoin upon you for the remission of your sins, to give pious alms and grateful charitable assistance to them, from the goods that God has bestowed upon you; so that their need may be cared for through your help, and you may reach eternal happiness through these and other good things which you may have done under God's inspiration.[105]

The indulgences must have helped a good deal, for hospitals abounded in medieval Europe. London alone possessed twenty by 1400; already seven had been founded in that city by 1200.[106] More than one thousand hospitals could be found in England and Wales together by the turn of the fifteenth century.[107]

Hospitals enjoyed the special patronage and protection of the ecclesiastical authorities, as in the statutes of the hospital of St. Gilles, Norwich:

> To all who observe this our ordinance, and who labor by counsel and aid that it may be kept, we impart the blessing of Almighty God and of Our Lord Jesus Christ. And we release them mercifully every year at the feast of St. Giles from forty days of enjoined penance. But those who shall labor for the subversion of this our ordinance, or shall procure anything whereby the said ordinance may obtain less effect in future, or who shall engineer anything against it maliciously, we bind them with the chain of excommunication by the authority of Almighty God, the Father, Son, and Holy Spirit.[108]

The despoilers of hospitals merited the severest condemnation, for their malefactions harmed the most pitiful and vulnerable.

The medieval hospital differed much from its modern counterpart. Many hospitals consisted merely of a chapel within a church, so that the masses and prayers offered within them might offer some consolation. Hospitals sometimes ministered to the sick, but more often were places where the poor retired to die and travellers, especially pilgrims, found shelter, such as the hospitals founded by the Knights of St. John, or Hospitallers, in the Holy Land. Popes and bishops were especially generous in granting indulgences to leper houses, a specialized kind of medieval hospital, of which there were ten in London by the end of the fourteenth century.[109] The imitation of Christ required service to the sick and to travellers, as the Savior himself had healed the ailing and washed the feet of travellers who gathered to hear his teaching; mercy shown to the sick and dying was mercy shown to Christ Himself. As Boniface VIII stated in a letter of indulgence for the hospital of Altopascio, whoever picks up a sick man and gives him aid nourishes Christ Himself. Nothing could be more pleasing to God than a contribution to a hospital, as Boniface remarked in another letter of indulgence dated 1299 for a hospital in Viterbo.[110] Hospitals also served other charitable purposes. Some were orphanages, where children were not only cared for, but sometimes educated.[111] Other hospitals cared for the blind, such as the foundation of Louis IX in Paris, to which Nicholas IV granted an indulgence of one hundred and forty days in 1291.[112]

Popes and bishops showered indulgences on many charitable endeavors. Pope Boniface VIII appropriated a custom of the city of Parma and granted partial indulgences to alms collectors who had taken the poor into their homes.[113] Special indulgences were granted for individual works of mercy. John XXII offered indulgences to Christians who housed poor pregnant women during their days of confinement, and another indulgence to benefactors who enabled women to leave the profession of prostitution.[114]

Indulgences were also employed to offer comfort during times of crisis and to encourage the people to pray for relief from God. At the height of the Black Death in 1349, Clement VI composed a new Mass for an end to the plague—*missa pro vitanda mortalitate*. He furthermore granted an indulgence of 260 days—a notably lengthy period—to those who attended such Masses.[115] The prefatory rubric, which contained the indulgence, promised that all who heard this Mass on five consecutive days while kneeling with a burning candle would be saved from sudden death; even if the disease was contracted, family and friends would have time enough to assemble and pray with the dying, and thus prepare the soul for God's judgement.[116] Other prelates followed suit. Bishop William of Eddington ordered the cathedral chapter of Winchester to say special prayers, especially "the long litany instituted against pestilence of this kind by the holy fathers." This litany called for the organization of penitential processions through the marketplace, wherein the people would march barefoot, with their heads bowed. They were required to fast and, during the procession, to recite the *Pater noster* and *Ave* as often as possible. The procession ended at the cathedral church with a Mass. Bishop Eddington extended an indulgence of forty days to encourage the execution of his mandate.[117] Indulgenced prayers, therefore, were believed to have especially great power against the forces of evil and darkness. Just as the crusades and roads and dams protected Christendom from harm inflicted by human and natural malefactors, prayers brought "healing and victory over evil, deliverance from sudden and unprovided death, and longing for assurance of salvation."[118] Medieval prelates endorsed all of these prayers by attaching pardons to them.

INDULGENCES, DEVOTIONALISM, AND CATECHESIS

Out of all the great variety and number of indulgences, most medieval Catholics knew best those pardons available at their own parish churches or confraternity chapels, which generally demanded that certain prayers be offered either while in the churches, or on the behalf of fellow members of the confraternities. In his brilliant, highly influential commentary on the decretals, Innocent IV noted that popes and bishops conceded remissions for hearing sermons, attending Masses, and participating in church services.[119] The popes granted many indulgences to confraternities—such indulgences would come to be considered "our indulgences" by their members. Alexander IV in 1258 granted a remission of one hundred days to a confraternity in Piacenza. This indulgence was granted to members who heard Mass each month in the confraternity chapel.[120]

Especially fashionable or powerful prayers, such as the rosary, were like-liest to be indulgenced, particularly if they were recited during the Mass. English parishioners so treasured the rosary indulgence that they donated rosaries to be left in the parish church for the benefit of worshippers who had none of their own, lest these parishioners be denied the benefit of the rosary pardon. Indulgences were offered to encourage worshippers at daily Mass to stay long enough to hear the reading of the "Second Gospel" (Jn 1.1–14), which was read just prior to the dismissal of the people at the *ite missa est*. These indulgences generally required that worshippers kiss a text, a religious picture, or even one's own thumbnail at the words "the Word became flesh."[121] A thirteenth-century indulgence offered remission to those who prayed the Our Father and Hail Mary during the consecration.[122] Guilds often provided money for liturgical candles, which, aside from their obvious symbolic importance, also illuminated the elevated Host. Bishops conceded indulgences for donations of these candles.[123]

In addition to the pardons granted for liturgical observances and partici-pation, late medieval prelates encouraged education in the faith by granting pardons for catechetical instruction and pastoral admonition. Indulgences were attached, for instance, to many of the numerous pastoral manuals that circulated in England. Most of the English manuals were put together from continental sources, which in turn imitated conciliar decrees. The *Lay Folks' Catechism*, used in every English diocese by the turn of the fifteenth century, contained an indulgence of forty days for those who would teach its lessons. That the *Lay Folks' Catechism* was in English most certainly means that not only priests but also the increasingly literate laity ought to be numbered among those who read and taught the book. The *Catechism* emphasized the necessity of learning the Ten Commandments, the *Pater noster*, the *Ave Maria*, and the *Credo*. Lessons on the seven vices and virtues, the seven works of mercy, and the seven sacraments filled its pages. In texts like the *Catechism*, indulgences patronized the teaching of prayer and of moral formation. These books also offered confessors a framework within which to examine parishioners' consciences and their knowledge of Catholic doctrine.[124] The *Lay Folks' Catechism*, which made its appearance in 1357, was a vernacular verse adaptation of the *Ignorantia sacerdotum*, a catechetical program formulated for the English Church by Archbishop Pecham and the Council of Lambeth in 1281. According to the canons of that council, the *Ignorantia sacerdotum* was to be taught to the laity four times each year. Pecham's program had in turn been inspired by the pastoral agenda of Lateran IV (1215). In particular, the decree *Omnis utriusque sexus*, which enjoined annual confession and communion, inspired many of the pastoral initiatives throughout Latin Christendom until the end of the Middle Ages. That decree also reconfirmed the ancient tradition whereby priests should be trained in the examination of conscience and imposition of penance. The council also commanded that the necessity of annual confession and communion be "frequently published in churches."[125] Indulgences, therefore, contributed significantly to the remarkable success of the series of pastoral reforms initiated by Lateran IV and promoted by those churchmen who embraced the council's spirit of religious renewal.

In addition to prayer and catechism, bishops eagerly and abundantly indulgenced new devotions, and thereby supported the era's Christo-centric and eucharistic spiritual focus. In the early thirteenth century, indulgences helped to popularize the new devotion to the Corpus Christi. This feast originated in the piety of Flemish nuns, among whom devotion to the Eucharist was especially strong.[126] Juliane of Liège (1192–1258), who "struck a chord with her idea of public, regular, concerted celebration of the Eucharist," sought the help of Hugh of St. Cher, cardinal legate for Germany, in popularizing the new devotion.[127] Hugh was especially sensitive to the pastoral needs of religious women and approved of Juliane's efforts. As a recognized visionary and mystic, Juliane had drawn the attention of Dominicans like Hugh to eucharistic devotion. In one vision, she saw the moon, of which a segment was darkened by a blemish. Twenty years later, a second vision revealed to her that that moon represented a Christian church not fully complete because it lacked the feast of Corpus Christi. Hugh was convinced that her visions were incontestable signs of divine approbation for her devotion.[128]

Hugh's enthusiasm for the new devotion matched Juliane's, and his help was generous and significant, for he declared that "we, in order to urge the faithful that they may more reverently celebrate and observe that feast [of the Blessed Sacrament]; to all penitent and confessed, who shall piously travel to a church where the office of the same feast is celebrated, on the same day and through the octave, mercifully relax one hundred days of enjoined penance."[129] Hugh's patronage, as expressed in his grant of pardon, was crucial for the spread of the popularity of the feast of Corpus Christi, enjoined on the universal Church by Pope Urban IV (1261–1265).[130] Prelates showered the observance of Corpus Christi with indulgences until the end of the Middle Ages. A fifteenth-century sermon preached for the occasion of the feast reads like a veritable roll call of indulgences:

On the occasion of this feast, great and numerous indulgences are granted to the faithful, namely, one hundred days to those who are present at the office of matins, in the church where it is celebrated; also to those who assist at the mass; also to those who assist at first or second vespers; forty days to those who assist at tierce, sext, nones, and compline; one hundred days remission to those who assist during eight days at matins, vespers, at mass and at the hours following, at each day of the octave.[131]

Through the feast of Corpus Christi, the veneration of the Blessed Sacrament went on to become one of the most important and characteristic devotional observances of later medieval and modern Catholicism.

The adoration of the suffering Jesus flourished well into the later Middle Ages, often with the support of the prelates in the form of pardons. Pope John XXII granted an indulgence of one hundred days to those who read and reflected upon the Passion of Jesus.[132] The influential conciliarist and reformer Pierre d'Ailly (1350–1420) granted remissions to the cult of the bleeding host of Christ.[133] Bishops likewise sponsored the extraordinarily popular late medieval devotion to the Five Wounds of Jesus, which probably originated in Italy and then spread to the rest of Europe. English manuscripts described how Jesus Himself, in a vision to an anchorite, recommended the veneration of the Five Wounds:

A woman solitari and recluse, covetyng to knowe hou many he suffrid for mankynde that he wolde schew en hem to hure. At last oure Lord spak to hure and sayde: say uche day in the yere 15 *Pater Noster* and *Ave* [with these orisons] . . . and at the yeres ende then shalt thou worship every wounde and fulfylle the nombre of the same woundus.[134]

The orisons that were to accompany the recitation of the Our Father and the Hail Mary were collects that began with "I adore you, Lord Jesus Christ," and continued with a reflection on the suffering of the crucified Jesus. According to the manuscript, Jesus himself promised forty days of pardon to its adherents.[135] The text also assured its readers that Pope Clement V had granted the indulgence—so they could be assured that the indulgence had the authority of the church.[136] While the suffering Jesus formed perhaps the most popular late medieval devotion to the human Christ, indulgences were attached to other reminders of his humanity, in particular, devotions to the Blessed Mother. Plenary indulgences were available for the feast of the Assumption.[137]

In addition to the devotions to the human Jesus, medieval prelates indulgenced the veneration of various saints. Since these remissions were usually granted for the visitation of a saint's shrine, they too originated in pilgrimage. Bishops rarely indulgenced a shrine built in honor of a long-venerated saint, such as a martyr, or an apostle, or a late antique bishop such as St. Martin of Tours, but eagerly promoted the adoration of the newly canonized.[138]

Honorius III (1216–1227) was the first pope to grant an indulgence for the occasion of a saint's canonization. He promulgated a remission of forty days in honor of St. Gerhard of Potenza, a significant figure in the Investiture Controversy of the early twelfth century.[139] Gregory IX (1227–1241) promoted the cult of St. Anthony of Padua (canonized 1233) and of St. Dominic (1234), each with an indulgence of one year, and promoted the cult of St. Elizabeth (1235) with an indulgence of one year and forty days.[140] Pope John XXII (1316–1334) indulgenced the veneration of Thomas Aquinas, who was canonized in 1323:

> So that a multitude of Christians may more ardently and profitably visit Thomas's venerable tomb, and that the feast of that confessor may be celebrated with joy, we, by the mercy of omnipotent God and by the authority of His saints and apostles Peter and Paul, remit one year and forty days of enjoined penance to all truly penitent and confessed, who shall make visitation there seeking Thomas's suffrages on the anniversary of the feast; and to pilgrims who visit the said tomb within seven days immediately following the feast in subsequent years, one hundred days of enjoined penance.[141]

John endorsed other saintly cults in the same way. In 1320, he approved the canonization of St. Thomas Cantilupe, the bishop of Hereford (d. 1282), granting two years and eighty days of indulgence in the first year and one hundred days in every following year for the visitation of Thomas's shrine.[142] For the rest of the Middle Ages, popes customarily attached indulgences to the celebrations of canonizations and their anniversaries.[143]

Church authorities likewise favored other services in honor of the saints. In 1309, Pope Clement V (1305–1314) presided at the translation of the relics of the reforming bishop Bertrand of Comminges (d. 1123) and granted an unusually liberal indulgence of fifteen years and fifteen *quarantaines* (one *quarantaine* equalled forty days) to those who venerated the relics on the day of the feast of the translation. The pope also granted seven years and seven *quarantaines* to pilgrims who visited his shrine during the octave of the translation, ten years and ten *quarantaines* to those who arrived on a Marian feast, and three years and three *quarantaines* to those who visited during the octave of these feasts.[144] In Bertrand's honor, Pope Clement granted a plenary indulgence to the cathedral in Comminges in each year that the feast of the discovery of the True Cross (May 3) fell on a Friday.[145]

Prelates less often rewarded the veneration of the saints of old with grants of remission, but such pardons were granted from time to time. In 1229, Henry of Braine, the archbishop of Rheims, granted an indulgence of forty days for the transfer of the relics of the martyrs Timothy and Apollinaris to the Church of St. Timothy. In so doing, however, Henry tied the veneration of Timothy and Apollinaris to a popular twelfth-century saint, Thomas Becket, by declaring "the said translation to be celebrated . . . on the morrow of the feast of the holy archbishop Thomas of Canterbury."[146] The popes Clement VI (1343) and Gregory XI (1376) granted indulgences to the relics of Martial of Limoges, a third-century bishop whose intercession, believed to be especially efficacious against malefactors, was still sought after by the people of the Limousin.[147] Devotions to ancient saints, then, tended to be indulgenced only if they could be linked to a recently canonized figure or if the saint's intercession was believed especially efficacious against some misfortune.

The rarest indulgences granted to honor the saints were bestowed on shrines where miracles—the most extraordinary manifestations of saintly power, because wrought by God himself—had been performed. In 1145, Pope Eugene III endowed the Church of St. James the Apostle in Pistoia with an indulgence of seven days because

> the church in Pistoia has demonstrated many splendid and various miracles at its altar by the merits of St. James, for the remorse of the faithful; for we have learned from our venerable brother Atto, the pious bishop of that town, and from other sources, that the blind, the lame, the feeble, and those afflicted by many other sufferings receive the complete restoration of health at that church and altar through the prayers and merits of St. James, as we have proclaimed. [148]

Indulgences of this kind were nonetheless unusual, and Eugene's grant of only seven days probably betrays a cautious response to the request of his fellow bishop Atto.[149]

By the mid-fourteenth century, then, bishops and popes had indulgenced a broad array of good and pious works. The wide range represented by pilgrimage, crusade, schooling, building, philanthropy, and prayer betrays the subtle distinctions medieval Christians made between the sacred and the secular, as well as the common thread that runs through all of them, namely, that they in some way served to construct, edify, or preserve the Church Militant. Christendom had deadly enemies—throughout the early medieval centuries, pagan and Muslim warriors invaded Christian lands, slew many believers, and occupied the holiest of Christian shrines; hence, remissions were granted to warriors who held off the infidel and drove him from the land of Christ's Passion and Resurrection. Christendom also had intellectual and ideological enemies, with whom learned advocates of the faith engaged in another sort of combat. Pardons were used to motivate learning. Christians needed roads and bridges to create the wealth that preserves life. Remissions were granted for their construction and maintenance. Above all, Christians ought to be occupied in the work of God—prayer, in all its various forms—and so bishops and popes conceded a great number of pardons for reciting especially favored or efficacious prayers. The concession of indulgences, then, went hand in glove with all the developments considered characteristic of high medieval Christendom. Indulgences were part and parcel of the spirituality and piety of the High Middle Ages, as well as that era's expansion, prosperity, thought, and culture.

NOTES

1. See Mansfield, *Humiliation of Sinners*.

2. *PL* 54:635.

3. *PL* 20:559. Translation from Paul F. Palmer, S. J., *Sacraments and Forgiveness* (Westminster, MD: Newman Press, 1959), 113.

4. Cf. Lk 12.47–48.

5. McNeill and Gamer, 90.

6. McNeill and Gamer, 88.

7. McNeill and Gamer, 88.

8. McNeill and Gamer, 91.

9. Pierre J. Payer, "The Humanism of the Penitentials and the Continuity of the Penitential Tradition," *MS* 46 (1984), 341.

10. H. A. Wilson, ed., *Liber sacramentorum romanae ecclesiae* (Oxford: Clarendon Press, 1894), 14, 63–66. Translation is from Palmer, 160.

11. Wilson, 63–66.

12. H. J. Schmitz, *Die Bußbücher und die Bußdisciplin der Kirche* (Mainz: Kirchheim, 1883), 82–83. Translation is from Palmer, 167.

13. Palmer, 168.

14. *Geschichte*, 1:69–70.

15. Hincmar of Rheims, *Epistola* 26 (*PL* 126:172–173). The translation is in Palmer, 326–327. See also Poschmann, *Der Ablaß*, 17.

16. *PL* 126:172. Palmer, 326.

17. McNeill and Gamer, 274.

18. McNeill and Gamer, 293.

19. McNeill and Gamer, 304–305.

20. *PL* 132:1092.

21. *PL* 78:447. Palmer, 325. Lanfranc, *Decreta pro ordine S. Benedicti*, c. 23 (*PL* 150:514): "Illi diligenter illud in sepulchro componant, et absolutione scriptam et a fratribus lectam super pectus ejus ponant et operiant." See also *Geschichte*, 1:35–36, and Poschmann, *Der Ablaß*, 113.

22. McNeill and Gamer, 320.

23. Mansi, 17:345–346: "Decreverunt hanc poenitentiam his qui bello Suessionis inter Robertum ac Carolum acto interfuerant injungendam: videlicet, ut tribus quadragesimis per tres annos agant poenitentiam: ita ut prima quadragesima sint extra ecclesiam, et coena Domini reconcilientur. Omnibus vero his tribus quadragesimis, secunda, quarta, et sexta feria, in pane, sale, et aqua abstineant, aut redimant. Similiter quindecim

diebus ante nativitatem S. Joannis Baptistae, et quindecim diebus ante nativitatem Domini Salvatoris, omnis quoque sexta feria per totum annum, nisi redimerint. . . ."
24. McNeill and Gamer, 400–402.
25. McNeill and Gamer, 402–403.
26. Tentler, 328–329.
27. See for instance, X 5.38.4 (*Quod autem*), a decretal of Pope Alexander III (1159–1181).
28. Cod. Theo. 9.38.5 and 9.38.6.
29. One of the first appearances of *indulgentia* was in Canon 62 of Lateran IV in 1215 (X 5.38.12), *Cum ex eo*.
30. Although the intercessory forerunners of indulgences survived for a long while in the theological memory; see Hödl, 336.
31. *Geschichte*, 1:97–109.
32. Jean Mabillon, ed., *Annales ordinis S. Benedicti*, (Lucca: L. Venturini, 1739), 4:355: "Fecerint absolutionem de omnibus peccatis minimis et maioribus, relaxando scilicet poenitentibus, qui ad illam ecclesiam convenirent, de tribus dies unum: ita ut si quis intra quadraginta poenitentiae dies mortuus esset, censeretur absolutus de omni peccato, quod presbytero confessus esset." See *Geschichte*, 1:98.
33. Jaime Villanueva, ed., *Viage literario a las iglesias de España*, (Madrid: Imprenta real, 1821), 8:262: "Et ego Wifredus sancte prime sedis Narbone archiepisco-pus, cum sanctissime vite merito sancte Arelatensis ecclesiae Raiamballo episcopo, cum aliis coepiscopis x et vii in concilio Narbonensi congregatis, rogatu Guifredi venerabilis viri, qui iam dicti loci noviter fundator extitit, pro Dei amore et beati Petri apostolorum principis honore, facimus constitucionem prephato loco, ut quicumque homo vel femina . . . venerit . . . pro remissione suorum peccaminum, vel ad iam dictam ecclesiam ex rebus propriis vel in lumine ecclesie adiutorium fecerit, quantum unius denarii precium potest estimari, de parte Dei et nostra maneat absolutus de I ex maioribus peccatis, quod plus timet, et unde maiorem penitentiam abet. Constituimus etiam ut in diebus xl quicumque fidelium ibi usque in Pascha in servicio dei perseveraverit, et lampada eius tota xl in ecclesia beati Petri apostoli arserit, sive ille qui toto tempore xl aliqua necessi-tate constrictus ibi perseverare minime potuerit, et tamen lampada ipsius per totum tempus xl in prephata ecclesia competenti tempore arserit, si penitentiam trium vel duorum aut certe unius diei tenuerit pro amore dei et honore sancti Petri, ex tribus vel duobus unum diem usque in capud xl, solvimus. Si quis autem pro remissione pecca-torum in penitentiam abet, ut ad ecclesiam sancti Petri Rome cupiat pergere, et ad iam dictum cenobium sancti Petri peregrinus cum propria candela septies venire studuerit, tantum illi prossit, quomodo si longi itineris peregrinationem tenuerit. Qui vero ad iam dictam ecclesiam tres magistros [*sic*] vel certe duos xl diebus in pane et vino atque redemptione detinuerit, tantum mercedis accipiat, quantum si sancti sepulcri desiderio ductus, illic pergere voluerit, et gratiam dei promereatur, et apostolica benedictione roboratus, nostra omnium adfirmatione et absolutione solvatur. Amen." See also *Geschichte*, 1:99. The original is the autograph of a charter in the archives of the monastery of St. Peter de Postilla, appended to a chronicle of the council of Narbonne of 1035. Ermengaude was bishop of Urgel from 1010 to 1035. Wifred was bishop of Carcasonne from 1031 to 1054.

34. Purcell, 36.

35. James Brundage, *Medieval Canon Law and the Crusader* (Madison: University of Wisconsin Press, 1969), 145.

36. S. Loewenfeld, ed., *Epistolae pontificium romanorum ineditae* (Leipzig: Veit, 1885), 43, no. 82: "Eos, qui in Ispaniam proficisci destinarunt, paterna karitate hortamur, ut, que divinitus admoniti cogitaverunt ad effectum perducere, summa cum sollicitudine procurent; qui iuxta qualitatem peccaminum suorum unusquisque suo episcopo vel spirituali patri confiteatur, eisque, ne diabolus accusare de inpenitentia possit, modus penitentiae imponatur. Nos vero auctoritate sanctorum apostolorum Petri et Pauli et penitentiam eis levamus et remissionem peccatorum facimus, oratione prosequentes."

37. Mansi, 20:816: "Quicumque pro sola devotione, non pro honoris vel pecuniae adeptione, ad liberandam ecclesiam dei Hierusalem profectus fuerit, iter illud pro omni poenitentia reputetur."

38. Jonathan Riley-Smith, "Crusading as an Act of Love," *History* 65 (1980), 177.

39. Jonathan Riley-Smith, *The First Crusade and the Idea of Crusading* (Philadelphia: University of Pennsylvania Press, 1986), 27–29. Purcell, 49, also believed that the various terms used for indulgences must have meant a great deal of confusion about indulgences' usefulness.

40. Marcus Bull, *Knightly Piety and the Lay Response to the First Crusade* (Oxford: Clarendon Press, 1993), 167–168.

41. Brundage, *Medieval Canon Law and the Crusader*, 148.

42. Jean Richard, "Urbain II, la prédication de la croisade et la definition de l'indulgence," in Ernst-Dieter Hehl, ed., *Deus qui mutat tempora: Menschen und Institutionen im Wandel des Mittelalters* (Sigmarigen: Jan Thorbecke Verlag, 1987), 133.

43. *PL* 151:483: "Poenitentiam totam peccatorum, de quibus veram et perfectam confessionem fecerit, per omnipotentis dei misericordiam et ecclesiae catholicae preces, tam nostra, quam omnium pene archiepiscoporum et episcoporum qui in Gallis sunt, auctoritate dimittimus, quoniam res et personas suas pro dei et proximi charitate exposuerunt."

44. Brundage, *Medieval Canon Law and the Crusader*, 149–150.

45. Joseph F. O'Callaghan, *Reconquest and Crusade in Medieval Spain* (Philadelphia: University of Pennsylvania Press, 2003), 24–26.

46. Robert of Rheims, "Historia Iherosolymitana," *RHC* 3:728.

47. R. Hill, ed., *Gesta francorum* (London: T. Nelson, 1962), 1. The translation is Riley-Smith's in "Crusading as an Act of Love," 178.

48. Guibert of Nogent, "Historia quae dicitur gesta dei per francos," *RHC* 4:137.

49. Riley-Smith, "Crusading as an Act of Love," 182.

50. Baldric of Dol, "Historia Jerusalem," *RHC* 4:12–13. Translation is from Edward Peters, ed. and trans., *The First Crusade: The Chronicle of Fulcher of Chartres and Other Source Materials* (Philadelphia: University of Pennsylvania Press, 1971), 6.

51. "Historia peregrinorum euntium Jerusolymam," *RHC* 3:173.

52. James Powell, *Anatomy of a Crusade, 1213–1221* (Philadelphia: University of Pennsylvania Press, 1986), 53.

53. Riley-Smith, *The First Crusade and the Idea of Crusading*, 47.

54. Riley-Smith, *The First Crusade and the Idea of Crusading*, 43.

55. Ralph of Caen, "Gesta Tancredi," *RHC* 3:605–606: "Eoque frequentior eum coquebat anxietas, quod militiae suae certamina praecepto videbat obviare dominico . . . at postquam Urbani papae sententia universis Christianorum gentilia expugnaturis peccatorum omnium remissionem ascripsit, tunc demum quasi sopiti prius experrecta est viri strenuitas, vires assumptae, oculi aperti, audacia geminata. Prius namque . . . animus ejus in bivium secabatur, ambiguus utrius sequeretur vestigia, Evangelii, an mundi."

56. B. E. C. Guérard, ed., *Cartulaire de l'abbaye de Saint-Père de Chartres* (Paris: Imprimerie de Crapelet, 1840), 2:428. The translation is in Louise and Jonathan Riley-Smith, eds. and trans., *The Crusades: Idea and Reality, 1095–1274* (London: E. Arnold, 1981), 99.

57. Powell, 55–56.

58. Wasserschleben, "Zur Geschichte der Gottesfrieden," *Zeitschrift der Savigny-Stiftung für Rechtsgeschichte* 12 (1891), 112–117.

59. *MGH* Legum 4, 1:615–616, no. 431.

60. Léopold Delisle, ed., *Recueil des historiens des Gaules et de la France*, vol. 14 (Paris: Palmé, 1877), 393: "Princeps autem et cuncti fideles . . . contra violatores pacis fideliter decertaverint . . . si in vera poenitentia in hoc Dei servitio decesserint, auctoritate Dei et domini Papae, et ecclesiae universalis, omnium peccatorum suorum indulgentiam et fructum mercedis aeternae se non dubitent habituros."

61. *Geschichte*, 1:141.

62. Jessalynn Bird, "Innocent III, Peter the Chanter's Circle, and the Crusade Indulgence: Theory, Implementation, and Aftermath," in Andrea Sommerlechner, ed., *Innocenzo III: Urbs et Orbis* (Rome: Instituto storico italiano per il medio evo, 2003), 1:523.

63. In canon 71, *Ad liberandam sanctam terram*.

64. Helena Tillman, *Pope Innocent III*, trans. Walter Sax (New York: North-Holland, 1980), 232.

65. Powell, 56.

66. John B. Freed, *The Friars and German Society in the Thirteenth Century* (Cambridge, MA: Medieval Academy of America, 1977), 147.

67. *Geschichte*, 2:21.

68. Extrav. comm. 3.11.1 (*CIC* 2:1284–1285).

69. Thomas Aquinas, *Commentum in IV libri sententiarum*, 4.20.1.3.3 I, in Opera Omnia (Parma: Peter Fiaccadori, 1863), 7:845.

70. Heinrich Denifle, ed., *Chartularium universitatis Parisiensis* (Paris: Delalain, 1891), 1:130, no. 72.

71. *Chartularium universitatis Parisiensis*, 1:424, no. 379.

72. *Chartularium universitatis Parisiensis*, 1:208–209, nos. 177–177a.

73. Extrav. comm. 5.9.1 (*CIC* 2:1303–1304): "Antiquorum habet fida relatio, quod accendentibus ad honorabilem basilicam principis Apostolorum de Urbe concessae sunt magnae remissiones et indulgentiae peccatorum . . . nos de omnipotentis Dei misericordia, et eorundem Apostolorum eius meritis et auctoritate confisi, de fratrum nostrorum consilio et apostolicae plenitudine potestatis omnibus in presenti anno millesimo trecentesimo, a festo Nativitatis Domini nostri Iesu Christi praeterito proxime inchoato . . . vere poenitentibus et confessis . . . non solum plenam et largitiorem, immo plenissimam omnium suorum concedemus et concedimus veniam peccatorum."

74. Herbert Thurston, S. J., *The Holy Year of Jubilee: An Account of the History and Ceremonial of the Roman Jubilee* (Westminster, MD: Newman Press, 1949), 12.

75. Extrav. comm. 5.9.1 (*CIC* 2:1304): "Qui voluerint huiusmodi indulgentiae a nobis concessae fieri participes, si fuerint Romani, ad minus XXX. diebus continuis seu interpolatis, et saltem semel in die, si vero peregrini fuerint aut forenses, simili modo diebus XV ad basilicas easdem accedant."

76. Dante, *Inferno*, 18.28–30 (trans. John Ciardi [New York: New American Library, 1954], 159).

77. Extrav. comm. 5.9.1 (*CIC* 2:1304): "in quolibet anno centesimo secuturo annis. . . ." 78. It is, for instance, quite obvious in the work of John of Dambach, an influential Dominican theologian. See Robert W. Shaffern, "A New Canonistic Text on Indulgences: *De quantitate indulgenciarum* of John of Dambach, O. P. (1288–1372)," *Bulletin of Medieval Canon Law* 22 (1991), 25–45.

79. Extrav. comm. 5.9.2 (*CIC* 2:1305): "Nos autem, attendentes, quod annus quinquagesimus in lege Mosaica [Lv 25.8–17] (quam non venit Dominus solvere, sed spiritualiter adimplere), iubilaeus remissionis et gaudii, sacerque dierum numerus, quo lege fit remissio, censebatur, quodque ipse quinquagenarius numerus in testamentis. . . ."

80. Thurston, *Holy Year of Jubilee*, 65–72.

81. Hippolyte Delehaye, "Les lettres d'indulgences collectives," *Analecta Bollandiana* 44 (1926), 357–358: "Universis sancte matris ecclesie filiis ad quos presentes littere pervenerint, nos miseratione divina frater Egidius patriarcha Gradensis, Lando Nolanensis, frater Bartholomeus Montis Corbini, Thomas Salvinensis, Nicholaus Semensis, Landulphus Brixinensis, frater Iacobus Calcedonensis, frater Maurus Ameliensis, Nicholaus Capritanus, Thomas Coronensis, Stephanus Opicensis et Nicholaus Turibulensis episcopi salutem in domino sempiternam.

Pia mater ecclesia de animarum salute sollicita devotionem fidelium per quedam spiritualia munera, remissiones videlicet et indulgentias, invitare consuevit ad debiti famulatus honorem deo et sacris edibus impendendum ut quanto crebrius et devotius illuc confluit populus christianus mutuis salvatoris gratiam precibus implorando, tanto celerius delictorum suorum veniam et gloriam celestis regni consequi mereatur eternam. Cupientes igitur ut monasterium ordinis sancte Clare iuxta Gandavum, Cameracensis dyocesis, congruis honoribus et iugi Christi fidelium frequentatione veneretur, omnibus vere penitentibus et confessis qui ad dictum monasterium in festivitatibus subscriptis, videlicet Nativitatis, Resurrectionis, Ascensionis domini nostri Iesu Christi atque Penthecostes, in quatuor festivitatibus gloriose virginis Marie, sanctorum Iohannis Baptiste et Evangeliste, beati Michaelis archangeli, beatorum Petri et Pauli aliorum omnium apostolorum, beatorum Laurentii, Vincentii, et Stephani martirum, beatorum Martini et Nicholay pontificum, beatarum Katharine, Margarete, Lucie, Cecilie, Agnetis et Clare virginum, beate Marie Magdalene, Omnium Sanctorum, in dedicatione ipsius et per octo dies feast predicta immediate sequentes, causa devotionis et in spiritu humilitatis accesserint aut qui pro sua fabrica, structura, luminaribus, ornamentis vel pro aliis suis necessariis manus porrexerint adiutrices, vel in extremis laborantes quicquid facultatum suarum donaverint, miserint seu procuraverint loco prelibato, pro singulis vicibus quibus hoc fecerint, nos de dei nostri salvatoris misericordia dulcisque matris sue gratia necnon et beatorum Petri et Pauli apostolorum auctoritate confisi, quilibet nostrum quadraginta dies de iniuncta sibi penitentia dummodo voluntas diochesani ad id accesserint et consensus, misericorditer in domino relaxamus. In cuius rei testimonium presens scriptum sigillorum nostrorum munimine duximus roborandum. Datum Anagnie, anno domine MCC nonagesimo IX, pontificatus domini Bonifacii pape octavi anno V."

82. Jürgen Petersohn, "Jubiläumsfrömmigkeit vor dem Jubelablaß: Jubeljahr, Reliquientranslation und 'remissio' in Bamberg (1189) und Canterbury (1220)," *Deutsches Archiv für Erforschung des Mittelalters* 45 (1989), 31–53.

83. Mansfield, 152.

84. Wilhelm Wiegand, ed., *Urkundenbuch der Stadt Strassburg*, (Strasbourg: J. H. Ed. Heitz, 1879), 1:135.

85. *Social Factor*, 43.

86. *Social Factor*, 44.

87. Neuhausen, 22.

88. Berthold von Regensburg, *Seiner Predigten*, ed. Franz Pfeiffer (Vienna: Wilhelm Braumüller, 1862), 1:190: "Der rîche sî, der sol almuosen geben unde messe frumen unde wege unde stege machen unde kloester rîchen unde spitâle unde den hungerigen etzen unde den durstigen trenken unde den nacheten kleiden."

89. Guibert of Nogent, *De vita sua sive monodiarum suarum libri tres*, 1.21, in John F. Benton, trans., *Self and Society in Medieval France* (Toronto: University of Toronto Press, 1984), 102.

90. Anonymous, *Summa sacramentorum, De indulgenciis et remissionibus* (Munich, Staatsbibliothek Clm 22233, fol. 44rb): "Item si indulgencia pro pontibus edificandis, pro viis sternendis, vel planiendis, vel alias meliorandis, sciendum quod licet unicuique dispensatorum conducere operarios ad agenda opera domini sui, sic licet prelatis ecclesiarum in huiusmodi opere laborantibus dare indulgencias, quas viderint expedire considerato fructu illius ecclesie, quia huiusmodi opera serviunt peregrinacionibus et alias propter pias causas iter agentibus. Magis est enim elemosina et etiam precepti dei litteralis obediencia *planum facere et eligere lapides* [Is 62.10]."

91. Anonymous, *Summa sacramentorum* (Munich, Staatsbibliothek Clm 22233, fol. 44va): "Agentes in malis passagiis et viis periculosis et laboriosis inpediuntur. Cespitant et leduntur et quadrige versantur, et vina effunduntur et equi occiduntur et homines irascuntur. Murmurant et maledicunt omnes illos qui viam reparasse debuerant, et deum et sanctos turpissime iurando blasphemantes mortaliter peccant."

92. X 5.38.4.

93. *Social Factor*, 79.

94. J. Kehr, *Regesta romanorum pontificum* (Berlin: Weidmann, 1908), 3:376.

95. August Potthast, *Regesta pontificum romanorum*, (Berlin: Rudolf Decker, 1874), 1:328, no. 3799.

96. *Social Factor*, 93.

97. *Social Factor*, 87.

98. Guillaume Mollat, ed., *Lettres communes de Jean XXII*, (Paris: E. de Boccard, 1919), 7:147, no. 40181.

99. Boniface VIII, *Les registres de Boniface VIII* (Paris: Thorin & Sons, 1906), 3:508–509, no. 4719.

100. Peter Passutti, ed., *Regesta Honorii papae III* (Rome: Ex Typographia Vaticana, 1895), 2:88–89, no. 4098.

101. Rudolf Philippi, ed., *Preussisches Urkundenbuch* (Königsberg: Hartungsche Verlagsdruckerei, 1882), 1:73, no. 98, and 1:123, no. 163.

102. *Social Factor*, 107.

103. Innocent IV, *Les registres d'Innocent IV*, (Paris: Ernest Thorin, 1897), 3:176, no. 6335.

104. G. R. Owst, *Preaching in Medieval England* (Cambridge: Cambridge University Press, 1926), 100. For the date of the *Summa predicantium*, see W. A. Pantin, *The English Church in the Fourteenth Century* (Cambridge: Cambridge University Press, 1955), 147, n. 2.

105. Tanner and Alberigo, 1:263.

106. Carole Rawcliffe, "The Hospitals of Later Medieval London," *Medical History* 28 (1984), 18–21.

107. David Knowles and R. N. Hadcock, *Medieval Religious Houses: England and Wales* (New York: St. Martin's Press, 1972), 310–410.

108. Carole Rawcliffe, *Medicine for the Soul: The Life, Death, and Resurrection of an English Medieval Hospital, St. Giles, Norwich, c. 1249–1550* (Stroud, England: Sutton Publishing, 1999), 248.

109. Nicholas IV granted indulgences of one hundred and forty days to leper hospitals in Tours, Perugia, and Assisi. Ernest Langlois, ed., *Les registres de Nicolas IV*, (Paris: Thorin & Sons, 1891), 2:681, nos. 4753, 4754, 4755. In 1303, Bishop Peter of Basel gave permission to the alms-collectors of the leper hospital outside the walls of Ulm to gather alms. Friedrich Pressel, ed., *Ulmisches Urkundenbuch* (Stuttgart: Karl Aue, 1873), 1:280, no. 233.

110. Boniface VIII, *Les registres*, 1:673–674, no. 1780.

111. Rawcliffe, "Hospitals of Later Medieval London," 2.

112. Langlois, ed., *Les registres de Nicolas IV*, 2:681, no. 4752.

113. Boniface VIII, *Les registres*, 1:758, no. 1981.

114. Mollat, ed., *Lettres communes de Jean XXII*, 3:94 (1906), no. 11351, and 4:124 (1910), no. 15749.

115. Francis Henry Dickinson, ed., *Missale ad usum insignis et praeclare ecclesiae sarum* (Oxford: J. Parker and Soc., 1861–1883), col. 886*: "Missa pro mortalitate evitanda quam dominus papa Clemens fecit et constituit in collegio cum omnibus cardinalibus, et concessit omnibus poenitentibus, vere contritis et confessis, sequentem missam audientibus, cclx dies indulgentiae."

116. Dickinson, ed., Missale, col. 886*: "Et omnes audientes sequentem missam debent portare in manu unam candelam ardentem dum missam audiunt per quinque dies sequentes, et tenere eam in manu per totam missam, genibus flexis: et eis mors subitanea nocere non poterit."

117. William J. Dohar, *The Black Death and Pastoral Leadership: The Diocese of Hereford in the Fourteenth Century* (Philadelphia: University of Pennsylvania Press, 1995), 4–5.

118. Duffy, 294.

119. Innocent IV, *Commentaria Innocenti quarti Pont. Maximi super libros quinque decretalium*, X 5.38.4 (Frankfurt: Sigismundus Feyrabendus, 1570, 543va): "Sunt et

aliae indulgentiae quae requirunt honorem et devotionem, ut sunt indulgentiae quae fiunt euntibus ad praedicationem et missas, et alia huiusmodi."

120. Potthast, ed., *Regesta pontificum romonorum*, 2:1412, no. 17322.

121. Duffy, 124.

122. Joseph A. Jungmann, S. J., *The Mass of the Roman Rite: Its Origins and Development*, trans. Francis A. Brunner (New York: Benziger, 1953), 2:215, no. 87.

123. Duffy, 56–57.

124. Thomas Frederick Simmons and Henry Edward Nolloth, eds., *The Lay Folks' Catechism*, EETS 118 (London: K. Paul, Trench, Trubner & Co., 1901), 3.

125. Tanner and Alberigo, 1:245.

126. Miri Rubin, *Corpus Christi: The Eucharist in Late Medieval Culture* (Cambridge: Cambridge University Press, 1991), 168.

127. Rubin, 172.

128. Rubin, 169–170.

129. *AS* April 1:462: "Nos enim ad invitandum fideles quod festum illud venerabilis celebrent et observent; omnibus poenitentibus et confessis, qui ad ecclesiam ubi officium agetur de eodem, ipso die et per octavas, accesserint reverenter, centum dies de iniunctis sibi poenitentiis misericorditer relaxamus."

130. Rubin, 174.

131. From Sémur, Bibliotheque municipale MS 42, fol. 195, in H. Martin, *Le métier de predicateur en France septentrionale à la fin du môyen âge, 1350–1520* (Paris: Éditions du Cerf, 1988), 419.

132. Oxford, Bodleian Library MS Rawlinson G 23, fol. 1: "Commemoraciones dominicae passionis facte a domino papa Iohannes xxii dicende post horas canonicas quicumque dixerit pro qualibet hora centum dies indulgencie auctoritate predicti pape possidebit."

133. Oakley, 311.

134. Oxford, Bodleian Library MS Lyell 30, fol. 41v.

135. Oxford, Bodleian Library MS Lyell 30, fol. 43r, and MS Tanner 407, fol. 42v. The pardon is written in dark, larger script in the Tanner manuscript.

136. Oxford, Bodleian Library MS Lyell 30, fol. 51v. The text of the indulgence itself is on fol. 93.

137. Oxford, Bodleian Library MS Bodl. 487, fol. 21r: "annis in festo assumptionis beate marie virginis a primis vesperis usque ad secundas est plena remissio et indulgencia omnium peccatorum concessa."

138. Bernard Guillemain, "Les papes d'Avignon, les indulgences, et les pèlerinages," in *Les pèlerinages* (Toulouse: E. Privat, 1980), 262.

139. *AS* Oct. 13:466 and 13:469.

140. *Magnum bullarium romanum a beato Leone mango usque ad s. d. n. Benedictum XIII*, (Luxembourg: Andreae Chevalier, 1727), 1:74, 1:78, and 1:79.

141. *Magnum bullarium romanum*, 1:204.

142. *Magnum bullarium romanum*, 1:200.

143. *Geschichte*, 2:176.

144. Guillemain, 257.

145. Herbert Thurston, S. J, and Donald Attwater, eds., *Butler's Lives of the Saints* (New York: Kenedy, 1956), 4:131.

146. Th. Gousset, *Les actes de la province ecclésiastique de Reims* (Reims: L. Jacquet, 1843), 2:355–356.

147. Goodich, 132.

148. *PL* 180:1063: "Plurima clara diversorum miraculorum genera, beati Jacobi apostoli meritis ad sacratissimum altare suum, ad compunctionem fidelium, in Pistoriensi ecclesia demonstravit; nam sicut venerabili fratre nostro Attone eiusdem civitatis religioso episcopo, et aliis pluribus referentibus, agnovimus, caeci, claudi, contracti, et alii diversis languoribus debiles, in eodem loco, per beati, ut diximus, Jacobi preces et merita, optata salutis remedia percipere."

149. D'Avray, "Papal Authority," 396.

Chapter 3

The Treasury of Merit

On January 27, 1343, Pope Clement VI (1342–1352) proclaimed the bull *Unigenitus*.[1] The pope addressed the bull to the bishop of Tarragona and his suffragans. The bull announced Clement's plan to hold another Jubilee in the year 1350. The idea of proclaiming another Jubilee, however, originated not in the mind of Clement VI but, rather, among a number of noble Roman families who wanted the Jubilee indulgence.[2] Bridget of Sweden and Petrarch both encouraged the pope to grant the request of the Roman aristocrats.[3] Thus, like most indulgences and church benefits, the beneficiaries of the pardon initiated the process whereby church authorities proclaimed a remission.

In the introduction to *Unigenitus*, Clement laid out the scriptural basis for indulgences. Jesus wrought the redemption of the human race, said the pope, not through the blood of goats and calves, which were the sacrifices of the Old Law, nor "by corruptible gold and silver, rather He redeemed us by the precious blood of that pure and immaculate Lamb."[4] In the great act of salvation, "the sacrificed Innocent shed no small drop of blood on the altar of the Cross, which because the union of God and man [in that Innocent] would nonetheless have sufficed for the redemption of the whole human race, instead, His Blood flowed copiously, indeed, just like a flood."[5] By His Passion, Christ:

> acquired the treasury (*thesaurum*) of the Church Militant, wishing to store up treasure for the sons of His Holy Father, such that there might now be an infinite treasure for men, through which those who draw upon it are made friends of God. Indeed, this treasure is not wrapped in cloth, nor hidden in a field, but committed to be dispensed to the faithful profitably through St. Peter, the bearer of the keys of heaven, and to his successors on earth, and applied mercifully for right and reasonable causes to the truly penitent and confessed, now for the plenary, now for the partial remission of temporal penalty owed for sin.[6]

Not only the merits of Christ, but also those of the Blessed Mother and of all the saints "from the early times until the latest times," are continually added to the stockpile of the church's treasure; consequently, the "consumption or diminishing of that treasury ought not to be feared in any way."[7]

Several generations earlier, Clement's predecessor Boniface VIII "wanted to open the unconsummable treasury in such a way as to arouse and reward the devotion of the faithful, and so he proclaimed the fullest remission of sin [in the year 1300] to those truly penitent and confessed who should visit and pray in the basilicas in Rome during that year."[8] But while Boniface had stipulated that a Jubilee should be celebrated once every hundred years, Clement noted a scriptural prefiguration of more frequent Jubilees: "In the law of Moses (which the Lord did not come to destroy, but to fulfill spiritually), every fiftieth year was reckoned a jubilee of remission and rejoicing [Lv 25.8–13], and by which law a holy number of days of remission is granted."[9] Furthermore, the number fifty "is especially honored in the Old Testament by allowance of the Law, in the New Testament by the visible sending forth of the Holy Spirit to the disciples [Pentecost], through whom the remission of sins is given."[10] But Clement granted the indulgence not only for these reasons, but also he hoped that there would be more partakers of this kind of indulgence, "since, consequently, few out of the many are able to arrive for the centennial years owing to the brevity of human life, by the advice of our brothers the lord cardinals, we order the interval between the aforesaid Jubilee indulgences to be reduced . . . to the fiftieth year."[11] Like his predecessor Boniface, Clement commanded that residents of Rome pray for thirty consecutive days at the basilicas to receive the indulgence. Pilgrims and foreigners had only to pray for fifteen days.

Fewer pilgrims took advantage of the Jubilee of 1350 than had done so in 1300. Many penitents, who would have welcomed the opportunity to make pilgrimage to Rome, had died of the Black Death, although the plague may have compelled many to make the journey, who in less terrifying circumstances would have remained at home.[12] Furthermore, wars in both Italy and France endangered all travelers to Italy. Nonetheless, penitents from all over Christendom endured inclement weather, hunger, and highwaymen to descend upon the Holy City and atone for their sins. So many pilgrims crowded into the city that some lacked accommodations. Many spent the nights in the cold outdoors, huddled in Rome's streets and alleys.

In *Unigenitus*, Clement confirmed a number of traditional teachings. First, as St. Peter taught in his first epistle, Jesus paid the price of humanity's ransom from the slavery of sin and the Evil One with his own blood. Indeed, that copious flow of Christ's blood had won for the Church Militant (the Church Triumphant having no need of it) an inexhaustible fund of merit, usually depicted as a treasure chest, to which were added the merits of the Blessed Mother and of all the martyrs and saints throughout history. Penitents in a state of grace—as in the words of Clement and theologians generally, those who were remade into "friends of God" because they had made a valid confession and received the grace of absolution in the sacrament of penance—could, with the approval of a pope or bishop, make withdrawals from the treasury to apply against their debt of sin. Finally, Christ entrusted stewardship of the treasury to the successors of Peter, who along with his brother bishops distributed its merits to the friends of God. The popes controlled one of medieval Christendom's most pregnant metaphors.

The origins of the belief in a treasury of merit has attracted research by both medieval and modern historians and theologians. Thirteenth-century Schoolmen were especially fond of one theory. In his commentary on the decretals, the canonist Hostiensis credited the French Dominican Hugh of St. Cher (c. 1200–1263), Cardinal of St. Sabina and sponsor of Juliane of Liège, with the invention of the treasury:

> Moreover, the martyrs shed their blood for the faith and the church, and they were punished beyond that for which they had sinned. It so occurs that in [Christ's] shedding of blood, all sin is punished, and this effusion of blood is the stored treasury in the cask of the church, the keys of which belong to the church. Hence, when the church wishes, she is able to open the cask, and will be able to grant to anyone her treasury, by granting indulgences and remissions to the faithful. And thus sin goes not unpunished, because it was punished in the Son of God, and by His holy martyrs, according to the Lord Cardinal Hugh.[13]

Other medieval writers acquiesed in the authority of Hostiensis, although they uncovered no evidence to corroborate the canonist's accreditation of Hugh. Neither has modern scholarship been able to confirm Hostiensis. No pertinent manuscript survives, nor does any extant medieval library catalogue list a treatise by Hugh in which he is likely to have elucidated the treasury of merit. The probability is that, had it existed in the first place, the manuscript tradition would have preserved Hugh's authorship of the treasury, given the treasury's ubiquity and popularity in the religious imagination of medieval Latin Christians. Perhaps Hostiensis was writing from undependable hearsay.

As for modern investigations into the origins of the treasury of merit, liberal Protestant historians, writing at the turn of the twentieth century, condemned the notion of the treasury as utterly perverse and unprecedented in the history of the Church. How could medieval Christians seriously portray the process of atonement and reconciliation in an image that was so crassly arithmetic, mercantile, and monetary? Furthermore, why should the metaphor of the treasury postdate the first indulgences by about a century and a half? What purpose did the teaching of the treasury serve? Henry C. Lea observed that the twelfth-century sacramental theologians of penance had little to say about indulgences.[14] In contrast the mendicant theologians of the mid-thirteenth century wrote a good deal. Lea then insisted that scholastic theologians invented the treasury to increase the power of the papacy, since they also taught that the pope had final authority over its distribution.[15] Lea argued not only that the treasury was a *mercantile metaphor* but also that acceptance of the treasury "led naturally to the *mercantile treatment* of sin and pardon . . . in which the sinner is taught that God keeps an account with him, which is to be paid, it matters little how,"[16] a judgment that barely veils the sixteenth-century Protestant witticism about the alleged selling of indulgences: "when the money in the box clinks, the soul from Purgatory springs." The possibilities for abuse angered Lea, certain as he was that the image of the treasury only whetted the avarice of friars and curialists, and corrupted the souls of countless late medieval believers. Since the convocation of Vatican II, some Catholic theologians and historians have admitted to sharing his misgivings.

However, most modern Catholic historians and theologians, like their medieval predecessors, also were interested in discovering who invented the doctrine of the treasury. Paulus believed, on the basis of the Cologne 1623 edition of book four of his *Summa theologica*, that the English Franciscan Alexander of Hales (c. 1185–1245) was the author of the treasury. According to the Quaracchi editors of the modern critical edition of this text, however, book four may no longer be considered to have been written by Alexander.[17]

What all the preceding theories share, of course, is the assumption that metaphor and the teaching of the treasury took place in a "top-down" manner, that is, that some intellectual fabricated the idea, and that his students and disciples popularized it. Barring the discovery of new evidence, dead ends are bound to greet this approach to the treasury's origins. Still, the question of the origins of the treasury remains a fascinating one, since in the treasury, Catholics had coined one of the most historiographically controversial metaphors in medieval religious culture. The treasury provides the basis for a fuller understanding of indulgences in medieval religion, if historians entertain a rather different approach—what might crudely be called the "bottom-up" perspective, for in the words of M. D. Chénu: "The economy of salvation is not defined exclusively in the reflective and cautiously reasoned understanding of a few licensed thinkers, but also in the concrete decisions, in the state of life embraced, in the ideals of sanctity, in the evangelical work which the church, in its head and members, approves, sets up, promotes—in sort, defines."[18] The treasury once again compels modern historians of medieval religion to reconsider the distinction often made in recent scholarly work between clerical, elite culture on the one hand and popular, folkloric culture on the other.

The brief comment of Praepositinus of Cremona (1140–1210), chancellor of the University of Paris from 1206 until 1209, suggests that, as far as the practice and imaging of indulgences was concerned, little separated the rustic parishioner who desired pardons from the bishops who granted them. He observed that indulgences were a custom of the universal Church:

> Now as regarding pardons (*absolutiones*)—they are only granted by bishops who proclaim "whoever shall give one *denarius* to such-and-such a place, shall be remitted a certain amount"—it is asked whether someone who gives because of devotion is absolved. This seems to be the case, as the Lord said [Mt 16.18]. When a bishop grants this absolution justly and without error, therefore, this contributor is absolved. Furthermore, this is a universal custom of the church (*consuetudo ecclesie*), against which it is not permitted to dispute. Therefore, this pardon is valid.[19]

Praepositinus's description of indulgences as a "universal custom of the church" carries great weight. He meant that the universal Church accepted their worth and power and, as a result, an indulgence was infallibly efficacious because that universal Church could not err. Latin Christians, then, had embraced a common set of ideas about indulgences *before* theologians and canonists began to write learned commentaries about them.

Furthermore, the theologians and canonists made descriptive, not prescriptive, remarks about indulgences. Their opinions about pardons should be thought about in the same way as their commentaries on other authorities (such as the Bible or the *Decretum*) in the Christian intellectual tradition. The authoritative texts as well as the authoritative commentaries had been handed down from previous generations, and the scholar's task was to contribute to the tradition of commentary. Scholars applied the same intellectual method to the dispensation and reception of indulgences as they had to the Mass. By the beginning of the thirteenth century, bishops and popes had long been conceding indulgences, and penitents had equally long been obtaining them. Both grantors and receivers must have believed in their validity and efficacy. The intellectuals explained how and why that validity worked, and they described that validity with a colorful metaphor. Any meaningful explanation of indulgences' benefits and powers depend *on what was generally imagined about them*. The academic commentaries, then, offer the modern student of medieval religion a keyhole through which the granting and receiving of indulgences might be better understood.

By the middle of the thirteenth century, theologians and canonists teased out a doctrine from ideas and images already current in Latin Christendom, which has ever since been the accepted theological explanation of indulgences' validity and efficacy. In the commentaries on the authoritative texts, the *summae*, and the pastoral manuals, theologians and canonists taught that indulgences were grants—some even used the term *payments*—from the infinite treasury of merit that Christ and the martyrs had gained for the church through their example, suffering, and good works. Thus Bonaventure said: "remissions or indulgences are granted from the superabundant merits which belong to the church, which indeed are unto its spiritual treasury."[20] In more Aristotelian terms, Thomas Aquinas stated: "Indeed, the cause of remission of penalty in indulgence is nothing other than the abundance of merits of the church."[21] The distribution of these merits by a bishop or his duly appointed agents to the confessed and contrite who had completed a good work could make vicarious satisfaction possible. No one commentator on the Christian tradition invented the treasury of merit. Instead, the metaphor's origins are better sought in Scripture and the scripturally inspired liturgy, as well as the daily routine of medieval life.

SOURCES OF THE IMAGE

In the treasury of merit, medieval Catholics undeniably conceptualized pardons in a mercantile image, but what must be remembered is that Scripture, as interpreted by the Fathers and proclaimed in the cycle of liturgy and paraliturgical dramas, constituted the source of that imagery. Indeed, before they became religious terms, the Latin words *redemptio* and *redimere* originally had secular and commercial meanings. The word *redemptio* denoted a buying back or ransom (*re-[d]-emptio*). The verb from which the noun was derived, *redimere*, referred in particular to the liberation by ransom of captives, prisoners, and slaves.

Scripture, of course, described God's rescuing of his people from captivity as a ransoming. The prophet Isaiah foretold: "those whom the Lord has ransomed will return and enter Zion singing [Is 51.11]." The people of Israel would regain their freedom, but only after God paid their ransom. Scripture also spoke of the price (*pretium*) of redemption and liberation. The psalmist thus lamented over God's abandonment of Israel to her enemies: "You have sold your people for no price (*sine pretio*) [Ps 43.13]." He also denied that any man could redeem himself: "A man may not give to God the cancellation of his debt or the price of the redemption of his soul [*pretium redemptionis animae suae*] [Ps 48.9]." The Fathers understood this Psalm as meaning that the giving of alms was the price of salvation. Augustine wrote that this psalm meant that "they, who do not cease to give alms, give the price of the redemption of their souls." In his commentary on the same verse, Jerome regretted that some did not give alms "through which sins are

THE TREASURY OF MERIT

forgiven."[22] Such comments, of course, draw mental pictures wherein the buyer uses coin to purchase a slave or captive.

The same language figured prominently in the New Testament. Paul contrasted the slavery of sinfulness with the freedom of faith in Christ, which he twice reminded the Corinthians had been purchased at a price (*pretio* [1 Cor 6.20 and 1 Cor 7.23]). In verses Pope Clement VI cited in *Unigenitus*, Peter likewise recalled that Christians' redemption came not from "corruptible things as gold or silver . . . but from the precious blood of Christ (*sed pretioso sanguine Christi*, [1 Pt 1.18–19])", that is, Christ's blood was *precious* precisely because it was the *price* of redemption—both words have the same Latin root. Peter thus contrasted coins minted in corruptible gold and silver with the incorruptible blood of Christ. Finally, the language of the *Pater noster*, which the canon law of the medieval Church required parents to teach to their children *in Latin*, encouraged mercantile images of atonement, since the prayer asked God the Father to forgive *debita nostra*—our "debts" as rendered in the Douay-Rheims, rather than "sins," as in modern translations of the word—as we forgive *debitoribus nostris*, our "debtors" [Mt 6.9–13].

The meaning of redemption in Christian teaching closely paralleled its secular and legal antecedents. As Scripture made clear, however, Jesus had satisfied a spiritual, not monetary, debt. Nonetheless, the Church Fathers could appropriate the juridical sense of *redemptor* to illustrate the salvific mission of Jesus as related in the New Testament. For Jerome, redemption in Christ mirrored the Trinity of which he was the Second Person. Christ, a Trinity Himself, is "the sanctification, without whom no one shall see the face of God, Christ is the redemption, as well as the redemptor and the price."[23] In Jerome's blatantly commercial metaphor, Jesus was the purchase itself, but he was also an agent participating in the purchase, as well as the money that exchanged hands because of the purchase.

In *Sermo* 130, Augustine even more plainly compared Christ the Redeemer to the buyer and seller of goods and wares:

The Merchant came to purchase the goods of our world, and since every merchant sells and buys, he sold what he possessed and acquired what he did not have. When a merchant buys something, he gives money in return for it, and he receives money when he sells something, just so has Christ in this [spiritual] market sold and acquired. But what did Christ purchase? The things that abound in this world: birth, toil and death. And what did he sell? Rebirth, restoration, and rule forever. O good Merchant, buy us! What else should I say? Buy us, for we ought to live in grace because you have bought us. You spend our price in us—we drink Your Blood; therefore, you spend your price in us. And we read the Gospel, our provision. We are Your slaves, we are Your creatures: You made us; you redeemed us. The Lord is indeed able to buy his slave; he is not able to create him a slave. The Lord indeed created and redeemed his slaves: he created, so that they might exist, he redeemed, lest they always be captives. For we fell to the prince of this world, who seduced and made Adam a slave, and with his fall the Evil One began to possess us as slaves. But the Redeemer came and the deceivor was conquered. And what did the Redeemer do in exchange for our captivity? To pay the price of our ransom he stretched out his arms on the Cross.[24]

Christ the Redeemer was also Christ the Merchant, who purchased the liberty of humankind from the servitude of sin. Christ had paid to the Great Slaver, the Prince of Darkness, the ransom of all humankind. The price of the ransom was Christ's own blood.

The imagery of the Bible and the Fathers would have reached most medieval Christians through the scripturally inspired liturgy and the paraliturgical plays, which enjoyed great popularity from the twelfth century on. Isaiah 51.11, for instance, was the Old Testament reading for the octave of Epiphany in the Sarum missal.[25] The cycle of the Divine Office required that monks sang Psalm 48 each Saturday at the hour of Matins. One of the oldest and most familiar hymns of the Advent season, the *Veni Emmanuel*, pleaded with God to "ransom captive Israel." This hymn, based on Is 7.14, is itself derived from the seventh-century O-Antiphons, sung at Vespers on the seven days preceding Christmas. Among the pertinent New Testament texts, 1 Cor 6.20 was read on the fourth Sunday after the octave of Epiphany, and 1 Cor 7.23 on the eleventh Sunday after Trinity Sunday in the Sarum missal.[26] Not only was 1 Pt 1.18–19 read on the second Sunday after Easter in the Sarum rite,[27] it also inspired numerous prayers for the Mass, such as the following: "Spare, O Lord, we ask you, spare Your people and now suffer those, whom You have *redeemed by the precious blood of Your Son*, to be beset by no adversities."[28] The prayer, which survives in forty manuscripts from all over medieval Christendom (twenty-three of which date from before the eleventh century), was invoked during the regular cycles of the liturgical seasons as well as in a variety of special petitions. Another prayer survives in a Fulda manuscript of about 975, which contains a rite of Mass for the cultivation of humility: "all-powerful and merciful God, who redeemed all people sold under sin, not by a payment of gold and silver, but by the precious blood of Your Son."[29]

In addition to the liturgy, Latin Christians of the High Middle Ages received the mercantile imagery of redemption from liturgically inspired religious drama. Medieval liturgical commentators themselves appreciated and highlighted the dramatic grandeur of the liturgy. According to Honorius of Autun (c. 1100), "our tragedian [i.e., the celebrant] represents to the Christian people in the theater of the church, by his gestures, the struggle of Christ, and impresses upon them the victory of his redemption."[30] The earliest of these plays, which date from the late eleventh century, extended and elaborated the liturgies for Christmas and Holy Week. The earliest dramas often excerpted dialogue verbatim from Scripture. Clerics performed them inside churches. In a twelfth-century play written in Beauvais, the two disciples to whom Christ appeared on the road to Emmaus remind the audience that Jesus was "our redemption (*nostra redemptio*)."[31] The midwives in a twelfth-century play from Fleury, probably sung at the end of Matins on Epiphany, show the baby Jesus to the magi and introduce him as "the redemption of the world (*redemptionis mundi*)."[32] In the *Ordo repraesentationis Adae*, written in Norman French and probably staged on the front steps of the church, the patriarch Abraham prophesies the birth of Christ, "by whom the world will be ransomed."[33] In the same play, the prophet Jeremiah proclaims that the Son of God will come down to earth for the sake of humankind, and "He will release Adam from prison, / Giving his own body as ransom."[34] In the famous twelfth-century Passion Play of Benediktbeuern in Germany, the boys of Jerusalem greet Jesus with the joyous shout: "This is he who is destined to come for the deliverance of the people, this is our salvation and the redemption of Israel (*redemptio Israhel*)."[35] Other plays, such as the early thirteenth-century Klosterneuberg *Ordo paschalis* and the twelfth-century Sicilian *De peregrino in die lune Pasche*, incorporated the hymn *Ihesu, nostra redemptio* into the performance itself.[36] That these plays were so eagerly produced, performed, and attended testifies to how successfully they captured the medieval religious imagination. By the thirteenth century, the staging of plays ceased to be the preserve of the clergy. Lay religious associations assumed the responsibilities for and cost of production of the plays. By the fourteenth century, the staging and performance of the liturgical plays created heated competitions between lay confraternities all over Christendom.

Hence, by the turn of the twelfth century, Scripture, the liturgy, homilies, and religious drama had for centuries regularly and consistently portrayed in the metaphors of ransom, price, chattel slavery, and precious metals the means by which God had chosen to reconcile a fallen humanity to Himself. The very imagery of Scripture taught Christians to understand the essential mysteries of their faith in language that compared Christ's salvific mission to the handing over of gold and silver to the powers of sin and death. As a consequence of Adam's sin, his children were cast into prison and had been delivered into bondage. The ransom, the cost of manumission, the price of humanity's liberation, was the Redeemer himself. This language and imagery— all undeniably and plainly Christian—was the most significant reason that, after indulgences had come to be distributed all over Latin Christendom, bishops and penitents imagined that they were making withdrawals from the inexhaustible treasury of merit that Jesus, Mary, the martyrs, and all other saints had won for the church through their suffering and death.

FURTHER REFINEMENTS

The development of the treasury of merit as a doctrine, however, did not rest on the language and imagery of Scripture and the liturgy alone. A confluence of other cultural and intellectual developments, unique to the High Middle Ages, also contributed to the theological teaching of the treasury of merit.

First, the transition, in the words of Michael Clanchy, from "memory to written record" in Latin Christendom, contributed to the emergence of the treasury as a teaching of the Church.[37] Prior to the twelfth century, the memory of legal transactions was preserved through image and ritual, rather than documentation. For instance, when land changed hands, parties to the transfer summoned villagers to witness the event. The handing over of a knife or a clod of soil from the previous to the new owner symbolized the agreement. In case of a legal dispute over ownership, litigants customarily presented these symbols as evidence of their claim to the land, as well as to serve as a mnemonic device for those who had witnessed the transfer of the land. The following anecdote, translated by Richard Southern, describes a record of enserfment:

> Be it known to all who come after us, that a certain man in our service called William, the brother of Reginald, born of free parents, being moved by the love of God and to the end that God—with whom is no acceptance of persons but regard only for the merits of each—might look favorably on him, gave himself up as a serf to St. Martin of Marmoutier; and he gave not only himself but all his descendants, so that they should for ever serve the abbot and monks of this place in a servile condition. And in order that this gift might be made more certain and apparent, he put the bell-rope around his neck and placed four pennies from his own head on the altar of St. Martin in recognition of serfdom.[38]

The text further records the witnesses to the event. In a gesture clearly intended to impress his own humiliation on mostly illiterate memories, William placed the rope of the monastery's bell around his own neck. Further, he left the price of his freedom upon the altar of the monastery; the four pennies he gave the monastery served as the symbol of his serfdom, not only for himself but for future generations of his family as well. Consequently, prior to the widespread employment of documentary records, symbol, ritual, and image preserved the memory of past events.

Indeed, as Clanchy has pointed out, rituals such as these survived long after documentary records had come into common use. For instance, in the fourteenth and fifteenth centuries, English testators asked that copies of the indulgences they had obtained should be placed in the grave with them, as if to show them to God or St. Peter at Heaven's gate as a ticket of admittance. Even if these testators could not read what was written on the parchment, they knew that the pardons were written in important and powerful words by the competent authorities. The document itself served as the symbol of the remission granted them by the authority of the Church Militant. As written record replaced memory, old habits of mind coexisted with new ones demanded by the increasing prevalence of written documentation in medieval life and law. As far as indulgences were concerned, the image of a treasury of merit, inferred from scriptural and liturgical language, served well to memorialize the spiritual benefits bishops and popes conferred upon penitents.

But the reliance on written documentation, upon which medieval businessmen and governments increasingly relied, contributed significantly to the treasury of merit as a theological conception. Many occupations of the twelfth and thirteenth centuries required either a growing acquaintance with the keeping of accounts or at least enough arithmetic ability to keep track of money. Merchants and financiers developed more sophisticated business records. "The great increase in the number of inventories and accounts after 1180, and the passion for numerical accuracy which they reveal, were partly the effects of a general cultural progress. But it also shows a greater familiarity with the use of money; masters and their agents gradually became conscious of values and more accustomed to appraising and accounting."[39] According to the thirteenth-century Dominican Giordano da Pisa, the merchant "did nothing day or night but calculate," and "thought arithmetically in and out of his countinghouse; and when he had children, whether they followed him into trade, or became friars or mathematicians, he would pass on to them a deep familiarity with number."[40] No medieval businessman could have survived long in the unforgiving world of medieval commerce without documentary records such as bills of sale or accounts of receipt and expenses.

Kings, popes, and bishops also decided that documentary records well served the needs of rule. By the reign of Henry II (1154–1189), the royal Exchequer in England tracked royal finances in several rolls. The pipe rolls of the bishop of Winchester date from 1208. Christ Church Canterbury began recording the profits made by its manors in 1224. Although rather less is known of the production or use of royal documents on the continent, what is known suggests that the trends at the French and papal courts mirrored those of England.[41] The rate of increase in the number of letters extant issued by the papacy, the French crown, and the English crown from the years 1080–1200 is virtually the same.[42]

The new dependence on documentation dovetailed with a transformation of royal militaries. Prior to the eleventh century, most armies, whether royal or otherwise, consisted of the feudal levy. Leaders granted their warriors *honores* in exchange for a generally very brief term of military service. By the beginning of the twelfth century, most kings discovered that, because they were often unreliable and obliged only to forty days of campaigning, feudal warriors no longer served the monarchs' military ambitions. The hired soldier, in contrast, served as long as he was paid. Their preference for paid soldiers compelled the kings and their ministers to fret continually about the collection of revenues and disbursement of military stipends. Like Giordano da Pisa's merchant, kings were also preoccupied with the sums of money—not, of course, to make profits, but to wage war.

By the end of the thirteenth century, rural estate managers, most of whom were rustics themselves, were likewise conscripted into the increasing reliance on account rolls and other written records. According to an English source, peasants paid taxes *after the beadle showed them writs of the Exchequer listing their obligations*; the peasants must have understood, then, that that written document served as an instrument of royal authority. The statute of Exeter (1285) commanded local bailiffs to supply the king's commissioners with the names, recorded in a roll, of every village, half-village, and hamlet within franchises as well as in the kingdom as a whole. The crown also ordered bailiffs to make lists of everything on the manor, from tools to the amount of milk given by the cows. "From at least the 1270s, seignorial stewards and bailiffs were meant to have written on rolls the names of all males (excluding clerics) over the age of twelve; these lists were read out twice a year when the sheriff or the franchise-holder visited the locality for the view of frankpledge."[43] The reeves, bailiffs, and beadles then must have acquired a pragmatic, if not polished, literacy— perhaps only in French—for as Clanchy points out, they read their accounts aloud to the cultivators of the manor. Furthermore, the numerous ways in which laity involved themselves in the liturgy suggests that many peasants also had some familiarity with Latin. The humblest plowman, then, need not have been literate to share the arithmetic and mercantile habits of mind acquired by beadles, reeves, merchants, bankers, priests, bishops, or officials of the Exchequer.

The pervasiveness of accounting and documentation affected Christians' imaginings of reconciliation and atonement. For the scholastic theologian William of Auvergne (c. 1190–1249), writing around the year 1230, crusade indulgences resembled the payment rendered mercenary soldiers:

> Moreover, if a king or a prince wages war, he gives to his generals the power of summoning and recruiting soldiers, and also the power of paying them with stipends. Now

because the King of kings and Lord of lords Jesus Christ has waged war from the time during which, I believe, the church began to fight the not only spiritual, but also literal, or physical, or material war against the heretics and other enemies of the Christian religion, namely the pagans, and from the time of Mahomet, the Saracens, by necessity he gave to his generals, that is to the prelates, the power of summoning worldly soldiers, and of recruiting them, and of paying them with appropriate wages. What else is it to proclaim indulgences?[44]

William pressed the analogy further. Just as kings free their soldiers from other obligations to the crown, the church excuses crusaders from fasting, almsgiving, and other penitential works. Unlike royal soldiers, "the stipends of these soldiers will be an eternal remuneration, for the greatest and noblest deeds on their part."[45]

Early scholarly writings on indulgences reflect the transition. Following the rhetorical logic of a "debt of sin," atonement came to be imagined as a spiritual account of debits (sins, with penalties) and credits (works of satisfaction, such as indulgences), an account which was never certainly paid in full; consequently, penitential works were to be constantly undertaken. According to the theologian Simon of Tournai (probably in the last quarter of the twelfth century), partial indulgences could never completely eradicate the debt of sin:

It is asked whether since public remission is granted to pilgrims or frequenters of dedications under this form—"Let them be absolved from a third or from a seventh part," or however so much the prelate expresses—the pilgrim or frequentor of a dedication may be loosed from all penance if a third have been proclaimed and the pilgrim visit the church often. It is answered: if one goes to the dedication with a humble and contrite heart, one is absolved from a third part of penance. When one goes to the second dedication, one is absolved from the third part of penance to which one is *still* held— since one goes to another dedication—not of that penance to which one *was* held, because one had gone to the first dedication. And so on with the third dedication and all others. Therefore, if one goes to many, one is not wholly absolved from penalty.[46]

Simon must have had the earliest grants of indulgence in mind here, for he assumed that indulgences expressed the magnitude of their remissions as a fraction of the total debt of sin.

Over time, penitents thought about a remission's amount as a fraction less frequently than as a unit of account. This transition in the reckoning of indulgences' benefits was underway by the mid-twelfth century, as the comment of Peter of Poitiers, chancellor of the University of Paris from 1193 until his death in 1205, makes clear:

Moreover, when a priest, either a bishop or not, is able to reduce some part of penalty, it ought to be known that if a bishop or other prelate indicates or announces that he will remit a third or a fourth fraction of penance for the dedication of some church, or forty days, or some other such thing, to all those who contribute their alms to the maintenance of some church.[47]

Peter must have had in mind an indulgence such as that which Pope Urban III and a number of bishops together conceded to the abbey of St. Nicholas of Angers in 1186. Pope Urban granted to visitors of the monastery remission of *one-seventh* their debt of sin, and so like those granted in the first half of the twelfth century, the magnitude of the pardon was cited as a fraction. In contrast, the archbishop of Tours, the bishop of Angers, and all the bishops of Brittany granted *forty days* of indulgence each.[48] The magnitude of the remission extended to penitents by the bishops came in the form of whole numbers—rather more countable and accountable, and in keeping with the era's increasing reliance on accounts and documentary records.

By the late twelfth century, bishops and popes increasingly cited the magnitude of a pardon's remission in whole numbers, rather more precise and arithmetic than the indulgences Simon of Tournai considered. Pope Alexander III conceded a typical indulgence in 1163:

> Alexander, bishop, servant of the servants of God, to all the faithful of God who dwell throughout the kingdom of France, greetings and apostolic blessing. It is certain and proven by the testimony of many passages in the Scriptures, the manner in which our Lord and Redeemer Jesus Christ gave the full power of binding and loosing to St. Peter, the bearer of the keys of heaven, in these words, through which he ordained that power, saying, "You are Peter, and on this rock I shall build my church, and whatever you shall hold bound on earth, shall be held bound in heaven, and whatever you shall hold loosed on earth, shall be held loosed in heaven." That this same power has been held by each of Peter's successors from the same Redeemer until us we believe to be unknown by no one who has knowledge of the Sacred Scriptures. Accordingly, from that power conceded to us, who, although unworthy, succeed to the chair of St. Peter, by the Lord Jesus Christ, we, since the Church of St. Germain of Paris, which properly belongs by right to the most holy Church of Rome, extend the benefit of dedication according to the common counsel of our brothers the bishops and cardinals, and remit *one year* of enjoined penance to each of the faithful of God travelling to there because of devotion from the day of the dedication until and octave of Pentecost, and to those who shall visit there on the anniversary of the same day of dedication, and for *three days* following, we also indulge *twenty days* of enjoined penance, urging and exhorting all your faithful in the Lord, so that with a contrite humble heart, having visited at that same place in each year, such that you shall be seen to go there for no other thing than only the reason of devotion, and by the omnipotent Lord you may merit indulgence of your sins.[49]

Alexander thus conceded an indulgence whose benefits were neatly subject to accounting—a whole number of years (one) and a whole number of days (twenty). The most common number of days of remission granted was forty, the length of the penitential season of Lent. New indulgences, better suited to keeping penitential account, were almost entirely rendered in whole numbers in a marriage of the new mental habits required by accounting documentation, on the one hand, and Christian images of redemption, on the other. Indeed, in a comment that parallels Simon of Tournai's, the Dominican theologian Guerric of St. Quentin, following the logic of the rhetoric, considered whether the treasury of Christ's merits might be exhausted by continual withdrawals made from it because of the numbers of indulgences granted: "it seems that the treasury of the church is able to be exhausted, because subtraction is always made from it without any recompense or restoration."[50] The debits to the account far exceeded the credits. Of course, Guerric went on to say that the treasury was inexhaustible.

Unlike many modern scholars, the moral theologians of the twelfth and thirteenth centuries discerned no inconsistency between the new, arithmetic imagery and their emphasis on a psychologically more sophisticated and humane administration of confession and penance. The moral theologian Peter the Chanter (d. 1197), one of the first to pioneer the new approach to pastoral care, believed that indulgences were actually better stipulated in a specific number of days, than as a fraction of total penalty owed for sin: "Bishops grant remission of a third, or a fourth, part of penance, or howsoever much in saying, 'If someone shall give to this church construction a *nummos*, or some other amount, we grant him relaxation of a third of his penance by our authority, and the authority of God, and of the Blessed Mother, and of all the saints.' It would be better to declare that it should be called ten days, or something similar."[51] Peter offered no reasons for his preference. Perhaps he thought that pardons stated in fractions were too large; other early scholastics sometimes expressed the same concern. However, he may also have decided that penitents would benefit more from the arithmetic imagery. Whatever the reasons, Peter's endorsement made arithmetic imagery authoritative for many subsequent thinkers.[52]

At the same time, commentators were aware that the analogy of treasury and account limped, for they could never completely capture the vastness of God's generosity towards the repentant. Pope Innocent IV reminded readers that God's generosity should always be trusted:

> But you ask whether he receives more remission who gives greater alms or labors longer than he who gives less or works less. I respond as above, that God, who evaluates all things in their number, weight, and length, *beyond the measure set by the bishop* in church, shall give by grace more to one, less to another; concerning these things not much care or thought should be given, unless one thinks, because it ought to be believed, that the Lord, whose nature is pious and generous, always provides from Himself, *beyond the measure of grace and justice.*[53]

Furthermore, in comments echoed by many other thinkers, William of Auvergne cautioned anyone against certainty that his debt of sin was fully paid. The pursuit of indulgences, he said, should only be one facet of the penitential life, for that account can never be assumed to be cancelled: "No one is sure that he is freed from his penances . . . therefore no one is certain that he understands indulgences in this way [that they completely liberate penitents from their penances]. However, it is certain for anyone to be the debtor of enjoined penance, or of penance to be enjoined in the future."[54]

INDULGENCES AND CONTRITIONISM
The indulgence of the High Middle Ages depended for its development not only on the penitential regimen inherited from antiquity and the growing prominence of documentation and accounting in the twelfth and thirteenth centuries. A number of developments in twelfth-century spirituality and sacramental theology also figured prominently in the medieval history of pardons. In particular, Christian intellectuals had to connect indulgences with the era's increased emphasis on interior conversion. They also had to explain, during a period of penitential fervor in the Western Church, what constituted valid confession, the first step in the process of atonement, which made possible indulgences' efficacy.[55] The answers, of course, came in the commentaries on the authoritative texts, the theological and canonistic *summae*, and the pastoral manuals.

By the twelfth century, the essentials of confession and reconciliation had been in place for eight centuries; sacramental theologians addressed the question as to why the Church demanded of serious sinners both confession and penance. They distinguished between two consequences of serious sin. Each serious sin incurred both guilt (*culpa*) and penalty (*pena*). The guilt of serious sin (sometimes also called "mortal," because such sins "killed" the soul) was so offensive to God that it merited eternal death—a permanent separation of the soul from God; that is, the one guilty of serious sin, through his own perversion, cut *himself* off from God. However, those who embraced God's grace, repented, and sought God's forgiveness would suffer only a temporal death—the separation of the soul from the body until the Last Judgement.[56] The grace of repentance invited sinners to confess to a priest, who in the sacrament of penance absolved the guilt (*culpa*) of the sin. Although God's mercy had been extended to the penitent through this ministration of the priest in the sacrament of penance, God's justice still demanded satisfaction—the slate was not yet wiped clean, but the confessed was now in a state of grace or, as often said, a state of friendship with God, which made possible the satisfaction of God's justice. Full atonement required that in addition to sacramental confession, penitents complete penances enjoined on them by confessors during administration of the sacrament. Completed penances made full restitution and also served—in a favorite metaphor of theologians and canonists—as preventative medicine against the disease of further temptations, transgressions, and perversions.

Valid confession thus opened the gates of heaven for a contrite sinner, and so the sacramental theologians grappled with another important issue, namely, what constituted valid confession? The debate on this issue paralleled another controversy in twelfth-century sacramental theology, namely, the essence of valid marriage. In both cases, the consensus of the theologians echoed high medieval spirituality. Whereas the free consent of the man and the woman to the union—which suggested a movement of interior disposition—constituted a valid marriage, contrition of heart (instead of the exact enumeration of sins to the confessor) made a confession valid. In the case of marriage, theologians rejected the opinion of the canonist Gratian— no small authority—who argued that consummation made a marriage valid. In the case of the sacrament of penance, the theologians rejected the idea that a correct recitation of sins committed made a confession valid. In both cases, the authoritative opinion emphasized the necessity of the right ordering of the inner person, in keeping with the Gospel teaching: "For out of the heart come evil intentions, murder, adultery, fornication, theft, false witness, slander [Mt 15.19, Mk 7.21–23]."

Theologians and canonists (who were, after all, moral theologians) continually stressed that the efficacy of a grant of pardon depended upon contrition and confession, just as the Church had required for the very first indulgences. In his theological lexicon, the *Alphabeticum morale*, Peter the Chanter taught that

> pardon is granted for the necessity of a place or a person, or for the relief of the Holy Land and Jerusalem, by an equal compensation of penance, so that if one is not able to fast, one may succor a poor man, in a way that shall burden the penitent to give alms as much as to fast. For a wasteful or a rich man would much prefer to give alms than to fast, just as a greedy man would prefer not to give alms. Again, relaxation is granted when permission is given by the confessor to the one accepting penance. Finally, indulgence is granted whenever charity, contrition, and devotion are magnified, and, if some of these conditions are lacking, the relaxation is not valid.[57]

The emphasis on interior conversion explains the many discussions that compared the benefits of indulgences obtained by the rich versus those gained by the poor. Did one of the most commonly conceded pardons, namely, monies given for church constructions, discriminate against the poor? Did the rich, who could give much money, benefit from such indulgences more than the poor, who could contribute only a little? Peter of Poitiers considered the issue thus:

> Does anyone believe that if some rich fellow gives as many coins or *oboli* as an old, poor man he will receive an equal remission? Nonsense! For God does not ask men to do what they are incapable of; he does not consider how much one gives [for an indulgence], but from how much sincerity, that is, from what intention.[58]

The exterior act any indulgence required must be accompanied by the proper interior disposition. Peter's reasoning was echoed in an anonymous treatise, *De relaxationibus*:

> That a rich man is better off than a poor man [because one can give more for an indulgence than the other can] does not follow, because if the rich man and the poor man are in a state of charity in so far as the crown of eternal life is concerned they shall have equal merits, yet if they both die with unequal satisfaction because of their almsgiving or devotion one shall be more liberated from Purgatory than another.[59]

Succeeding generations of scholars upheld and refined the opinions of the late twelfth-century theology masters. Indeed, William of Auxerre, whose *Summa aurea* was written between 1215 and 1220, argued that indulgences probably removed more penalty from the debt of a poor man than of a rich one:

> In so far as pardon of penalty is concerned, a poor man's situation is worse than a rich man's; yet the poor man is not simply of the worse condition, rather, he is of the better condition. For although the rich man seems in an advantageous position in terms of the remissions which are granted for contributions of money, still the poor man is better off in so far as the pardon, which is granted to those in contrition. For the poor man is forgiven more certainly and efficaciously than the rich man, all other things being equal, for through contrition, rather than the contribution of alms, is the penalty of sin reduced more efficaciously.[60]

Again, the deeper contrition of the poor man merited a greater pardon than the sum given by the rich man.

Even in the work of the twelfth-century theologians, then, little may be found that was new; rather, they systematized and organized what had been believed about efficacious indulgence for quite some time into textbook form. Their commentaries and arguments made explicit what had been implicit in a bishop's concession and a penitent's reception of pardon. By the end of the twelfth century, for instance, proclamations of indulgence included the reminder that indulgences were efficacious only for those "truly penitent and confessed" (*vere poenitentibus et confessis*) or "heartily sorry and orally confessed" (*corde contritis et ore confessis*). All others were wasting their time. Only one who had turned away from sin and accepted Christian discipline gained the full benefit of remission. Finally, that indulgences were understood to apply to penalty, and not guilt, is made clear in a text of Godfrey of Poitiers, who said that "the *relaxatio* or indulgence granted by the pope must be related to sins that have been confessed; this is clearly his view because he says the indulgence does not apply to sins that have been forgotten (and not confessed)."[61]

The close connection that the Schoolmen drew between indulgences and penitential fervor was highlighted in manuals for confessors, a genre of religious literature that enjoyed great popularity until the end of the Middle Ages. Raymond of Peñafort (1175–1275), compiler of the *Decretals* and author of the thirteenth century's authoritative pastoral manual, *Summa de poenitentiis et matrimonio*, argued that the rewards of indulgences enhanced the reception of grace: "They have the power in a sinner making an offering out of pious devotion . . . for a bestowal of grace."[62] He asserted that three factors determined the magnitude of the remission gained: "It must be known that how much more or how much less of the remission of penance is reckoned according to three factors, namely, according to the zeal of the penitent himself, according to the amount of remission granted by the prelate, and according to the number of prelates granting the pardon."[63] In his widely popular *Summa confessorum*, which was completed around 1298, John of Freiburg reaffirmed the notion that the depth of the penitent's contrition increased the amount of remission gained through indulgences. Since zeal varied from penitent to penitent, the cancellation of debt must also vary, even if all received forty days of pardon:

> Therefore, indulgences are not valid for all equally, but according to how penitents are better or lesser disposed through conviction for the remission of sins, not simply to save their souls. For just as forty days of canonical penance is more valid to one penitent with greater fervor and labor than another who has less, so I say that forty days of indulgence is worth more for the one who disposes himself better for it, namely, by labor or fervor or discipline or by the quantity of his gift.[64]

So, the visitors to a monastery may all receive forty days of indulgence, but that did not mean that each received the same remission, lest interior conversion and devotion mean nothing in the reception of an indulgence.

THE AUTHORITY OF THE CHURCH

Contrition and confession, the learned commentators agreed, were not the only necessary requirements for a grant of efficacious indulgence. The commentators also taught that only bishops or their duly authorized agents could grant valid remissions. Abelard, who scolded bishops for being "prodigal in relaxing penances, remitting to all in common now a third, now a fourth, part of their penance under some pretext of charity," had argued that repentance alone reconciled sinners to God.[65] The Council of Soissons condemned his radical contritionism in 1122 and reaffirmed the traditional role of the ministrations and mediations of the Church in the process of human salvation. In 1215, Lateran IV upheld an old precept, namely, that among the prelates of the church, only bishops possessed the ordinary power to grant indulgences.[66] That no pardon, conceded by an abbot, survives from the medieval era for instance, must mean that either the law was obeyed or violations of the law were successfully nullified and erased from memory and the documentary record.

Hence, intellectuals also had to consider the church's authority to grant indulgences. By what power did the church grant cancellations of temporal penalties for sin? Of course, the answers invoked Scripture and the traditions of the church. Among a host of texts, two most commonly justified the church's ability to grant indulgences. The first and probably more authoritative was Jesus's command to Peter in Mt 16.19: "And I will give to you [Peter] the keys of the kingdom of heaven. And whatsoever you shall bind on earth, it shall be bound also in heaven: and whatsoever you shall loose on earth, it shall be loosed also in heaven." According to the ordinary gloss on Scripture, Peter here represented the whole church (not the pope), and so the efficacy of indulgences rested upon the unfailing, intercessory powers of the universal Church.[67] Another favorite text was Jn 20.23: "Whose sins you shall forgive, they are forgiven them; and whose sins you shall retain, they are retained." For the canonist Huguccio (c. 1190), this text proved conclusively the Church's power to grant pardons: "How is it then, that there are those who say that the remissions granted by the church, and which are granted daily in church, are not valid . . . for Christ Himself said: Whose sins you shall forgive, etc."[68] These two biblical texts continued to be the most authoritative on the issue of indulgences until the end of the Middle Ages and beyond.

The theologians Stephen Langton (1150/55–1228), Godfrey of Poitiers, and Robert Courson (1158/60–1219) produced other texts that testified to the church's authority to pardon a penitent's debt of satisfaction. Like the gloss on Mt 16.18, the commentaries of Langton, Godfrey, and Courson on these texts highlight the authority of the universal Church, as wielded by the bishops, who may apply the merits of one Christian to the debt of another, assuming that the beneficiary was in a state of charity and grace. For Langton, in 2 Cor 2.10, Paul explicitly declared that the apostles had the power to pardon satisfaction owed for sin: "If you forgive someone anything, so do I. For, what I have pardoned, if I have pardoned any thing, for your sakes have I done it in the person of Christ." Langton argued that this verse applied especially to the dispensation of indulgences, since Paul here was writing of the debt of sin, not the guilt:

> Here we have the authority of daily pardons, for in this text the apostle does not speak of the pardon of guilt (*condonacione culpe*) nor of the foulness of the soul, because here the apostle granted pardon without anyone's request; hence he speaks of the pardon or relaxation of satisfaction (*relaxatione satisfactionis*). For since the apostle pardoned satisfaction at the request of the community, and so he desired that it be granted to them, pardon of satisfaction is able to be granted at the request of some learned and honest man, and especially at the request of the saints, through whom pardons are granted every day for church consecrations, or the establishing and meeting of associations. And these Paul made in the person of Christ, as if Christ himself pardoned, because no one, here in this case Paul, could have done such a thing without the spirit of God, because he says he did so in the person of Christ, lest a pardon of this sort, which he granted for his friends, be empty.[69]

For Langton, Paul, who acted in the place of Christ and invoked the power of Christ, established the precedent whereby bishops grant pardons. Such an invocation, however, assumed a friendship between God and sinner; after all, while friends render each other all manner of kindnesses, strangers rarely give each other favors or affectionate greetings. After they confessed their serious sins, penitents once again became the friends of Christ.

Godfrey of Poitiers was a student of Langton's, an advisor to Pope Innocent III, and also an influential voice at Lateran IV. In his comments on 2 Cor 2.10, he argued that when *the pope in particular* granted indulgences, he acted in the stead of Christ, because as the ordinary gloss on Mk 6.28 ("the head of John the Baptist was given to the girl") stated, the headship of the church had been given to the Roman Church: "Therefore, the head of the grace of God was given to the Roman Church."[70] Godfrey's slight departure from the view of his teacher may well reflect the leadership of Innocent III as implemented in the reform decrees of Lateran IV, along with the longstanding tradition that only the pope had the power to concede plenary indulgences. A generation later, Thomas Aquinas interpreted the same text in the same way, but added that the pope has no less authority in the church than had the Apostle Paul.[71]

Godfrey's contemporary, the Englishman Robert Courson, was another advisor to Innocent who presented other examples from Scripture to support the authority of the church in general and of the pope in particular to grant pardons. While he appealed to the Petrine commission to prove the pope's authority to grant indulgences, he located the source of that power in the faith of the church, as attested by numerous scriptural texts. The pope was like unto Daniel, he said, whose prayers liberated the people of Israel from captivity (Dn 9.17–25), to say nothing of the plea of Moses, which removed the wrath of God against Israel (Ex 32.7–14). In the New Testament, the unceasing prayers of the church freed Peter from imprisonment (Acts 12.5), and the apostle James exhorted his readers to pray for each other (Jm 5.16), "for the continual prayer of a just man avails much." The relevant scriptures showed that the pope, by the commission granted to Peter in Mt 16.19, could pardon the penalty of the confessed by invoking the faith and prayer of the church, which numerous verses of Scripture proved could be efficaciously applied to a penitent's debt of sin.[72] Just as Innocent IV wrote confidently about indulgences as an example of God's generosity, Robert assured his readers that the faith and prayers of the church ensured the validity of the church's ministrations, even if thieves and murderers filled the episcopate, or corruption stained the Church Militant:

> Three things are duly noted here which are certain, which in themselves retain an invariable efficacy for the Church Militant: the power of words, the power of the sacraments, and the petition of the church; because although the entire church may be in mortal sin, still these three would be valid for those for whom suffrage is made, namely, the power of words, like those of certain psalms which have special virtue no matter who chants them, such as Ps 115.16: *"Sunder my bonds and I shall sacrifice to you."* Similarly, the power of the sacrament of the eucharist is valid by whomever priest it is offered for those for whom it is offered, if it is done devoutly. Again, the petition of the Church Militant is valid for those for whom it is offered, because of the whole church one part journeys on earth, the other glories in heaven and for the former it is said all together, "let us pray" several times [in the liturgy].[73]

The faith and prayers of the Church Triumphant, along with those of the Church Militant, underwrite the validity and efficacy of pardons as well as the other suffrages mediated to penitent Christians. The Church Militant knows the prayers of the Church Triumphant because the two are united in the liturgy; consequently, Christians should have the greatest confidence in the ministrations of the church.

This confidence in the church's power to remit the debt of sin featured prominently in the commentaries of the Schoolmen. The canonist Huguccio insisted that penitents must be certain of the church's authority to remit the debt of sin: "But if one believes that the church is able to grant him such remission, that which invites that penitent to complete a good work, the cause of the devotion, as if in compensation of that penalty which is removed from him, then such remission is valid for him."[74] Thomas Aquinas echoed the same sentiments: "The universal church cannot err, since he who in all things *'was heard because of his reverent submission* (Hb 5.7)' said to Peter upon whose confession the church was founded: *'I have prayed for you that your faith may not fail* (Lk 22.32).' But the universal church approves and grants indulgences."[75] Thomas likewise argued that the church's faith and steadfast obedience, as evidenced by the prayers and petitions she submitted to God, ensured the validity of indulgences. Learned fourteenth-century commentators such as the Augustinian Thomas of Strasbourg and the Dominican John of Dambach, as well as compilers of important pastoral manuals such as the Dominican John of Freiburg, likewise inherited and handed down the ideas of Stephen Langton, Godfrey of Poitiers, Robert Courson, and Huguccio.[76] The myriad indulgenced devotions of the thirteenth century and later testify that the unschooled shared with their more learned brethren the same confidence in the church's administrations.

Over the course of the thirteenth century, however, the learned were inclined to emphasize the authority of bishops and popes more often than that of the universal Church, as necessary to the validity of a grant of pardon. This point of view is plainest in a *quodlibet* of Aquinas. No one doubted that crusaders who journeyed to the Holy Land and fought against the Muslim foe received full remission, but what about the many *crucesignati* who took crusading vows yet died on the way to Palestine? Or what about Christian warriors who intended to make a crusade but died before they could depart for the East? Many *crucesignati* must have perished without ever having raised a sword, spear, or ax against the infidel.

Thomas answered that the proclamation of the crusading indulgence, drawn up at the pleasure of the pope, determined who received its benefits. If the document required only intention and embarkation, then even crusaders who died en route received its remission, because they had met the conditions for the indulgence. If the proclamation required departure for the Holy Land, then those who died before leaving received no remission:

> Therefore, it must be said in answer to the proposed question, that if, according to the form of the papal letter, indulgence is granted to those who take up the cross for the liberation of the Holy Land, the crusader immediately receives the indulgence, even if he should die before arriving in the Holy Land, because the cause of the indulgence is not the crusader, but the vow of the crusader. But if in the form of the letter it shall be stated that indulgence is given to those who travel to the Holy Land—he who dies before he departs receives no indulgence, because the cause of the indulgence is not present.[77]

In Thomas's view, the pope, successor to St. Peter and steward of the goods of the universal Church, determined who received the benefits belonging to the universal Church. His view, which of course maintained the necessity for interior conversion, was prompted by the imagery of indulgences, for if remissions were drawn from the treasury, they were also a nearly tangible good—indeed, a benefice—and only the stewards of that good had the authority to distribute them.

Consequently, in the midst of all these developments, strong continuities with the Church's past endured. Like their patristic ancestors, Catholics of the High Middle Ages generally believed that their offenses against God incurred so much debt that alone they had little chance of balancing the scales of God's justice. Therefore, penitents relied upon the help of both the Church Militant and the Church Triumphant, much like a frightened little boy who seeks the comfort of his mother's embrace, as in the anonymous treatise *Summa breves dies hominis sunt*, written about 1210: "When one shall see oneself that one is insufficient [for completion] of enjoined penance, and that infirmity crush under one's own burden, then one is honestly able to turn back to the ecclesiastical suffrages and, as it were, to return to the maternal breasts."[78] Medieval Catholics calculated their debt of sin much like their antique forebears, and they sought out the aid of their coreligionists. The form of that aid is what differed.

THE MID-THIRTEENTH-CENTURY SYSTEMATIZATION

In the 1250s, theologians and canonists wove the arithmetic and mercantile imagery for indulgences into the systematic swatch of the treasury of merit. Franciscan and Dominican Schoolmen, sent forth to preach especially to the growing numbers of Christian faithful living in towns and cities, dominated this intellectual enterprise. These preachers illustrated in handy language the teachings of the Christian faith. In the words of Humbert of Romans, who became master-general of the Friars Preachers in 1254, Dominican friars should preach to the people "usefully, about things relevant to them."[79] The mendicant Schoolmen, in following the logic of the imagery, added parallel images to illustrate further the church's authority to concede indulgences. Thus, a striking characteristic of the learned discussions of the treasury (generally in commentaries on the *Sentences* of Peter Lombard, 4.20) is the gathering together of the metaphors of family, body, and commonwealth, along with that of the treasury.

An early instance of this combination may be found in the Dominican theologian Guerric of St. Quentin, regent master at Paris from 1233 to 1242, who explained the pope's power over the treasury by invoking the traditional nuptial and parental metaphors for papal power. In *De relaxatione*,

Guerric suggested that "the spouse of the church, and especially of the universal church, namely the pope, ought to succeed to Christ in all goods which pertain to the education of the children of the church."[80] A generation later, Guerric's fellow Dominican, Thomas Aquinas, argued that priests could not grant pardons because only a bishop, to whom that power rightfully belongs, "is properly called a prelate of the church, and so only he receives the ring of the church, as if he were her spouse."[81] Bonaventure offered a similar depiction: "Moreover, the reason why the treasury of the church is only entrusted to bishops to be distributed is because the church possesses that treasury by betrothal to Christ, who is man and her spouse, and with whom she raises sons and daughters, perfect and imperfect, for the education of whom Christ wants these goods to be of service."[82] The traditional images of parent and spouse, moreover, highlighted the uniqueness of papal authority, which, unlike the coercive authority of secular rulers, was most perfectly exercised in charity.[83] The images of spouse, parent, and child also reinforced the necessity for a charitable disposition in those who sought the reduction of their debt of sin through the authority of the church.

The metaphor of the mystical body likewise was linked to that of the treasury. Bonaventure suggested that the mystical body must resemble animal bodies, and since "we see in the case of an animal's body that one member exposes itself to sustain an injury or hurt to another member, as is clear when the arm exposes itself to shield the head: if then there is a connection and likeness between the mystical body and the natural body, it seems that one member can and should bear the burdens of the other."[84] Thomas Aquinas agreed that the power of pardons rested upon "the unity of the mystical body, in which many pay out in penitential works much more than the debts they owe; and they also patiently sustain numerous unjust tribulations, through which a multitude of penalties is able to be expiated."[85] Just as one member of the physical body helps another, so the members of the mystical body of Christ aid each other. The merit gained by some members may be applied to the debt of others.

Third, to underscore the need for indulgences to serve the common good, the scholastics of the mid-thirteenth century also described the church as a commonwealth. Like its secular counterpart, the Christian commonwealth had rulers—Christ, the pope, and the bishops. The pope's authority to grant pardons, according to Guerric of St. Quentin, resembled a steward's authority over the goods of his lord: "The pope is the minister and steward of the church. Hence, just as a steward is only able to distribute the goods of his lord for the usefulness of that lord, so the pope is only able to distribute the goods of the church for the usefulness of the church."[86] Bonaventure also pointed out the meaning of the church as a commonwealth:

> It must be said that, just as we observe in the polities and communities of human beings, the treasury of the commonwealth is customarily distributed and spent for two reasons—so also is it understood for the spiritual treasury. In the first instance, the treasury is spent in order to advance the glory of the prince, such as royal courts display, like Ahasuerus did in the first chapter of the Book of Esther. In the second instance, the treasury is spent because of the need or usefulness of the community, so that when the community is attacked, stipends or rewards are given to soldiers, so that they may go to war. Thus, the treasury of the church ought to be distributed by those to whom it is entrusted for two reasons, namely, for the glory and praise of the prince. And the praise and honor of God is in his saints, and the saints are honored by the construction and visitation of basilicas, and by the commemoration of the saintly virtues—all these are also recommended in preaching and sermons, therefore, indulgences are rightly granted to all persons for these deeds. However, in the case of the church the common need is the defense of the Holy Land, the defense of the faith, and the encouragement of studies and related endeavors, and therefore indulgences ought also to be granted for these endeavors. And since these services to the church consist in exterior acts, indulgences ought especially to be granted for them.[87]

The religious commonwealth closely mirrored the worldly commonwealth. While dukes, counts, and margraves ruled earthly principalities, the only ruler of the church is God. Like secular princes, ecclesiastical princes could use the treasury belonging to their monarch to honor those who served God or their fellow citizens. The treasury also could be used for the common defense, and so remissions also were granted to crusaders, scholars, and others who protected doctrinal, as well as territorial, integrity of Christendom.

The religious commonwealth constituted a more perfect community, however, than its secular counterpart. Both commonwealths were ordered to preserve peace and justice; however, the Christian commonwealth was ordered also to the loftier aims of charity and salvation. In Christendom all goods—both spiritual and secular—served spiritual ends. So in the words of Thomas Aquinas, the pollution of simony never tainted a grant of pardon, even if it was offered for the contribution of money:

> It must be said that temporal things are ordained for spiritual goals—that we ought to use temporal things because of spiritual goals. And therefore indulgence is not able to be granted simply for temporal things, but for temporal things ordained for spiritual goals, like the repression of the enemies of the church, who disturb the peace of the church, or for the construction of churches and bridges, and for the collection of alms. And it is clear that simony is not committed by these acts, because a spiritual thing is not given in exchange for a temporal thing, but for a spiritual thing.[88]

The logic of the rhetoric employed by the mendicant scholar-preachers of the mid-thirteenth century suggested that the treasury was a spiritual bene-fice over which—as the canon law had recognized since Lateran IV—only bishops could exercise jurisdiction.[89] Just as dukes, counts, and castellans retained jurisdiction over grants of land, the princes of the church retained similar powers over grants of remission. Of course, the pope, as prince of the bishops, had the fullest power to grant indulgences:

It must be said that the pope has the plenitude of pontifical power, just as a king in his kingdom. But bishops are endowed with a part of his power, much like the ruling magistrates in individual towns. Because of this, bishops alone the pope calls "brothers" in his letters; all others he calls "children." And therefore the power of granting indul-gences resides fully in the pope, because he is able to grant indulgences as he wishes, of course, with an existing, legitimate reason. But for bishops, the power to grant indulgences is distributed by the ordination of the pope.[90]

Here again Aquinas conflated two metaphors. The church is a common-wealth, with the pope ruling as Christ's vicar. But the church is also like unto a family, for the bishops are the brothers of the pope, and all other Christians are his sons and daughters (the mother of these children being the church herself). As in the secular commonwealth, where counts and dukes exercised royal powers appropriate to their rank, the lesser princes of the church could grant pardons, like the pope. But while their powers of dispen-sation were limited to their own dioceses, the pope could grant remissions anywhere in Christendom. Furthermore, only the pope had the power to grant plenary indulgences, while bishops could concede only partial remis-sions, according to the canon law, of forty days for the visitation of churches, and up to one year for the occasion of the dedication of a church.[91] Insofar as candidates to the episcopacy had to be approved by the pope, the powers vested in the bishops could be exercised only through his commissioning. The treasury thus lay under direct authority of the pope; at their consecration, bishops received a share of his authority.

Thus did the theologians and canonists of the thirteenth century systematize the traditions inherited from the twelfth. *Unigenitus* was certainly not the "first full elaboration of the church's doctrine of indulgences."[92] Instead, that bull well may be understood as representing the end and also the endorsement of two centuries of learned theological and canonistic speculation concerning indulgences. Behind this intellectual enterprise lay the scriptures, liturgy, and penitential traditions of the church. The mendicant Schoolmen, like their intellectual predecessors, illustrated their thought in imagery proclaimed in the rhythms of the liturgy. Jesus Christ had paid the ransom of a humanity shackled in the bondage of sin. The price of that ransom was His Precious Blood. Since Christ was blameless, His sacrifice won for His Church a superabundant trove of spiritual treasure, the stewardship of which now belonged to the successors of Peter, whom Christ himself chose as head of His Church. The princes of the church distributed that treasure to the friends of Christ.

To these ideas, however, the mendicant Schoolmen contributed a series of parallel images with which they further illustrated the unique intersection between church power and divine mercy represented in each grant of pardon. Ultimately, Augustine's presentation of the two cities inspired one image; church authorities presided over the Christian commonwealth much as princes governed the secular commonwealth. When pope or bishops granted indulgence, they exercised power over the treasury of the church in much the same way that secular rulers exercised authority when they distributed land and magistracies. But, since the Christian commonwealth was ordered to higher ends than the secular commonwealth, so also were the relations within the church between ruler and ruled more noble. While secular princes used power to confer favors on supporters and friends (which need not necessarily be the same), only friends received the benefit of the church's treasury. A pardon thus served not only as an application of ecclesiastical jurisdiction but also as an episcopal or papal gesture of charity towards a "son" or "daughter," who was also a "friend of God." The mendicant Schoolmen interwove the metaphors of treasury, body, marriage, commonwealth, and kin, but they hardly can be credited with the invention of the doctrine of the treasury of merit. They merely expressed in scholastic fashion ideas long present in the high medieval religious imagination.

NOTES

1. Extrav. comm. 5.8.2 (*CIC* 2:1304–1306).

2. Diana Wood, *Clement VI: The Pontificate and Ideas of an Avignon Pope* (Cambridge: Cambridge University Press, 1989), 90.

3. Thurston, *Holy Year of Jubilee*, 55.

4. Extrav. comm. 5.8.2 (*CIC* 2:1304): "Non per sanguinem hircorum aut vitulorum, sed per proprium sanguinem . . . redemptionem inventa. Non enim corruptibilibus auro et argento, sed sui ipsius agni incontamini et immaculati pretioso sanguine nos redemit."

5. Ibid.: "In ara crucis innocens immolatus non guttam sanguinis modicam, quae tamen propter unionem ad verbum pro redemptione totius humani generis suffecisset, sed copiose velut quoddam profluvium."

6. Ibid.: "Quem quidem thesaurum non in sudario repositum, non in agro absconditum, sed per beatum Petrum coeli clavigerum, eiusque successores suos in terris vicarios, commisit fidelibus salubriter dispensandum, et propriis et rationabilibus causis,

nunc pro totali, nunc pro partiali remissione poenae temporalibus pro peccatis debitae . . .
vere poenitentibus et confessis misericorditer applicandum."

7. Ibid.: "De cuius consumptione seu minutione non est aliquatenus formidandum."

8. Extrav. comm. 5.8.2 (*CIC* 2:1304–1305): "Bonifacius papa VIII praedecessor
noster . . . inconsumptibilem thesaurum huiusmodi pro excitanda et remuneranda
devotione fidelium voluit aperire . . . dum tamen vere poenitentes et confessi exsis-
terent, personaliter visitarent, suorum omnium obtinerent plenissimam veniam
peccatorum."

9. Extrav. comm. 5.8.2 (*CIC* 2:1305): "Quod annus quinquagesimus in lege Moysica
(quam non venit Dominus solvere, sed spiritualiter adimplere), iubilaeus remissionis et
gaudii, sacerque dierum numerus, quo lege fit remissio, censebatur."

10. Ibid.: "Veteri quidem ex legis datione, novo ex visibili Spiritus sancti in discipulos
missione, per quem datur peccatorum remissio, singulariter honoratur."

11. Ibid.: "Cum pauci multorum respectu propter vitae hominum brevitatem valeant
ad annum centesimum pervenire, de fratrum nostrorum consilio praedictam concessionem indulgentiae . . . ad annum quinquagesimum duximus reducendam."

12. Thurston, *Holy Year of Jubilee*, 57.

13. Hostiensis, *Summa aurea*, 5.67 (Lyons: Iacobus Guinta, 1537, 288v): "Et preterea
martyres pro fide et ecclesia sanguinem suum fuderunt et ultra quam peccassent puniti
fuerunt. Restat quod in dicta effusione omne peccatum punitum est, et hec sanguinis
effusio est thesaurus in scrinio ecclesie repositus cuius claves habet ecclesia. Unde quando
vult potest scrinium aperire, et thesaurum suum cui voluerit communicare, remissiones et
indulgentias fidelibus faciendo. Et sic peccatum non remanet impunitum quia punitum fuit
in filio dei et martyribus sanctis suis secundum dominum Hugonem cardinalem."

14. Lea, 3:17–23.

15. Lea, 3:21–22.

16. Lea, 3:28.

17. Alexander of Hales, *Summa theologica* (Quarrachi: Ex typographia Collegii
S. Bonaventurae, 1948), 3:lix–lx.

18. M. D. Chénu, *Nature, Man, and Society in the Twelfth Century*, trans. J. Taylor
and L. K. Little (Chicago: University of Chicago Press, 1968), 202–203.

19. Praepositinus of Cremona, *Summa* (Todi, Biblioteca communale MS 71, fol.
133rb): "Item queritur de absolutionibus; que fieri per episcopos qui dicunt: Quicumque
tali loco dederit denarium unum, remittatur ei etc., utrum aliquis ibi dans ex devotione
intelligatur absolutus. Quod videtur, quia Dominus dicit: quicumque solveritis super
terram erat solutum in celis. Sed hanc absolutionem facit episcopus iuste et sine errore,
ergo iste dans absolutus est. Item generaliter est consuetudo ecclesie, contra quam
disputare non licet. Ergo talis absolutio valet."

20. Bonaventure, *Commentaria in IV libros sententiarum*, 4.20.1.3 (*Opera omnia*,
[Quarrachi: College of St. Bonaventure, 1882–1902], 4:534): "Relaxationes sive indulgentiae fiunt de meritis supererogationis, quae sunt in ecclesia, quae quidem sunt sicut
thesaurus spiritualis eius."

21. Thomas Aquinas, *Summa theologiae, supplementum*, 25.2 (Ottawa: Studia Generalis
O. Pr., 1945), 5:97b: "Causa autem remissionis poenae in indulgentia non est nisi
abundantia meritorum ecclesiae."

22. Augustine, *Enarrationes in Psalmos*, 48.9 (*PL* 36:549): "Illi dant pretium redemptionis animae suae, qui non cessant eleemosynae facere." Jerome, *Breviarium in Psalmos*, 48.9 (*PL* 26:967): "Non fecit eleemosynam per quam peccata delentur."

23. Jerome, *Epistola* 66.8 (*CCSL* 54:658): "Christus sanctificacio est, sine qua nemo videbit faciem dei, Christus redemptio, idem redemptor et pretium."

24. Augustine, *Sermo* 130.2 (*PL* 38:726): "Ad tales merces Mercator ille descendit. Et quoniam omnis mercator dat et accipit; dat quod habet, et accipit quod non habet; quando aliquid comparat, dat pecuniam, et accipit quod emit: etiam Christus in ista mercatura dedit et accipit. Sed quid accipit? Quod hic abundat, nasci, laborare, et mori. Et quid dedit? Renasci, resurgere et in aeternum regnare. O bone Mercator, eme nos. Quod dicam, eme nos, cum gratias agere debeamus, quia emisti nos? Pretium nostrum erogas nobis, sanguinem tuum bibimus; erogas ergo nobis pretium nostrum. Et Evangelium legimus, instrumentum nostrum. Servi tui sumus, creatura tua sumus: fecisti nos redemisti nos. Emere potest quisque servum suum, creare non potest. Dominus autem servos suos et creavit et redemit: creavit, ut essent; redemit, ne semper captivi essent. Incidimus enim in principem huius saeculi, qui seduxit Adam et servum fecit, et coepit nos tanquam vernaculos possidere. Sed venit Redemptor, et victus est deceptor. Et quid fecit Redemptor noster captivatori nostro? Ad pretium nostrum tetendit muscipulam crucem suam."

25. Dickinson, ed., col. 89.

26. Dickinson, ed., col. 105.

27. Dickinson, ed., col. 394.

28. Eugenio Moeller, *et al.*, eds. *Corpus oracionum* (Turnholt: Brepols, 1995), 6.4132 (*CCSL* 160, 6:193): "Parce, domine, quaesumus, parce populo tuo et nullis iam patiaris adversitatibus fatigari, quos pretioso filii tui sanguine redemisti."

29. *Corpus oracionum*, 6.3753 (*CCSL* 160, 6:25): "Omnipotens et misericors deus, qui genus humanum, sub peccato venditum, non auri argentique pondere sed pretioso filii tui redemisti sanguine."

30. David Bevington, ed., *Medieval Drama* (Boston: Houghton Mifflin, 1975), 9: "Sic tragicus noster pugnam Christi populo Christiano in theatro ecclesiae gestibus suis repraesentat, eique victoriam redemptionis suae inculcat."

31. Bevington, 45.

32. Bevington, 65.

33. Bevington, 114: "Par cui serra li mond salvez."

34. Bevington, 118: "Adam trara de prison, / Son cors dorra por rançon."

35. Bevington, 205.

36. Karl Young, ed., *Drama of the Medieval Church* (Oxford: Clarendon Press, 1933), 1:428 and 1:459.

37. M. T. Clanchy, *From Memory to Written Record: England 1066–1307*, 2nd ed. (Oxford: Blackwell, 1993).

38. Richard Southern, *The Making of the Middle Ages*, (New Haven, CT: Yale University Press, 1953), 98–99.

39. Georges Duby, *Rural Economy and Country Life in the Medieval West*, trans. Cynthia Postan (Columbia, SC: University of SC Press, 1968), 232.

40. Alexander Murray, *Reason and Society in the Middle Ages* (Oxford: Clarendon Press, 1978), 194.

41. Marcia L. Colish, *Medieval Foundations of the Western Intellectual Tradition, 400–1400* (New Haven, CT: Yale University Press, 1997), 365.

42. Clanchy, 60.

43. Clanchy, 46–47. See also David L. D'Avray, *The Preaching of the Friars: Sermons Diffused from Paris before 1300* (Oxford: Clarendon Press, 1985), 42.

44. William of Auvergne, *De sacramento ordinis*, c. 13 (*Opera omnia* [Paris: Andrea Pralard, 1674], 1:551): "Si rex, vel princeps bellum habeat, dat potestatem ducibus suis perquirendi et conducendi bellatores dignisque stipendiis remunerandi. Quia ergo rex regum et dominus dominantium Christus bellum habuit a tempore, quo caepit ecclesia bellum, inquam, non solum spirituale, sed etiam literale, seu corporale, sive materiale contra haereticos, et alios Christianae religionis inimicos, videlicet paganos, et a tempore Machometi, sarracenos, necessario dedit potestatem ducibus suis, id est, praelatis, perquirendi bellatores materiales, et conducendi eos, et congruis stipendiis remunerandi. Quid autem est praedicare indulgentias."

45. Ibid.: "Stipendia hujusmodi bellatorum pro maxima ac nobilissima sui parte remuneratio aeterna erit."

46. Simon of Tournai, *Institutiones theologicae* (Paris, Bibliothéque Nationale, Cod. lat. 14886, fol. 60va–vb): "Queritur an, cum publica sit remissio peregrinantibus vel dedicaciones frequentatibus sub hac forma: Absolvantur a tertia vel a septima vel quotamlibet prelatus expressit, peregrinus vel dedicacionis frequentator, si tertia pars sit expressa et tres frequentaverit, dedicaciones, a tota poenitentia sit absolutus. Redditur: Si corde contrito et humiliato ad primam dedicacionem accedit, absolvitur a tertia parte poenitentie, qua tenetur tunc, cum accedit, ad eam, non eius, qua tenebatur, cum accederet ad primam. Idem iudicium de tertia et omni alia. Ergo si accedat ad innumeras, non prosus absolvetur a poena."

47. Peter of Poitiers, *Sententiarum libri quinque*, 3.16 (*PL* 211:1076): "Item, cum sacerdos, sive sit episcopus sive non, possit aliquid de poena subtrahere, sciendum est quod si episcopus vel alius prelatus indicat et publicet se in dedicatione ecclesiae dimissurum tertiam vel quartam partem poenitentiae, vel quadraginta dies, vel aliquid tale omnibus illis qui ad fabricam illius ecclesiae contulerint eleemosynas suas."

48. Lea, 3:171.

49. Loewenfeld, ed., *Epistolae pontificium*, 133, no. 240.

50. Guerric of St. Quentin, *De relaxatione* (Todi, Biblioteca communale MS 71, fol. 44vb): "Videtur quod posset thesaurus Ecclesiae exhauriri cum semper fiat subtractio et nulla fiat recompensatio sive restauratio."

51. Peter the Chanter, *Alphabeticum morale* (Munich, Staatsbibliothek Clm 22283, fol. 91rb): "Relaxant quidam terciam partem vel quintam vel huiusmodi dicendo: si quis dederit huius ecclesie fabrice nummum vel huiusmodi, terciam partem penitenciarum auctoritate dei et beate Marie et omnium sanctorum et nostra ei relaxamus. Discretius esset determinare, ut si diceretur: x dies vel huiusmodi." On Peter's significance for the new pastoral theology, see Leonard E. Boyle, "Summae confessorum," in *Les genres littéraires dans les sources théologiques et philosophiques médiévales. Definitions, critiques, et exploitations* (Louvain-la-neuve: Institut d'Études Médiévales, 1982), 229–237.

52. Such religious imaginings lasted until the end of the Middle Ages. See Thomas Lentes, "Counting Piety in the Late Middle Ages," in Bernhard Jussen and Pamela

Selwyn, eds. and trans., *Ordering Medieval Society: Perspectives on Intellectual and Practical Modes of Shaping Social Relations* (Philadelphia: University of Pennsylvania Press, 2001), 55-91.

53. Innocent IV, *Commentaria*, X 5.38.4, 543: "Sed dices, nunquid tantum habebit, qui plus dederit, vel laboraverit quantum qui minus? Respondeo ut supra, quod Deus, qui omnia moderatur in numero pondere et mensura, ultra metam in ecclesia a praelato impositam, de gratia dabit alii plus, alii minus, nec in his multum curandum vel cogitandum, nisi quia credendum, quod dominus cuius natura pie est et liberalis, de suo semper adijcit ultra gratiam et justiciam."

54. William of Auvergne, *De sacramento ordinis*, c. 13 (*Opera omnia*, 1:550b): "Nulli autem est certum, quod immunis sit . . . nulli ergo certum est quod indulgentias huiusmodi percipiat. Certum est autem unicuique se esse debitorem injunctae sibi poenitentiae, vel injungendae."

55. The classic account of twelfth-century penitential theology is Paul Anciaux, *Le théologie du sacrément de pénitence au XIIe siècle* (Louvain: E. Nauwelaerts, 1949).

56. Cf. Augustine, *De civitate dei* 13.12 (*CCSL* 48:394–395).

57. Peter the Chanter, *Alphabeticum morale* (Munich, Staatsbibliothek Clm 22283, fol. 91rb): "Relaxatio fit necessitate loci vel persone vel ad succerendam terram sanctam, ut Iherosolimitanam, equa reconpensatione, ut si quis non potest ieiunare, pauperem reficiat, ita tamen, quod tantum gravet eum dare ut ieiunare. Prodigus enim vel dives mallet multum dare quam ieiunare, sicut avarus econverso. Quando penitenti accipienti penitentiam conceditur licencia ab illo, a quo iniunigitur penitentia. Quomodo caritas, contricio, devocio augmentatur, et nisi aliquis istorum modorum intervenerit, non fit relaxatio."

58. Peter of Poitiers, *Sententiarum libri quinque*, 3.16 (*PL* 211:1076): "Item, cum sacerdos, sive sit episcopus sive non, possit aliquid de poena subtrahere, sciendum est quod si episcopus vel alius prelatus indicat et publicet se in dedicatione alicuius ecclesiae dimissurum tertiam vel quartam partem poenitentiae, vel quadraginta dies, vel aliquid tale omnibus illis qui ad fabricam illius ecclesiae contulerint eleemosynas suas, non ideo quicunque suam ibi attulerit eleemosynam, promissam consecutus est veniam. Si enim dives aliquis det tantum nummum vel obolum, sicut vetual pauperrima, credit tantum dimissum esse? Absit! Deus enim non quaerit ab homine quod non potest, non considerat quantum detur, sed ex quanto, id est ex qua voluntate."

59. Anonymous, *De relaxationibus* (Erlangen, Universitätsbibliothek MS 260, fol. 72r): "Ergo melior est condicio divitum quam pauperum non sequitur, quia si dives et pauper sunt in pari caritate quantum ad coronam vite eterne paria habebunt merita, tamen si impari affectu ambo decedant ex virtute eleemosinarum et devotarum citius liberabitur unus quam alius a poena purgatorii." Cf. the anonymous treatise, written c. 1201–1206, *Summa breves dies hominis sunt* (Bamberg, Staatsbibliothek Cod. lat. Patr. 136, fol. 77va [cited in Hödl, 258]): "Deus enim attendit non quantum sed ex quanto, licet non saccum sed animum."

60. William of Auxerre, *Summa aurea*, 4.14.2.2 (Paris: Éditions du Centre national de la recherché scientifique, 1985, 4:356): "Quantum ad relaxationem pene, peioris condi- tionis est pauper quam dives; sed simpliciter non est peioris, immo simpliciter melioris. Licet enim dives melioris sit conditionis quam pauper in relaxationibus que fiunt per

dationem elemosinarum, tamen pauper est melioris quantum ad relaxationem, que fit in contritione. Cicius enim et efficacius conteritur pauper quam dives, aliis paribus, et per contritionem efficacius dimittitur pena peccati quam per elemosinarum largitionem."

61. Principe, 67–68.

62. Raymond of Peñafort, *Summa de poenitentiis et matrimonio*, 3.63 (Rome: John Tallini, 1603, 496b): "Valent peccatori offerenti ex pia devotione . . . ad gratiae impetrationem."

63. Raymond of Peñafort, *Summa de poenitentiis et matrimonio*, 3.64 (ed. Tallini, 496a): "Sciendum quod maioritas et minoritas remissionis paenitentiae attenditur secundum tria, scilicet, secundum maiorem et minorem devotionem ipsius paenitentis, et ipsorum, qui suffrangantur, et secundum maiorem numerum eorundem suffragantium."

64. John of Freiburg, *SC* 3.181: "Ideo non valent indulgencie omnibus equaliter, sed secundum quod sunt magis vel minus dispositi per meritum remissionis pene, non adeptionis vite. Unde sicut xl dies penitencie canonice valent uni perficienti eam cum maiori fervore et labore quam alteri qui cum minori, scilicet labore et fervore seu afflictione seu dati quantitati." John of Freiburg wholly excerpted this text from the influential Dominican moral theologian Peter of Tarentaise, *Commentaria in IV libros sententiarum*, 4.20.3.3. Peter became pope in 1276 as Innocent V.

65. D. E. Luscombe, ed. and trans., *Peter Abelard's Ethics* (Oxford: Clarendon Press, 1971), 107–109.

66. X 5.31.12, *Accedentibus* (*CIC* 2:840–841).

67. Hödl, 336.

68. Huguccio, *Summa decretorum*, De pen. D. 1 c. 88 (Admont, Stiftsbibliothek 7, fol. 484va): "Ubi ergo sunt illi, qui dicunt quod remissiones facte ab ecclesia que fiunt cotidie in ecclesia, non valent? Ipse enim Christus dixit in evangelio: si cui peccata remiseritis, remitteretur ei."

69. Stephen Langton, *Commentarium in 2 Corinthios* (Salzburg, Stiftsbibliothek St. Peter, Cod. lat. a X 19, fol. 93): "Hic habemus auctoritatem cotidiane relaxationes. Non enim loquitur hic apostolus de condonacione culpe vel rancoris anime, quia hec donaret apostolus sine prece alicuius, immo loquitur de condonacione sive relaxatione satisfactionis. Cum ergo apostolus ad preces subditorum condonaret satisfactionem, et idem peteret fieri ab eis, potest fieri relaxatio satisfactionis ad preces alicuius magistri et honesti viri et maxime ad preces sanctorum, pro quorum ecclesiis sanctificandis vel collegiis instituendis et utandis fiunt hodie relaxationes. Et hoc feci in persona Christi, id est si Christus condonaret, quia nemo in talibus sine spiritu dei agebat, apostolus hic autem scilicet, quia fecisse scilicet in persona Christi dicit, ne vana huius videatur condonacio quae fit propter amicos."

70. Godfrey of Poitiers, *Questiones de relaxationibus* (Bruges, Stadtbibliothek Cod. lat. 220, fol. 117vb): "Romane ergo ecclesie datum est caput gracie dei."

71. Thomas Aquinas, *Summa Theologiae Suppl.*, 25.1 (ed. Studia Generalis, 5:95a): "Sed Christus poterat relaxare absque omni satisfactione poenam peccati, ut patet, Ioann. VIII de muliere adultera. Ergo et Paulus potuit. Ergo et Papa, qui non est minoris potestatis in Ecclesia quam Paulus fuerit."

72. V. L. Kennedy, "Robert Courson on Penance," *MS* 7 (1945), 328.

73. Kennedy, 329: "Tria sunt diligenter hic annotanda que immobilia sunt, que in presenti ecclesia invariabilem sui retinent efficaciam: virtus verborum, virtus sacramentorum,

desiderium ecclesie; quia quamvis tota ecclesia presens esset in mortali peccato tamen ista valent hiis pro quibus suffragatur, scilicet virtus verborum sicut psalmi qui specialem habent virtutem a quocumque decantentur, ut versus ille: dirupisti vincula mea tibi, etc. Similiter virtus sacramenti eucharistie a quocumque offeratur valet illis pro quibus offertur si devote assint. Similiter desiderium ecclesie militantis valet illis quia ecclesie generalis una pars militat in terris, alia triumphat in celis et pro illis insimul dicitur in ecclesia *oremus* pluraliter."

74. Huguccio, *Summa decretorum*, De pen. D. 1 c. 88 (Admont, Stiftsbibliothek 7, fol. 484va): "Set si credit, quod ecclesia possit ei talem remissionem facere, que illum ad aliquod bonum faciendum invitat, causa devotionis quasi in recompensationem illius, quod sibi relaxatur, valet eis talis remissio."

75. Thomas Aquinas, *Summa Theologiae Suppl.*, 25.1 (ed. Studia Generalis, 5:95a): "Ecclesia generalis non potest errare, quia ille qui in omnibus exauditus est pro sua reverential, dixit Petro, super cuius confessione Ecclesia fundata est: 'Ego pro te rogavi, Petre, ut non deficiat fides tua,' Luc. xxii. Sed Ecclesia generalis indulgentias approbat et facit."

76. Thomas of Strasbourg, *Commentaria in IV libros sententiarum*, 4.20.4 (Venice: J. Ziletti, 1564, 130rb); John of Dambach, *De vir. indul.*, q. 1 (Heiligenkreuz [Austria], Stiftsbibliothek 208, fol. 84v), and John of Freiburg, *SC*, 3.180.

77. Thomas Aquinas, *Quodlibet*, 2.8.2 (*Opera omnia* 9:484): "Est ergo dicendum in questione proposita, quod si secundum formam papalis litterae indulgentia concedatur accipientibus crucem in subsidium terrae sanctae, crucesignatus statim habet indulgentiam, etiamsi decedat antequem interarripiat; quia sic causa indulgentiae erit non iter, sed votum itineris. Sed autem in forma litterae contineatur quod indulgentia detur his qui transierunt ultra mare; ille qui decedit antequam transeat, non habet indulgentiam, quia non habet indulgentiam causam."

78. Anonymous, *Summa breves dies hominis sunt* (Bamberg, Staatsbibliothek Cod. lat. Patr. 136, fol. 77va [Hödl, 268, n. 2]): "Cum viderit se insufficientem esse poenitentie iniuncte et sub eius onere suam infirmitatem succumbere, tunc honeste recurrere potest ad ecclesiastica suffragia et velut ad materna ubera respirare."

79. Alexander Murray, "Religion among the Poor in Thirteenth-Century France," *Traditio* 30 (1974), 287.

80. Guerric of St. Quentin, *De relaxatione* (Todi, MS 71, fol. 45vb): "Sponsus ecclesiae et maxime ecclesiae universalis, scilicet papa, debet succedere ipsi Christo in omnibus bonis quae ad educationem ecclesiae filiorum pertinent."

81. Thomas Aquinas, *Summa Theologiae Suppl.* 26.1 (ed. Studia Generalis, 5:110a): "Solus episcopus proprie praelatus ecclesiae dicitur; et ideo ipse solus, quasi sponsus, anulum ecclesiae recipit."

82. Bonaventure, *Commentaria in IV libros sententiarum*, 4.20.1.3 (*Opera omnia*, 4:534): "Ratio autem, quare thesaurus ecclesiae solis episcopis committitur dispensandus, est quia ecclesia thesaurum istum habet ex desponsatione sui cum Christo, qui est vir et eius sponsus, et cui generat filios et filias, id est perfectos et imperfectos, ad quorum educationem Christus vult servari haec bona."

83. On this issue, see Robert W. Shaffern, "*Mater et magistra*: Gendered Images and Church Authority in the Thought of Pope Innocent III," *Logos* 4 (2001), 65-88.

84. Bonaventure, *Commentaria in IV libros sententiarum*, 4.20.1.ad 3 (*Opera omnia*, 4:530). Translation from Palmer, 341.

85. Thomas Aquinas, *Summa Theologiae Suppl.* 25.1 (ed. Studia Generalis, 4:95b): "Unitas corporis mystici, in qua multi in operibus poenitentiae supererogaverunt ad mensuram debitorum suorum; et multas etiam tribulationes iniustas sustinuerunt patienter, per quas multitudo poenarum poterat expiari."

86. Guerric of St. Quentin, *De relaxatione* (Todi, MS 71, fol. 44vb): "Papa minister est ecclesiae et dispensator. Ergo sicut minister bona domini sui non potest distribuere nisi ad eius utilitatem, ita nec papa bona ecclesiae nisi ad utilitatem ecclesiae."

87. Bonaventure, *Commentaria in IV libros sententiarum*, 4.20.1.4 (*Opera omnia*, 4:537): "Dicendum, quod sicut videmus in politicis et communitatibus humanis, quod thesaurus reipublicae propter duo maxime consuevit proferri et communicari exterius; sic in spiritualibus intelligendum. Profertur namque thesaurus extra ad dispergendum propter gloriam prinicipis, sicut faciunt reges curiales, sicut fecit Assuerus Esther primo; alio modo propter utilitatis communitatis sive necessitatem, ut quando laeditur communitas, proferuntur stipendia et donativa militibus, ut eant ad pugnam. Sic thesaurus ecclesiae ab his qui habent dispensare, duplici ex cause debet distribui, scilicet propter gloriam principis et laudem; et laus et honor dei est in sanctis suis, et sancti honorantur in constructione basilicarum, visitatione basilicarum, commemoratione virtutum suarum, et idem fit in praedicationibus et sermonibus: ideo pro his omnibus indulgentiae recte fiunt. Communis autem utilitas est defensio terrae sanctae, defensio fidei, promotio studii et consimilia; et ideo adhuc pro talibus debent fieri. Et quoniam haec consistunt in actibus exterioribus, ideo maxime pro actibus exterioribus debent fieri indulgentiae."

88. Thomas Aquinas, *Commentum in IV libri sententiarum*, 4.20.1.3.3 (*Opera omnia*, 4:537): "Dicendum quod temporalia ad spiritualia ordinantur: quia propter spiritualia temporalibus uti debemus; et ideo pro temporalibus simpliciter non potest fieri indulgentia, sed pro temporalibus ordinatis ad spiritualia, sicut repressio inimicorum ecclesiae, qui pacem ecclesiae perturbant; vel sicut constructio ecclesiarum et pontium, et aliarum eleemosynarum collatio. Et per hoc patet quod non fit ibi simonia, quia non datur spirituale pro temporali, sed pro spirituali." Cf. Peter of Tarentaise (Innocent V), *In IV libros sententiarum commentaria*, 4.20.3.2.5 (Toulouse: Arnald Clomerium, 1672), 4:232.

89. X 5.31.12. Canon 60 of Lateran IV (*Accedentibus*) forbade abbots from exercising powers belonging to bishops, among which was the granting of indulgences.

90. Thomas Aquinas, *Summa Theologiae Suppl.* 26.3 (ed. Studia Generalis, 4:101a): "Dicendum quod papa habet plenitudinem pontificalis potestatis, quasi rex in regno. Sed episcopi assumuntur in partem sollicitudinis, quasi iudices singulis civitatibus praepositi; propter quod eos solos in suis litteris papa fratres vocat, reliquos autem omnes vocat filios. Et ideo potestas faciendi indulgentias plene residet in papa; quia potest facere prout vult, causa tamen existente legitima. Sed in episcopis est taxata secundum ordinationem papae." Cf. Bonaventure, *Commentaria in IV libros sententiarum*, 4.20.1.3 (*Opera omnia*, 4:534). Albert, *Commentarii in IV libri sententiarum*, 4.20.21 (*Opera omnia* [Paris: Louis Vives, 1894], 29:857–858).

91. X 5.38.12.

92. Wood, *Church and Sovereignty*, 36.

Chapter 4

Indulgences, the Saints, and Devotionalism at the End of the High Middle Ages

Critics often have said that indulgences bankrupted late medieval religion. In particular, the dispensation of remissions fostered a piety of fear, in that penitents believed that pardons would cancel penalty for sin that otherwise would have to be served in Purgatory, the torments of which resembled those of Hell itself. The thesis of a piety of fear originated in later nineteenth-century historiography and has had both Catholic and Protestant defenders. Its influence may be discerned in much of today's scholarly investigations of medieval religion.

If this thesis is correct, the spiritual vanguard of the later medieval centuries, namely the saints, should have condemned with outraged voices the distribution and reception of indulgences, for the great religious person-alities of the era, such as Bridget of Sweden, Catherine of Siena, Peter of Luxembourg, and Henry Suso, represent a great flowering of mystical ecstacy, not a dark brooding over the punishments of the afterlife. If indul-gences had been damaging to spiritual renewal, these saints especially should have had no regard for them. With that thought in mind, Richard Kieckhefer, the author of the magisterial study of fourteenth-century saintli-ness, suggested that fellow historians of medieval religion explore the con-nection between saintly piety and indulgences in the later Middle Ages.[1]

In the main, the saints of the thirteenth and fourteenth centuries treasured pardons as desirable cancellations of the debt of sin, the burden of which they lamented time and again. The saints did not denounce pardons, although some confessed to having occasional doubts about their efficacy. In many thirteenth- and fourteenth-century *vitae*, no references to indul-gences are made, but in the *vitae* in which pardons are mentioned, the saints' enthusiasm for remissions mirrored that of their less celebrated con-temporaries.[2] For instance, Louis IX (1235–1270), king of France and leader of the Seventh and Eighth Crusades, heroically pursued indulgences.

On his deathbed, he exhorted his son and successor Philip III (1270–1285) to obtain indulgences constantly.[3] One of Louis's biographers, in fact, testified that, even though the king was assured of the plenary indulgence for the crusade, while on campaign he undertook other indulgenced works:

> Besides, when he was in North Africa—because he desired to gain the indulgences granted by the papal legate there to those who carried building stones, or gave help with the works that had to be done—Louis sometimes carried stones and other similar things, and performed the works of humility.[4]

Louis, then, received the plenary, crusading indulgence, as well as this partial indulgence, which the papal legate conceded to soldiers of the crusading army for participating in the construction of a building. The king's acceptance of penitential works agreed with the recommendations of the canonist Hostiensis, among other intellectuals of that generation, who counselled that no one should rest from penitence or the seeking of indulgences.

THE CANCELLATION OF "PURGATORIES"

Of course, Louis admonished his son to obtain indulgences so that his successor's debt of sin might be cancelled in this life, rather than after death in Purgatory, which by the mid-thirteenth century (if not sooner) figured more explicitly (perhaps not more significantly) in the religious imagination. Ideas about indulgences reflected this increasing prominence. Early accounts of pardons seem to indicate that they could be applied against penances imposed in confession, but according to the *Summa de poenitentia et matrimonio* of Raymond of Peñafort, indulgences should be applied against purgatorial penalty, rather than penances imposed in confession. No penitent could be sure that his confessor had imposed a penance severe enough to equal his debt of sin; in many cases, penitents died before they could complete their penances.[5] Still, better to complete penances imposed in confession (which were growing less severe and time-consuming) and use remissions for what might await in Purgatory.

For some historians, the prominence of Purgatory in the medieval religious imagination served as the prime example of the era's spiritual degradation. For Jacques Le Goff, Purgatory encapsulated the moral and spiritual emptiness of later medieval Christianity. He claimed that the Schoolmen of the late twelfth and thirteenth centuries invented the doctrine of Purgatory. Then, mendicant preachers and pastoral manuals spread the new teaching. In his view, the "glorious moments in the history of Purgatory belong to the period between the fifteenth and nineteenth centuries," after the church had a chance to spread the idea of Purgatory among the ranks of ordinary believers, who, prior to the twelfth century, had no familiarity with the idea.[6] For Le Goff, the civilization of the Middle Ages was "a native culture subjected to the propaganda of Christian missionaries." Thus, Purgatory damaged medieval spiritual life as a kind of feral species that led to the extinction of natural, folkloric popular piety. André Vauchez added that the spread of "clerical" culture failed, except for a few ephemeral manifestations of enthusiasm. The masses "seem to have remained relatively indifferent to the religious program that the clergy was trying to draft for them . . . the pastors, increasingly influenced by the culture of the university, now claimed to be the sole repositories of true Christianity, and tended to think of the minds of their flocks as soft wax on which they needed only to leave their own impression."[7] Consequently, in the view of these two historians, an almost foreign, elite clerical culture impressed the quest for pardons and the prominence of Purgatory on the wax of the "popular" religious imagination.

Other historians have gone somewhat further and characterized Purgatory as an instrument of religious terrorism. These historians have argued (as noted in Chapter One) that the sufferings of Purgatory terrified late medieval Christians into the quest for indulgences. For many medieval Christians, the tortures inflicted on the souls in Purgatory inspired a hysterical fear of the afterlife. Other believers, perhaps of healthier dispositions, made pilgrimages, observed fasts, and obtained indulgences, but still for a base, rather than noble, motivation. In any event, the preoccupation with Purgatory poisoned the wellsprings of later medieval Christianity.

In contrast, John Van Engen, among others, has cast much doubt on a dualistic modelling of medieval religious culture into opposing "clerical" and "popular" subcultures. He presented evidence that in fact shows churchman and layman held the same religious ideas. In his words, "medieval Christianity is better conceived as comprised of complex and diverse elements spread across a very wide but more or less continuous spectrum."[8] Moreover, Christians since antiquity had prayed for the souls of the deceased and, for just as long, had understood that prayers could not avail the damned and were pointless for the blessed. They only benefitted the deceased, who in one important respect were like those yet alive, that is, still on the pilgrimage towards Heaven.

Furthermore, the portrayals of Le Goff and Vauchez ignore important diversities among later medieval Catholics, who, for instance, visualized Purgatory in no single way. Instead, a broad spectrum of views may be found in the sources. Of course, one of the theologically most sophisticated medieval discussions of Purgatory is Dante's, in *Il Purgatorio*, the second part of *La divina commedia*. According to Dante's vision, the mount of Purgatory served as the antechamber of Heaven, not Hell. Before he began his ascent, the pristine dew in the healthy air of Purgatory cleaned Dante's face, which the fetid air of Hell had made grimy. Dante observed that souls in Purgatory suffer but are consoled in the knowledge that they are cancelling the debt of sin they failed to satisfy while still alive. They understand why they are unready for Heaven, which is nonetheless their destination. The souls Dante encountered there rejoice in the assurance that they numbered among the saved; they even rejoice in their toil, because they know that their labors heal as well as punish. In both Hell and Purgatory, Dante encountered the lecherous, the gluttonous, and the wrathful; however, the souls in Purgatory had *repented* of their sins *before death*, while the souls in Hell refused to acknowledge, much less repent, their evildoing. Consequently, Dante ought to be read as saying that Purgatory simply completed the healing and purification begun in earthly life; indeed, since they yet belonged to the Church Militant, the souls in Purgatory still were strongly attached to the living. Purgatory, then, need summon not fearful trembling but, rather, a happy anticipation of the beatitude to come.

Other contemporaries shared Dante's essentially benign visualization of Purgatory. The story, for instance, of the ghost named Guy enjoyed great popularity throughout the fourteenth century. *De spiritu Guidonis* (*On the spirit of Guy*), the work of a French Dominican named Jean of Gobi, was translated into English verse as *The Gast of Gy* soon after its original composition in Latin, in the form of a letter to Pope John XXII. The tale of Guy's ghost survives in over sixty manuscripts and three incunabula. Medieval prose and verse translations were rendered also in French, German, Italian, and Dutch, so the story had a broad lay as well as clerical audience.[9] On Christmas day in the year 1323, clerks and laymen asked Jean to investigate a spirit that haunted the house of Guy, a recently deceased citizen of the southern French town of Alès. John and his confrères were eager to discover whether the spirit who called out from the beyond was good or evil. They set out for the house with the most learned members of the convent in tow. Important secular officials joined them on the way.[10] Upon reaching the house, they began to recite the office for the dead. As they prayed, an apparition passed before their eyes. The brothers asked the widow to ask the spirit who he was. The spirit replied that his name in life had been Guy of Corvo. After satisfying themselves that the ghost was not only real but also a good spirit intent on making satisfaction for sins committed in life, the brothers questioned him about his condition. Guy's spirit replied that he suffered a Purgatory of fire alone, in this house.

Guy's ghost haunted his wife because she had done little to reduce his suffering in Purgatory. Guy told the Dominicans those suffrages that most alleviated his suffering—the celebration of Masses (in particular, the Mass of the Holy Spirit) and the recitation of the seven penitential Psalms (6, 32, 38, 51, 102, 130, 143), as well as indulgences.[11] Jean and his confrères eagerly listened to Guy's description of Purgatory. Guy tells them that "All payn es gud (that prove I the) / that ordaind es in gud degre, / that es to say, that punysch syn / Of tham, that in erth wald noght blyn."[12] Guy assured them that demons torment none of the souls in Purgatory, since nothing infernal could touch something destined for Heaven.[13] The demons would like to submit these souls to torture, but a good angel accompanied and protected them:

> His gud aungell sais to him sone:
> "Comfort the wele, I sall the were,
> That the devels sall the noght dere;"
> And to the fendes than sall he say:
> "Yhe wicked fendes, wende hethen oway,
> For yhe have na part in this man."[14]

Like the souls Dante encountered on the mount of Purgatory, Guy knew well that his toils were ordained for his own good and would eventually make him fit to enter Heaven. Still, a bit of help from living relatives and friends would quicken his route to Heaven. He wanted the help of his wife, in particular, not because his suffering was horrible but because the end of his journey was so desirable.

Other literary figures also possessed a relatively benign view of Purgatory. That view survived until the end of the Middle Ages and may be found in the English pastoral manual *The Arte or Crafte to Lyve well and dye well*. Like *The Gast of Guy*, *The Arte or Craft* was a translation, made in 1505 by Wynkyn de Worde (from another earlier French original). *The Craft* assured readers that good angels occasionally comfort and encourage the souls in Purgatory.[15] In her *Spiritual Dialogue*, the mystic Catherine of Genoa (1447–1510) taught that souls in Purgatory could not even remember their wrongdoing yet were fully cognizant of God's mercy: "They cannot remember the good or evil in their past nor in that of others. Such is their joy in God's will, in his pleasure, that they have no concern for themselves but dwell only on their joy in God's ordinance, in having him do what he will. They see only the goodness of God, his mercy toward men."[16]

In contrast, other medieval writers held more hair-raising views of Purgatory. For Thomas Aquinas, whom Dante had studied carefully,

Purgatory formed the vestibule of Hell, rather than the antechamber of Heaven. Thomas thought that Purgatory resembled Hell more than Heaven. He believed that the same fire that torments the souls in Hell also burns the souls in Purgatory, such that souls in Purgatory shared some of the punishments of the damned: "the place of Purgatory is an infernal region joined to Hell, such that the same fire which torments the damned also cleanses the just in Purgatory."[17] While he agreed with Dante that no demons tortured the souls in Purgatory, Aquinas entertained the idea that demons led souls to Purgatory and delighted in the suffering of the souls there:

> As after the Judgment Day, the divine justice will kindle the fire by which the damned are punished eternally, so also now are the elect purged solely by the divine justice, not by the ministration of the demons, nor by the ministration of the angels, who would not distress their fellow-citizens so dreadfully. Yet, it is possible that the demons take them to the place of punishment; also that the demons, who rejoice in the punishment of man, stand by while the elect are purged.[18]

Whereas the souls in Dante's Purgatory rejoice in their labors as a preparation and purgation, Thomas believed that suffering in Purgatory exceeded the pain of any punishment imaginable in earthly life. He thought that the frustrated desire of the disembodied soul to go to God intensified the distress of Purgatory. In Purgatory, the soul's delay in going to God caused torment, as did the infernal flames:

> In Purgatory there will be a twofold pain; one will be the pain of loss, that is the delay of the divine vision, and the pain of sense, namely punishment by corporeal fire. With regard to both, the least pain of Purgatory surpasses the greatest pain of this life. For the more a thing is desired the more painful is its absence. And since after this life the holy souls desire the Sovereign Good with the most intense longing . . . it follows that they grieve exceedingly for their delay. Again, since pain is not hurt, but the sense of hurt, the more sensitive a thing is, the greater the pain caused by that which hurts it: wherefore hurts inflicted on the more sensible parts cause the greatest pain. And, because all bodily sensation is from the soul, it follows of necessity that the soul feels the greatest pain when a hurt is inflicted on the soul itself . . . therefore, it follows that the pain of Purgatory, both of loss and of sense, surpasses all the pains of this life.[19]

Many shared Thomas's vision of Purgatory.[20] For instance, John of Dambach (1288–1372), a fellow Dominican, described the punishments of Purgatory in his treatise, *On the power of indulgences* (*De virtute indulgenciarum*), which was the very first independent theological treatise on indulgences; thus John's was also the first text wherein a description of Purgatory was included within a theological discussion of pardons. Clearly, Thomas's Supplement to the *Summa theologiae* and his commentary on the Sentences, where his visualization of Purgatory followed his analysis of pardons, influenced John of Dambach. John, who hailed from Alsace, was a famous teacher of theology in the Dominican province of Germany. *On the power of indulgences*, probably written in the 1340s, survives in five manuscripts of central European provenance, which may suggest that the tortures of Purgatory especially captured the religious imagination of southern Germans.

Like Thomas, John equated the fires of Purgatory with those of Hell. However, since John described Purgatory in more colorful imagery than did Thomas, his visualization was also more frightful. John agreed that the suffering of Purgatory exceeded anything imaginable in this life, but added that "some saints confessed that they would rather suffer ulcerous sores, or any other terrific pain in this life for ten years, rather than spend one year in Purgatory."[21] To emphasize the proximity of Purgatory to Hell, John described Hell, Purgatory, and Limbo within the framework of Aristotelian physics. Hell, Purgatory, and Limbo consist of concentric circles. Hell, which is located in the center of the earth, forms the core circle of these concentric circles. Purgatory is sited on the circumference of Hell, and the Limbo of unbaptized children sits on the circumference of Purgatory. John explained that Hell must be in the center of the earth, and therefore the center of the universe because, as Aristotle taught, the immobile earth was at the center of the cosmos because all heavy things descend to earth. In contrast, Heaven is the resting place of light things:

> Just as we observe in corporal things, so we must imagine it is with spiritual things. Now in corporal things, light things naturally move upwards, such as light itself, and fire, and on the other hand, heavy things move in the opposite way, such as a stone. So it is with spiritual things—by fervent charity they move up and away from sins; indeed, sinners *descend* in various ways to sin. Man is in a way set aflame by love, and he is inflamed, and he is taken heavenward, but sinners are weighed down by sins. And so [after death] sinners descend down towards Hell, because things which are heavy naturally move downward to the center of the earth, where all heavy things have their resting place in the infernal regions. And this is the center of the earth.[22]

Since lightness tends to rise, Purgatory is closer to Hell than it is to Limbo, where "the penalties are most lenient, without affliction or remorse of conscience."[23]

While the infernal flames did indeed torment some of the souls in Purgatory, John also visualized Hell as a place of great confusion, terror, and awful stench. Like a sewer, Hell was "where the dung of all the universe has descended and collected."[24] The penalty of the damned is to dwell forever in this powerful vortex of terror, stink, and cosmic crap. John enumerated eight infernal torments: "worms and darkness, scourging, freezing cold, flames, demonic visions, a variety of wickednesses, confusion, and sorrow."[25] The damned brought these penalties upon themselves because "it is in this place that the one who dies in mortal sin owes eternal penalty, which is infernal, since, deserted by God, that sinner lacks grace and despairs for his entire condition."[26]

John followed his description of Hell with a history of its neighboring region, Purgatory. During the time of the Old Law, even the righteous awaited the coming of the Redeemer in what John called the "Limbo of the Patriarchs." The Passion and Resurrection of Jesus either destroyed the Limbo of the Patriarchs or joined it to Heaven (John entertained both opinions as possible). The souls who had awaited the coming of the Christ in the Limbo of the Patriarchs then were admitted into Heaven. John seems to have thought that Purgatory existed before the Passion and Resurrection of Jesus, but what purpose Purgatory may have served under the Old Law he did not say:

After Christ opened the gates of Heaven, then the place which before the coming of Christ was called the Limbo of the Patriarchs could now in a way be called the place of glory or Heaven because it was then the place of the blessed. Thus it is clear that there are several dwelling places of the soul after it has been separated from the body, such that one is the place of glory. There had before the Passion been four places of punishment, but now that Christ destroyed the fourth [the Limbo of the Patriarchs], there are now three places of punishment [i.e., the Limbo of the unbaptized, Purgatory, and Hell]. And after the Final Judgement, Purgatory shall cease to exist because then temporal penalty shall be no more.[27]

Thus Purgatory—despite its proximity to the flames of Hell—most properly belonged to the *time of grace*, unlike the Limbo of the Patriarchs, which Jesus ended by His Passion and Resurrection. Although souls were purged and punished in Purgatory, as Dante emphasized in the *Purgatorio*, John did not think they ever despaired. He reminded readers that only those who had died confessed and contrite, but had not yet completed their debt of satisfaction, entered into Purgatory: "it ought to be borne in mind that in the place which is called Purgatory enter only those who perished with venial sins or confessed and contrite mortal sins."[28] Since punishment in Purgatory was very much like that in Hell, John's discussion of the afterlife, like many other medieval discussions of the infernal regions, served as an exhortation to reject sin. Furthermore, *On the power of indulgences* also explained to his mostly Dominican readership the benign power of indulgences. Through pardons, the hellish punishments of Purgatory could be avoided either entirely or, more probably, in part.

Other fourteenth-century accounts described Purgatory as like unto Hell, but not always with the consoling reminder that no demons terrorized the souls there; consequently, these depictions of Purgatory were in fact terrorizing. The Dominican tertiary Catherine of Siena (d. 1380), one of Christendom's great fourteenth-century spiritual masters, received a vision of Purgatory that, since it followed closely upon a vision of Hell, scarcely differed from it. St. Bridget of Sweden (c. 1303–1373), the Swedish visionary and foundress of the Brigittines, received a vision of souls in Purgatory punished for their lies and pride. This vision appears in Bridget's *Liber celestis*, which enjoyed great popularity in English translation:

> Than methoght that thar was a bande bonden abowte his hede so faste and sore that the forhede and the nodell mete togiddir. The eyn were hingande on the chekes; the eres as thai had bene brent with fire; the brayne braste out at the nesethirles and hys eres; the tonge hange oute, and the teth were smetyn togyddir: the bones in the armes were broken and wrethyn as a rope; the skyn was pullid of hys hede and thai were bunden in hys neke; the breste and the wombe were so clo[n]gen togiddir, and the ribbes broken, that one myght see the herte and the bowelles; the shuldirs were broken and hange down to the sides; and the broken bonys were drawen oute as it had bene a thred of a clothe.[29]

Far from being Dante's steep mount, Purgatory amounted to a torture-chamber. If most late medieval Catholics subscribed to Bridget's imaginings of Purgatory, how could it not have created a piety of fear?

THE PIETY OF THE SAINTS AND INDULGENCES

Contrary to much historiography, in which the infernal punishments of Purgatory terrorized everyone, the range of imaginings of the place must also mirror a host of attitudes taken by medieval Catholics towards Purgatory. While one depiction suggests essentially a place of purification, the other indicates an abode of punishment. To be sure, the more dreadful visions, which may well have been entertained by the majority of medieval Catholics, must at least have caused some misgivings, if not terror. Catherine of Siena, for instance, fretted especially about what awaited members of her family in Purgatory, for they had sinned by insisting she marry, rather than follow her spiritual inclination for celibacy. After she had despaired of her father's recovery from illness, Catherine asked God

> to grant him the further grace of entering straight into glory without passing through the pains of Purgatory. But in reply to this she was told that justice must of necessity be done, at least in one way or another; it is impossible for a soul that has not been fully cleansed to enter into a possession of that resplendent glory.[30]

In a vision, she learned that God was at first reticent to grant her wish. Catherine, however, continued to plead with the Almighty and promised that she would make satisfaction for her father's transgressions. God then agreed, but told her that henceforth he would "transfer his penalty to your account, and you must bear it till the day you die."[31]

God's justice, however, along with its accompanying penalties, was indeed intimidating, to say the least. Yet, medieval Catholics could, and clearly often did, know that penalties did not compose the whole picture. Like her contemporaries, Catherine relied on the power of pardons to cancel the debt of sin, not only for herself but also for her loved ones. When the Dominican friar Raymond of Capua, her hagiographer and admirer, fell seriously ill, he asked Catherine to pray for the forgiveness of his sins. She obliged, and took the further step of requesting an indulgence from the Curia.[32] The document that recorded the pardon was in all likelihood a *confessionale*, which enjoyed great popularity during the late Middle Ages. A *confessionale* gave its bearer's confessor the right to grant a plenary indulgence at the moment of death.[33] When Catherine herself languished in her deathbed, and after having made her last confession and communion, she "asked for the plenary indulgence which had been graciously granted in her favor by the two popes, Gregory XI and Urban VI."[34] Gregory had given her an indulgence in gratitude for the prayers he asked her to offer on behalf of himself and the universal Church.[35] That Catherine, whose life was by any measure (except, of course, her own) blameless, possessed *two plenary indulgences*, reflects the medieval Catholic's estimate of the bill of satisfaction owed for sin, not to mention her reliance on the church's aid. That Catherine asked to be handed the indulgences granted her by the two popes testifies to the consolation she sought not only in what those pardons promised but even in the ink and parchment on which they were written.

In seeking some consolation from pardons, Catherine had plenty of saintly company. Fourteenth-century saints especially treasured deathbed plenary remissions. In his last illness, the Sicilian hermit St. William Gnoffi (d. 1317)

> perceived that the day of his death had now arrived, because he was stricken with fever, and because he was tormented by a pain in his chest; he took to his bed. He quickly asked that a priest be summoned, from whom he often received valid indulgence of sins, and then most devoutly the most sacred viaticum of the body and blood of our Lord Jesus Christ, which he had always faithfully believed in and humbly adored.[36]

William eagerly received indulgences throughout his life, and even ended his life acquiring them. Similarly, the *vita* of the boy cardinal Peter of

Luxembourg (1369–1387), which described a brief life rich in humility, filled with prayer, harsh ascetic discipline, and constant veneration of the cross, also mentioned his desire to obtain a plenary indulgence at the hour of death: "Happy, they say, the most devout cardinal, about to go forth from this world to God, wishing to be absolved so that he would be with Christ, deserved to obtain by apostolic authority a plenary absolution from penalty and guilt at his hour of death."[37] That such plenary indulgences had to be petitioned from the pope in advance of the final illness suggests that for some at least such pardons had become part of the late medieval ritual of dying.

The examples of Catherine, William, and Peter suggest, moreover, that whether imagined as an essentially benign place of purgation, or as a raging outpost of Hell, few, if any, of the saints were obsessed with the fear of what many imagined as an immensely fearsome place.[38] The saints' lives countermand Umberto Eco's suggestion in the 1980s best-selling novel *The Name of the Rose* that the fourteenth century "replaced the penitence of the soul with a penitence of the imagination, a summons to supernatural visions of suffering and blood," a piety characterized by spiritual paralysis rather than conversion to a more blameless life.[39] Instead, numerous beacons of hope and consolation fill the pages even of those *vitae* and revelations wherein Purgatory was most petrifying. The lesson learned was that the souls in Purgatory were being punished for what they had failed to do in earthly life—their fate was not inevitably visited on all the contrite and confessed. God's Church offered a way out, literally and figuratively! The knight who in Bridget of Sweden's *Liber celestis* had seen Purgatory promptly resolved to amend his life.[40] Raymond of Capua insisted that Catherine's prayers had delivered two criminals from Purgatory.[41] John of Dambach's *On the power of indulgences* instructed Dominicans to remind the faithful that through amendment of life and reception of pardons Purgatory could be avoided altogether.

The sources, then, support no necessary connection, often made in the historiography, among pardons, Purgatory, and a piety of fear. Nor do they buttress the connection generally made between indulgences and the bankruptcy of late medieval Catholicism; rather, the opposite picture sometimes emerges. In the *vitae* of the later medieval centuries, wherein St. Francis was the single great example of the *imitatio Christi*, the saints either obtained indulgences, or indulgences are simply not mentioned. In no *vita* does a saint condemn indulgences as corrosive of zeal or penitence; instead, generally indulgences served as modest incentives to conversion, prayer, and works of charity. The Sienese saint, John Colombino (c. 1304–1367), for instance, was a rich merchant who spent much of his young adulthood in dissolute living. Marriage failed to soften his heart, for he and his devout wife often argued. On one particularly quarrelsome day, his wife gave him a copy of the *vita* of St. Mary of Egypt. She hoped that the saint's example might sweeten her husband's sour disposition. She got more than she bargained for, as that reading provoked a conversion experience that ultimately led John to leave his wife and adopt a life of voluntary poverty and service to the poor. His hagiographer wrote that after his conversion experience John "did penance anywhere *there were indulgences*, for they effected a liveliness in embracing conversion, eagerness in listening to God's word, and promptness in doing good work."[42] John heard sermons or gave alms because of the indulgences attached to these good works. Pardons, then, could encourage the adoption of Franciscan piety, the hallmark of which was joy, hope, and optimism.

Indulgences also served as the occasion for other fourteenth-century saints to follow Francis's model of the *imitatio Christi*. Pardons fostered the participation of Jane Mary of Maillé (1332–1414), the daughter of Baron Hardouin IV of Maillé, in Christ's Passion and Death. Religious zeal distinguished even Jane's childhood; indeed, family and friends were convinced that Jane's prayers had rescued her childhood playmate Robert—later her husband—from death. The Hundred Years' War devastated the estates and fortunes of Jane's family. Robert fought beside King John I (1350–1364) of France, whom Edward, "the Black Prince," of England defeated utterly at the battle of Poitiers (1356). Robert was maimed in the battle and accompanied his monarch into captivity (1356–1360). During Robert's imprisonment, English soldiers destroyed the family castle at Silles and slew forty-six local nobles. The English captured hostages from Robert's lands; his own captors demanded a ransom of three thousand florins. Her estates devastated, Jane failed to pay the ransom on time, and Robert's jailers tortured, starved, and threatened him with death. They even forced him to drink his own urine. Jane relied on all that remained to her—her prayers to the Blessed Virgin Mother, whom the couple credited with Robert's eventual release. Although crippled, he had survived the ordeal and returned to his wife. Robert and Jane then devoted themselves to the relief of other victims of the war. They negotiated the release of prisoners and pleaded for the lives of the condemned.[43] Jane suffered another series of misfortunes following upon Robert's death in 1362. Convinced that suffering had driven her mad, family and acquaintances drove Jane out of her home.[44] Rather than complain or succumb to discouragement, Jane instead rejoiced in the freedom from worldly cares and embraced the life of a Franciscan tertiary, which included the quest for indulgences:

> Thus made truly poor and truly needy, from then on she was not able to get shelter or lodging either by purchase or lease, for when charity grows cold iniquity flourishes, and her enemies, at the devil's instigation, spoke with her host; he, bent on gain, forgot all mercy and rather harshly threw her out of her ancient residence, in which she had lived honestly and devoutly for many years. Thus freed from worldly cares she visited churches, so that she began visiting the tombs of the saints, and thus would she receive the indulgences.[45]

Jane Mary's quest for indulgences led her all over France, even to the royal chapel, where she often prayed at the standards of the Redeemer.[46]

Other saints, less heroic but equally pious, also sought indulgences. The peasant girl Zita of Lucca (c. 1218–1278), who made a living as a household servant, obtained many of the devotional indulgences then available. She visited a great number of churches, monasteries, and hospitals and was sure to be one of the worshippers at the liturgy, "in order to obtain remission and customary indulgence."[47] Encouraged by a correspondence with Catherine of Siena, the fifteen-year-old Pisan widow Clare Giambacorta determined never to marry again. She sought out the indulgences attached to the hearing of sermons and worship at Mass on certain feasts in the liturgical calendar. She visited monasteries where indulgences were offered. To her surprise, she found that one monastery where she had gone was not Franciscan, but Dominican, and the memory of St. Bridget was revered there. She was so impressed that instead of becoming a Franciscan, she became a Dominican.[48] As Clare's *vita* shows, what unified the fourteenth-century Latin Christians superceded their divisions into legal statuses and religious orders.

For the Flemish nun Ida of Louvain (d. c. 1300), the possibility of gaining indulgence served as an annual incentive to penitential reflection. One year, on the feast of St. Thomas the Apostle (21 December), Ida anxiously recalled her sins and transgressions and, fearful that she might not be fit for remission and indulgence, she all the more sorrowfully and fervently confessed her wrongdoing.[49] Ida was "mother" to a spiritual "family" of associates, confidants, and followers. They all welcomed the itinerant preachers who urged them to receive indulgences:

> There was in that time a certain friar of the Order of Preachers, on close and friendly terms in Christ with Ida, the said servant of Christ. This friar, invested by the authority of the Apostolic See and of the most high Pontiff, in order to win for the Lord a faithful and worthy people, the seekers of good works, devoted himself assiduously to the office of preaching, through the grace given to him: and those whom he taught internally by the word of preaching, he marked externally by the sign of the living

cross; he set out for them the indulgence available for their sins. Indeed, he was given
such a grace from the Lord in this work that there was scarcely anyone, however hard
their heart, who could help himself from taking the cross of the Lord.[50]

The good will exhibited between this Dominican and Ida's followers can
only mean that, like the preacher, she taught her family that indulgences
might well aid the quest for holiness.

Like Ida, Peter of Foligno purged himself of worldly desires, grieved his
past sins, and desired to live in grace, expressly to make himself fit for the
reception of pardons: "Therefore he began with bitter sorrow to reflect upon
the sins he committed, and by his meditations, recitations, and works which
he completed in time, he began to have the greatest contrition, and because
of these exercises sorrowfully and humbly to seek divine mercy and indulgence with great tears, sighs, and sobs."[51] Having recognized his sinfulness
and dependence upon the mercy of God, he was barely able to receive the
sacrament of penance, because his weeping interrupted his confession.
Nonetheless, Peter persisted in penitence: "Finally, the confessor of God, in
shedding a great quantity of tears of the greatest sadness, such that, coming
to the priest he was barely able to express himself, confessing all sins fully,
he efficaciously obtained indulgence and full remission of sins from
the Lord."[52]

The sources contain yet other examples. After her conversion experience, the Englishwoman Margery Kempe (c. 1393–1439) made several
long pilgrimage journeys, first to Canterbury, then to Compostela, and on
to the Holy Land. She made the pilgrimage to Rome in 1415 to attend the
canonization of Bridget of Sweden.[53] While in Italy she made the trip to
Assisi to get the Portiuncula plenary indulgence, which was traditionally
available, "on Lammes Day (November 3), when there is great pardon of
plenary remission, for to purchase grace, mercy, and forgiveness for herself,
for all her friends, for all her enemies, and for all the souls in Purgatory."[54]
The people of Perugia detained the Franciscan tertiary Cicco of Pesaro
(d. 1350), during his return trip from the famous pardon of the Portiuncula.
He wished to continue with his journey, but the Perugians insisted that
such a spiritual celebrity stay with them a bit longer and partake of their
hospitality. His celebrity rested upon his having obtained the Portiuncula
indulgence.[55]

Bridget of Sweden and her daughter Catherine (c. 1321–1381) likewise
journeyed to the holy places in Rome to receive the numerous indulgences
available in that city. In fact, the Roman pardons sometimes occasioned
quarrels between the mother and daughter. Rome could be a dangerous
city in the best of times but was especially lawless in the mid-fourteenth

century. The absence of the popes in Avignon stirred up the tumult in a perpetually tumultuous city. Criminals terrorized certain streets and preyed upon pilgrims. Bridget and Catherine, who enjoyed the advantages of wealth and rank, could afford armed bodyguards. Nonetheless, Bridget strictly forbade Catherine from visiting the shrines without an escort, which was not always available when Catherine desired. Catherine pouted when she could not go to the indulgenced shrines and churches, and felt quite sorry for herself: "Here I lead a miserable life. Others profit from and enjoy the rewards of their souls; they visit the tombs of the saints, and they take part in the divine mysteries, but I am sequestered from all spiritual goods by brutal practice."[56] Catherine was allowed to visit the holy places outside the city walls—which may have been even more dangerous than the city streets—when Bridget received visions indicating that gaining the indulgences was safe. After she and her mother had been in the Eternal City twenty-five years, Bridget and Catherine ventured far from Rome to visit more holy places, even travelling to other kingdoms and places, "hoping to do God's will in [all] these undertakings."[57] At long last, they journeyed to Jerusalem, where they prayed in the Church of the Holy Sepulchre.

Of course, in gaining the pilgrimage indulgences, the saints were much like other fourteenth-century penitents. Unlike their fellows, their celebrity meant that they could petition bishops and popes for grants of indulgence with which they could promote their devotions and reforms. St. John Colombino (1304–1367) founded a community of lay brothers whose piety and daily regimen resembled the communities of the Devotio Moderna in Holland. He sought papal approval of his community in the form of a grant of pardon for members of the community and their benefactors, much as the popes approved new devotions through grants of indulgence. That the remission should come directly from the pope, rather than from one of his legates, was important to John, for a direct grant would express a stronger confirmation of his new community.[58] Similarly, Ursulina of Parma (c. 1385–1410) was told in visions to work for the end of the Great Schism (1379–1417). Twice she travelled to Avignon to convince Clement VII (1379–1394) to renounce his claim to the papal throne. She failed, of course, and in the meantime endured much "for the reconciliation of the Catholic faith." Her reputation for sanctity, however, spread throughout the neighborhood of Avignon, where many who suffered in mind and body came to her for direction and comfort. Although Ursulina believed that the Avignonese pope must resign to end the Schism, she nonetheless asked Clement for indulgences and other privileges for her home, including the right to build an oratory there.[59]

For the famous German Dominican mystic Henry Suso (d. 1365), devotion to the Passion of Christ included the quest for indulgences.[60] As a young, aspiring mystic, Suso brutalized his body as a participation in the suffering of the Savior. From his eighteenth until his fortieth year of age, he scourged himself bloody. He wore a hair shirt, an iron chain, and a barbed cross under his scapular. His feet bled as he stood in choir with his brothers, for he refused to warm them or wear shoes even in the coldest weather. Two decades of ascetical severity nearly ruined his health. "After the servant [Suso] had led a life filled with the exterior penitential exercises . . . his whole physical being had been so devastated that the only choice open to him was to die or to give up such exercises. And so he gave them up." In fact, God Himself told Suso in a vision that such exercises were not the final steps on the path to spiritual fulfillment.[61] Instead, Suso turned to contemplation, which led to detachment from worldly concerns. He even counselled those charged to his pastoral care to avoid excessive ascetic discipline.[62] Above all, Suso now cultivated a daily spiritual regimen that focused on Christ's Passion and prescribed works of satisfaction for the debt of sin. He found part of his desires in the quest for pardons:

> Eternal Wisdom: My stern justice requires that in all of nature any injustice, be it great or small, has to be atoned for and corrected. Now how should a sinner, who perhaps has committed more than a hundred serious sins—and, according to theological writings, each serious sin requires seven years of atonement or else the unaccomplished atonement has to be performed in the scorching furnace of grim Purgatory—alas, when should this miserable soul have finished its penance? When should its long period of anguish be over? How long this would last! Yet look! It can easily do penance and make amends through my innocent and noble suffering. *The soul can simply reach into the precious treasure of the merit I earned and draw on it for itself.* Even if it were supposed to burn in Purgatory for a thousand years, it has removed the guilt and done its penance in a short time so that it enters into eternal joy without any Purgatory.[63]

For Suso, receiving an indulgence was an exterior exercise like those he had undertaken in his younger days, but without the severity. The pardons also served as outward signs of his interior conversion and devotion to the crucified Christ:

> [Drawing upon the treasury of merit] is accomplished as follows: 1. A person considers with a sorrowful heart very carefully and often the seriousness and number of his offenses, for which he has so clearly deserved angry looks from his heavenly Father. 2. He should then consider as nothing his own acts of atonement because, compared to his sins, they are a drop in the ocean. 3. He should then joyfully consider the immensity of my atonement because the smallest drop of my precious blood that flowed

abundantly all over out of my loving body could atone for the sins of a thousand worlds. And yet each person draws this atonement to himself only to the extent that he identifies with me by suffering along with me. 4. Finally, a person should humbly and beseechingly sink his small self into the immensity of my atonement and cling to it.[64]

Suso also linked pardons and Christocentric piety in his later Latin revision of the *Little Book of Eternal Wisdom*, entitled the *Horologium sapientiae*, wherein he encouraged daily prayer for the protection of the church and increased devotion to the Savior. Of course, the *Pater noster* most powerfully served this purpose; yet another prayer also possessed great power: "Blessed be the name of our Lord Jesus Christ, of God, and of the glorious Virgin Mary, his mother for ever and ever. Amen. And for this prayer indulgences are granted. The purpose of this prayer, addressed to this name, is . . . so that this marvelous name may be revived in some way and take its place and be renewed in the hearts of the faithful."[65] In Suso's mysticism, then, indulgences encouraged good works, such as the recitation and repetition of especially efficacious prayers, and outwardly manifested the movement in interior disposition from religious indifference to the sincere desire to grow closer to Jesus.

SAINTLY VISIONS AND INDULGENCES

Perhaps, however, the most striking endorsements of indulgences in fourteenth-century saintly piety come from saints who had received commands to obtain indulgences in visions or whose quest for indulgences had led to visions. Visions, which were unmistakable and extraordinary affirmations of holiness, were the signs of God's grace working within a man or woman, such as the Prussian wife and mother, Dorothy of Montau (1347–1394).[66] Dorothy and her husband Albert had nine children, of whom only one survived into adulthood. Dorothy frequently made pilgrimages to both local and far-distant shrines. Her husband, whose zeal fell short of her own, accompanied her on three short pilgrimages from their home near Aachen to a nearby monastery, where the monks erected a shrine dedicated to the Virgin Mary. After her husband's death around the year 1390, she became a famous pious recluse. Dorothy, who soon gained some celebrity for holiness, was petitioned for visions and cures by the fearful and ailing. She came out of seclusion to make the pilgrimage to Rome for the plenary indulgence. She spent six months in the city, during which she had visions "of supernatural apparitions; she saw saints and heard the voices of Christ, of the most blessed Virgin, and of some saints."[67] The Jubilee indulgence thus served as the occasion for this vision, one of the most vivid Dorothy ever had.

Visions sometimes confirmed the great power of indulgences. Christ appeared to Bridget of Sweden in a vision, and commanded her to make the Jubilee pilgrimage to Rome (for 1350) because "there is a compendium— i.e., a shorter way—to heaven because of the indulgences that the holy pontiffs have merited by their prayers." Jesus told Bridget that she would make the pilgrimage not only as a penitent but also as his envoy and voice to the pope and emperor.[68] Bridget made the journey and thereafter resided in the Eternal City, "not only because of the indulgences but also because of the promises to be fulfilled," namely, "that she would go to Rome and would stay there until she saw the pope and the emperor," namely Innocent VI (1352–1362) and Charles IV (1346–1378).[69] Bridget received other revelations that assured her of the worthiness of indulgences. She was told that seekers of indulgences who intended to abandon sin and live according to the will of God will gain remission of sin, or at least will be led to confession and contrition. While this vision may seem to put the theological cart before the horse, the benefits of pardons often were expressed in this seemingly confused way. God told Bridget that a man who had died one thousand times for God's sake would yet be unworthy of the Beatific Vision, but indulgences would enable that man to participate fully in the divine glory. In a life lasting a millenium, no man could suffice for his sins, yet indulgences remove the debt; one with indulgences who dies in perfect charity and true contrition will be forgiven guilt and remitted penalty.[70] In another vision, Christ and his Blessed Mother assured Bridget of the efficacy of the church's ministrations. Before she journeyed to the Holy Land, a troubled Franciscan friar confided to her that he doubted whether sinful priests and prelates had the power to grant absolution and remission. Mary later appeared to Bridget and told her that God forgives all the truly contrite, even the Franciscan who had confessed his doubts to her. Mary reassured her that a pope who is without heresy possesses full and complete authority to bind and to loose from God through his succession to Peter.[71]

Margaret of Cortona (1247–1297), "the mother and mirror of sinners," also received a vision prompted by her desire to gain indulgence.[72] She was a beautiful woman from a peasant family, and a local noble fell in love with her. Although she returned his affections, Margaret's lowly birth rendered marriage out of the question. Instead, the couple lived together until a rival murdered Margaret's lover. The slaying occasioned Margaret's conversion to a harshly penitential life.[73] She much regretted her liaison and devoted herself to the veneration of St. Francis of Assisi, to whom she prayed "with precious tears" that she would be made worthy of a plenary indulgence before she died. Her prayers moved St. Francis to intercede with the Lord for her, such that she was fully absolved of all penalty, *so she had no need of the pardon she so coveted*! In a vision, Margaret learned from the Redeemer himself that both her guilt and her penalty were completely absolved:

> One day, with prayerful tears, Margaret asked her Father, Blessed Francis, that by his merits for her she might become fit to receive plenary indulgence of all her sins. By his intercessory merits, that saint obtained from the Lord for his beloved daughter Margaret that she be fully indulged through the revelation of the divine voice. Expressly speaking to her soul, the Most High indeed gave that gift to Margaret, saying: I, Jesus Christ, Son of the great and eternal Father, crucified for you, absolve you fully from all your sins.[74]

The zeal that made Margaret desire a plenary indulgence, then, won for her a full remission of guilt and penalty. Though the sources at this point do not permit, it would be interesting to know just how many cases mirrored Margaret's, where God's generosity as exemplified by the treasury of merit prompted a change of heart and adoption of a holier life.[75]

The full cancellation that St. Francis obtained for Margaret was neither the only plenary remission he won on the behalf of others nor the most famous. The celebrity of the indulgence of the Portiuncula perhaps exceeded that of any other pardon in later medieval Christendom. Margery Kempe travelled far to receive it, as did Bridget of Sweden, who wept when doubts about the validity of the pardon crept into her mind. Christ, however, appeared to her and asked why she was so troubled. She answered that she worried because of those who said that St. Francis had fabricated the indulgence. Jesus assured her that he himself had granted it and that no pope would ever recall it.[76]

The Portiuncula was the little church near Assisi that St. Francis had rebuilt. In 1334, Francesco Bartoli, a Franciscan friar, wrote a history of the indulgence. According to Francesco, in a vision, Christ told Francis that he wished the church to be given to his mother Mary.[77] In great excitement, Francis bought the church from the Benedictines and repaired it. Francis then had a revelation that Christ, Mary, and the angels could be seen in the Portiuncula. He hastened to the church, and there met the Savior and his mother. Francis thus spoke to Jesus:

> Our most holy Father, I, a sinner and a wretched thing, humbly beseech that you may deign to grant this grace to humankind, namely, that you concede mercy and indulgence of all sins to each and every person coming to this place and entering this church, by whom confession shall have been made to a priest and penance shall have been taken up. And I ask of the most blessed Mary, your Mother, the advocate for the

whole human race, that she may deign to aid me in this request, and shall see fit to intercede with your most pious and clement Majesty.[78]

Mary graciously obliged and asked her son to grant Francis's request. Jesus granted his wish, and told him to seek out Pope Honorius III (1216–1227). The Lord bade Francis tell the pope that the Savior wanted a plenary indulgence to be granted to the Portiuncula. Honorius first hesitated, and the cardinals fretted that a plenary indulgence given to this church might mean the end of the crusades. Francis persisted. Honorius finally consented and granted the church a plenary indulgence one day out of the year (Lammas Day, August 1), and asked Francis what proof of the grant of pardon he desired. Francis replied that the wishes of Christ were all the proof he needed.[79]

Modern scholars have already well documented the medieval controversy involving the validity of the Portiuncula pardon.[80] Francesco Bartoli's treatise was merely one polemic Franciscans used to defend its legitimacy while their rivals cast doubts upon it. By the 1290s, critics were challenging the validity of the indulgence, and that encouraged Franciscan apologists like Bartoli and Peter of John Olivi to write treatises in defense of the pardon. The weight of medieval opinion favored the Portiuncula's validity, for to naysay it was tantamount to insulting the memory of the beloved Francis.

Modern authorities have been more skeptical. Paulus pointed out that although early lives of Francis contain no mention of the Portiuncula, as time made of Francis a greater legend, anything connected with him became more wonderful and sometimes fantastic. He believed that the Portiuncula pardon added to the legend of the *Poverello*, but that did not mean the indulgence was licit.[81] The editor of Bartoli's treatise, the Calvinist Paul Sabatier, was certain that the indulgence was apocryphal. He pointed out, first, that the Portiuncula pardon was unheard of until 1267, and second, given the professionalism of the papal chancery, the fact that no document survives to prove its validity raises serious doubts about the remission's authority. Another student of the Portiuncula has observed that the best evidence on the behalf of the indulgence is a notary's deed, wherein Benedict of Arezzo, whom St. Francis received into the order, testified that Brother Masseo, one of Francis's companions, told him that Pope Honorius III had granted the indulgence at Perugia.[82] This deed, however, was drawn up in 1277, a half-century after the death of Francis! All in all, hardly any evidence at all suggests that the proper church authority, namely the pope, ever granted a plenary indulgence to the Portiuncula.

While the origins of this remission have been examined with some acumen, its overall historical significance, however, has yet to be presented.

Such a study would represent a major digression, so only a few relevant comments may here be ventured. The story of the Portiuncula indulgence encapsulates most of high medieval Christianity, as it involves a piety of penitence, the vision of a much-loved saint, the veneration and intercession of Mary, the genius of St. Francis, and the authority of the church. As the cult of Francis and the influence of his order grew, so did the crowds which visited the Portiuncula each year; by 1295 those crowds were a measure for large assemblies.[83]

By the 1330s the fame of the Portiuncula indulgence—as well as the misgivings about its authenticity—had spread throughout Latin Christendom.[84] Bridget traveled from faraway Sweden to receive it, and she wept copiously when its authenticity was doubted. Since documents proving its efficacy could not be produced, some of its advocates invoked another demonstration of the Portiuncula's validity—a miracle, the proof of saintliness and divine approbation. In this case, any miracle that could be connected to the indulgence must prove its validity. The Franciscan James of Porta, anxious that the Portiuncula pardon should be verified, prayed fervently for miracles that would prove its efficacy. He believed that the very serious illness of a confrère provided the chance for just such a miracle. Although other friars had despaired of the sick brother's life, James pleaded, "Sweet Lord Jesus, you have admonished me in a dream to comfort the infirm. If it is your will that this sick brother, who lingers as if in death, should be cured, and healed, and restored to health, this plain sign shall prove the efficacy of [the Portiuncula] indulgence."[85] With much fear and sadness in his heart, James waited long and patiently for the recovery of his brother's health. For four hundred days he knelt in prayer before a wooden cross made with his own hands. During each of those four hundred days James genuflected one hundred and forty times. Each time, he recited one hundred and five *Misereres*, six hundred and nine *Ave Marias* with eighty four collects each day, and seven penitential orations twice a day. No miraculous recovery, however, rewarded the persistence of his prayer.

His vigil and quest for a miracle seemingly ended, James one day took a walk, which led him past a house belonging to a peasant named Conrad. Conrad and his wife Catherine were seated in front of the house. They were comforting their baby son John. James asked the couple about the child's health. With tears in their eyes, the grieving father and mother answered that the boy had not urinated for four days, and they feared for his life. They asked James for a saint to whom they could pray and save his life. James told them to expect happy developments that evening, after compline. Having returned to the convent, James knelt before a picture of Mary and Jesus.

He vowed to Mary that if the child should recover, this miracle would serve as a proclamation of the truth of the Portiuncula indulgence to the whole world. The boy then passed a great stone and much urine. James marvelled that so small a boy could pass so large a stone. Although so near death, the child was now contented, as if he felt no pain at all. Other miracles confirmed the one wrought on behalf of the sick baby boy. To prove the validity of the Portiuncula indulgence, the Blessed Mother also worked the recovery of two notaries and one magistrate of the city of Basel, and of two Franciscan friars. James rejoiced in these miracles as signs that Mary and her Son wanted the Portiuncula indulgence to serve as an announcement that they desired the conversion and contrition of sinners and the salvation of the repentant. With this divine approbation and endorsement, James believed, the power of the Portiuncula indulgence should be proclaimed throughout the world.[86]

Other indulgences mimicked the Portiuncula pardon. A plenary visitation indulgence attached to the Franciscan Church of St. John of the Desert in Cremona attracted a similar controversy around the year 1380. Its defenders cited the legitimacy of the Portiuncula in support of the Cremona indulgence.[87] The critics of the Cremona pardons, like those of the Portiuncula, failed to undermine the indulgence. Church authorities cancelled neither of them (indulgences were rarely nullified in the medieval centuries), and both continued to attract estimable numbers of pilgrims until the end of the Middle Ages. Significantly, both the Portiuncula and Cremona indulgences resembled the vast majority of other indulgences granted during the Middle Ages in that they originated in the zeal of penitents. Their popularity, however, silenced neither orthodox nor heretical detractors.

Clearly, fear had very little, if anything, to do with the popularity of either the Portiuncula indulgence or its daughter pardon in Cremona. Rather, as the Provencal Franciscan Peter of John Olivi (1248–1298), who wrote the earliest defense of the pardon (a *quaestio* composed 1279–1285) first observed, the Portiuncula celebrated the piety and devotion of St. Francis. That devotion should be learned through the imitation of Francis, who in turn had imitated Christ:

> It is valuable to consider zealously, as though an eyewitness, the imitation of the passion of Christ wrought in the mind and flesh of St. Francis, and that one experience the vastness of the divine mercy flowing from the passion of Christ, just as one experiences that mercy in the reception of the indulgence and in the change of heart that accompanies it.[88]

Margery Kempe and Bridget of Sweden, who must represent many others, travelled great distances, primarily because the Portiuncula represented the piety and example of Francis and the powers of his intercession, which were so great they had superceded any documentary proprieties. While Bridget clearly visualized Purgatory in awful images, she was not terrorized into making the journey. Thus, the Italian historian Ovidio Capitani has suggested that important as the authority of the hierarchical church was to the dispensation of indulgences, in the minds of most ordinary faithful, the communication of the treasury of merit which took place in a grant of indulgence was even more vital. Capitani exaggerated only a little when he argued that "the indulgence had not an arithmetic sense, nor a procedural one, but an eschatalogical one."[89] That the Portiuncula undoubtedly had an eschatological sense need not at the same time exclude an arithmetic one. The pardon had both.

The literature about the saints, whether in the form of *vitae* or otherwise, quite clearly present no case for the view that preoccupations with Purgatory and indulgences necessarily created a piety of terror. Relatively benign visualizations of Purgatory may be found in the sources from the thirteenth century onward. At the very least, such imaginings of Purgatory could have been only so fearsome to people who suffered much in life before death. Fear there may have been, but fear was also not the only piece of the religious puzzle. Indeed, that Purgatory, not Hell, assumed such a prominent place in the religious imaginations of Catholics from the early thirteenth century is important, for the souls who endured the former had hope, because release and consulation awaited. The souls in Purgatory were still members of the Church Militant and tied to "fellow Christens" in a bond of charity. Of course, indulgences were rooted in that charity and formed part of that consolation. Cut off from the community of charity and cast into eternal despair and isolation were those whose refusal to embrace the grace of repentance served as their admission ticket to Hell and for whom nothing could be done.

In contrast, as the instances of the Portiuncula and Cremona pardons testify, the religious imagination and penitential fervor sometimes got ahead of the jurisdictions of the church authorities. While the vast majority of pardons were granted according to canonical protocols, that is, in a formal bull of indulgence, some, which were noteworthy for their celebrity, were not. At the same time, few of these irregular pardons were ever officially renounced. Indulgences, then, resembled many other impulses in medieval religion after the twelfth century. In the vast majority of instances, the church authorities managed them rather well. In rare instances, however, popes and bishops struggled to maintain control. Church authorities had to take care when presented with jurisdictional curiosities like the Portiuncula or Cremona pardons, lest they inhibit the piety they desired to patronize. The irony in the tension created in these situations was not that the masses rejected the program of the hierarchical church but that they embraced it.

NOTES

1. Richard Kieckhefer, "Holiness and the Culture of Devotion," 304.

2. Twenty-five of the seventy saints' lives I consulted report that a saint obtained indulgences.

3. *AS* August 5:756.

4. *AS* August 5:585: "Praeterea, quando erat trans mare, quia lucrari cupiebat indulgentias, quas legatus Romani pontificis trans mare largiebatur illis, qui saxa portabant, operibusque faciendis ferebant auxilium, hac de causa lapides quandoque portabat, aliave similia, operaque humilitatis exercebat. Id etiam faciebat, uti creditur, ut bonum aliis praeberet exemplum."

5. Raymond of Peñafort, *Summa de poenitentia et matrimonio*, 3.65 (ed. Tallini, 497a–b).

6. Jacques Le Goff, *The Birth of Purgatory*, trans. Arthur Goldhammer (Chicago: University of Chicago Press, 1984), 356.

7. Vauchez, *Laity*, 105.

8. John Van Engen, "The Christian Middle Ages as an Historiographical Problem," *American Historical Review* 91 (1986), 528–531.

9. Thomas Kaeppeli, O. P., ed., *Scriptores ordinis praedicatorum medii aevi* (Rome: Polyglottis Vaticanis, 1975), 2:444–446.

10. Gustav Schleich, ed., "The Gast of Guy," lv.

11. Schleich, ed., lv–lix.

12. Schleich, ed., 16.

13. Schleich, ed., 29–30.

14. Schleich, ed., 39–40.

15. Duffy, 345.

16. Catherine of Genoa, *Purgation and Purgatory: The Spiritual Dialogue*, trans. Serge Hughes (New York: Paulist Press, 1979), 71.

17. Thomas Aquinas, *Summa Theologiae Supplementum tertia pars appendix, De purgatorio* 2 (ed. Studia Generalis, 5:516a): "Locus purgatorii est locus inferior inferno coniunctus, ita quod idem ignis sit qui damnatos cruciat in inferno, et qui iustos in purgatorio purgat."

18. Thomas Aquinas, *Summa Theologiae Suppl., De purgatorio* 5 (ed. Studia Generalis, 5:518b): "Dicendum quod sicut post diem iudicii divina iusticia succendet ignem quo damnati in perpetuum punientur; ita etiam nunc sola iustitia divina electi post hanc vitam purgantur, non ministerio daemonum, quorum victores extiterunt; nec ministerio angelorum, qui cives suos non tam vehementer affligerent. Sed tamen possibile est quod eos ad loca poenarum deducant. Et etiam ipsi daemones, qui de poenis hominum laetantur, eos comitantur, et assistunt purgandis."

19. Thomas Aquinas, *Summa Theologiae Suppl. tertia pars appendix, De purgatorio* 3 (ed. Studia Generalis, 5:517a–517b): "Dicendum quod in purgatorio erit duplex poena: una

damni, inquentum scilicet retardantur a divina visione; alia sensus, secundum quod ab igne corporali punientur. Et quantum ad utrumque poena purgatorii minima excedit maximam poenam huius vitae. Quanto enim aliquid magis desideratur, tanto eius absentia est molestior. Et quia affectus quo desideratur summum bonum, post hanc vitam in animabus sanctis est intensissimus, quia non retardatur affectus mole corporis; et etiam quia terminus fruendi summo bono iam advenisset nisi aliquid impediret; ideo de tardatione maxime dolet. Similiter etiam cum dolor non sit laesio, sed laesionis sensus, tanto aliquid magis dolet de aliquo laesivo, quanto magis est sensitivum; unde laesiones quae fiunt in locis maxime sensibilibus, sunt maximum dolorem causantes. Et quia totus sensus corporis est ab anima, ideo si in ipsam animam aliquod laesivum agat, de necesssitate oportet quod maxime afffligatur. Quod autem anima ab igne corporali patiatur, hoc ad praesens supponimus . . . ideo oportet quod poena purgatorii, quantum ad poenam damni et sensus, excedat omnem poenam istius vitae."

20. Robert of Flamborough, *Liber poenitentialis*, 5.16 (ed. J. J. Francis Firth, C. S. B., Studies and Texts 18 [Toronto: Pontifical Institute of Mediaeval Studies, 1971], 277): "Incomparabiliter autem gravior est poena purgatorii quam aliqua in hac vita." Robert's work, written 1208–1213, was one of the earliest contributions to the genre of pastoral manuals.

21. John of Dambach, *De vir. indul.*, q. 2 (Heiligenkreuz [Austria], Stiftsbibliothek MS 208, fol. 86v): "Unde aliqui sancti dixerunt quod carius hic vellent esse 10 annis ulcerosi, et in miseria cuiuscumque doloris, quam unum esse in purgatorio."

22. John of Dambach, *De vir. indul.*, q. 2 (Heiligenkreuz MS 208, fol. 87v): "Sicut est in corporalibus, ita ymaginandum est in spiritualibus. Sed in corporabilibus lema ascendunt naturaliter sursum sicut lumen, et flamma, et gravia deorsum, sicut lapis. Sic ergo in spiritualibus fervida karitate ascendunt a gravia. Vero a peccato descendunt cuiusmodi peccatores. Modo per karitatem homo ignit, et inflammatur, et ascendit sursum, et peccatores agravantur per peccata. Et sic descendunt deorsum, quia naturaliter qui graves sunt descendunt usque ad centrum terre, ubi omnia gravia habent quiescere in locis inferius. Et hoc est centrum terre." Cf. Schleich, ed., 33.

23. John of Dambach, *De vir. indul.*, q. 2 (Heiligenkreuz MS 208, fol. 87v): "In quo limbo est pena mitissima—sine afflictione et sine remorsu consciencie."

24. John of Dambach, *De vir. indul.*, q. 2 (Heiligenkreuz MS 208, fol. 87v): "Eciam patet ille locus est turpissimus, quia ad illum locum feces omnium elementorum habent confluere et descendere."

25. John of Dambach, *De vir. indul.*, q. 2 (Heiligenkreuz MS 208, fol. 87r): "Unde octo sunt pene in inferno . . . vermis et tenebre, flagellum, frigus, et ignis, demonis aspectus, scelerium, confusio, luctus."

26. John of Dambach, *De vir. indul.*, q. 2 (Heiligenkreuz MS 208, fol. 87r): "Et huic est quod decedenti cum mortali culpa debetur pena eterna, que pena est infernalis, quia desertus a deo, caret gracia et ex toto statum miserendi."

27. John of Dambach, *De vir. indul.*, q. 2 (Heiligenkreuz MS 208, fol. 86r): "Sed postquam Christus ianuam celi aperuit, tunc ille locus qui prius ante adventum Christi limbus sanctorum patrum vocabatur, ille modo vocatur locus glorie seu celum empyreum quia ibi est nunc locus beatorum. Sic igitur patet quod diversa sunt loca animarum; postquam recedunt a corporibus, ita quod unus est locus glorie. Quattuor

sunt loca penarum, et quia Christus quartum destruxit, ideo sunt modo tantum tria loca penarum. Sed post iudicium non est locus purgatorii quia tunc cessabit pena temporalis."

28. John of Dambach, *De vir. indul.*, q. 2 (Heiligenkreuz MS 208, fol. 86r): "Ubi diligenter est advertendum quod in locum qui purgatorium dicitur intrant solum illi qui decedunt cum culpis venialibus vel cum mortalibus contritis et confessis, sed nondum satisfactis."

29. R. Ellis, ed., *The Liber Celestis of St. Bridget of Sweden*, EETS 291 (Oxford: Oxford University Press, 1987), 1:298.

30. Raymond of Capua, *Life of St. Catherine*, 2.7.220 (trans. Conleth Kearns [Wilmington, DE: Glazier, 1980], 209).

31. *Life of St. Catherine*, 2.7.222 (trans. Kearns, 210).

32. *Life of St. Catherine*, 1.9.88–89 (trans. Kearns, 80–82).

33. Oakley, 118.

34. *Life of St. Catherine*, 3.4.364 (trans. Kearns, 338).

35. Suzanne Noffke, O. P., ed. and trans., *The Letters of St. Catherine of Siena* (New York: Center for Medieval and Early Renaissance Studies, State University of New York at Binghamton, 1988), 1:81.

36. *AS* April 2:466: "Cum sibi iam mortis diem superesse conspicaretur, tum febri correptus, tum pectoris angore extortus, lecto decubuit. Sacerdotem ocius accersiri mandat a quo pluries obtenta peccatorum indulgentia, sacratissimum denique corporis et sanguinis domini nostri Jesu Christi viaticum tam devotissime suscipit, quam fidelissime semper credidit et humilime adoravit."

37. *AS* July 1:454: "Felix, inquam, cardinalis devotissimus, ex hoc mundo ad deum transiturus, dissolvi cupiens et esse cum Christo, authoritate apostolica absolutionem plenariam a poena et a culpa in mortis articulo meruit obtinere."

38. Richard Kieckhefer, *Unquiet Souls: Fourteenth-Century Saints and Their Religious Milieu* (Chicago: University of Chicago Press, 1984), 130–131.

39. Umberto Eco, *The Name of the Rose*, trans. William Weaver (New York: Warner Books, 1984), 119.

40. *Liber celestis*, ed. Ellis, 298. Marguerite Tjaden Harris, ed., *Birgitta of Sweden: Life and Selected Revelations* (Mahwah, NJ: Paulist Press, 1990), 187–188.

41. *Life of St. Catherine*, 2.7.228–230 (trans. Kearns, 215–218).

42. *AS* July 7:392: "Atque indulgentiae usquam poeniteret, effecerunt alacritas in reduce complectendo, aviditas in audiendo, promptitudo in exsequendo."

43. André Vauchez, "Influences franciscaines et réseaux aristocratiques dans la val de Loire: Autour de la bienhereuse Jeanne-Marie de Maillé (1331–1414)," *Revue d'histoire de l'église de France* 70 (1984), 95–105.

44. Kieckhefer, *Unquiet Souls*, 54–55.

45. *AS* March 3:738: "Sic vere pauper et vere mendica effecta, deinceps domum vel hospitium per locatum sive conductum habere non valuit: nam frigescente caritate abundavit iniquitas, et aemuli eius, diabolo procurante, cum suo hospite locuti sunt: qui lucro intendens, omnis miserationis oblitus, eam eiecit de domo satis dure, in qua remanserat annos multos honeste et devote. Sic igitur a curis mundalibus expedita ecclesias visitabat ut coeperat, loca sanctorum visitans, ut indulgentias consequeretur."

46. *AS* March 3:741.

47. *AS* April 3:509.

48. *AS* April 2:506.

49. *AS* April 2:179.

50. *AS* April 2:174: "Erat eo tempore frater quidam ordinis predicatorum, eidem Christi famuli satis in Christo familiaris et intimus: qui sedis apostolicae summique pontificis auctoritate subnixus, officio praedicationis, ad acquirendum domino fidelem populum et acceptabilem sectatoremque bonorum operum, assidue per datam sibi gratiam instabat attentius: et quos verbo praedicationis erudiebat interius, hos exterius vivificae crucis triumphali signaculo, praemissa sibi peccatorum indulgentia, consignabat. Tantam enim a domino gratiam assecutus fuerat in hoc opere, quod vix aliquis illo tempore, quantumcumque duri cordis existeret, a suscipiendo salutari signo crucis dominicae se potuerit."

51. *AS* July 4:665: "Coepit igitur de perpetratis peccatis cum dolore peramaro cogitare et de cogitationibus, locutionibus, atque operationibus suis per eum secundum tempora operatis, atque habitis in particulari et in generali maximam contritionem habere, ac de ipsis cum maximis lacrymis, suspiriis, et singultibus apud divinam misericordiam lamentabiliter et humiliter indulgentiam petere."

52. *AS* July 4:665: "Tandem dictus dei confessor plenus lacrymis cum dolore permaximo, atque uberrimo flens in tantis, ut vix valeret verba exprimere ad sacerdotem veniens, et peccata sua plenissime confitens indulgentiam, et remisionem plenariam obtinuit peccatorum a domino plenarie."

53. Kieckhefer, *Unquiet Souls*, 184.

54. Sanford Brown Meech, ed., *The Book of Margery Kempe*, EETS 212 (Oxford: Oxford University Press, 1940), 79. The translation is mine.

55. *AS* May 6:159, and August 1:657.

56. *AS* March 3:506: "Ego hic miseram vitam duco, alii proficiunt et commoda lucrantur animarum suarum, visitant loca sanctorum, intersunt mysteriis divinis: ego vero brutali more ab omnibus bonis spiritualibus sequestrata sum."

57. *AS* March 3:506: "In laboribus magnis fervens dei desiderio."

58. *AS* July 7:385: "Nimirum noverat, magnae prudentiae ac experientiae antistes, regulae ac instituti approbationem rem esse gravissimam earum, quae a Christi vicarii indulgentiae exspectari solent, et periculo affine, ut vel tunc negaretur, vel in aliud tempus differretur, quo adulta iam congregation suis consistens viribus seipsam probaret, quod esset a deo, et facile impetraretur a pontifice, quod aegre tunc a legato fuisset impetratum."

59. *AS* April 1:721.

60. Kieckhefer, *Unquiet Souls*, 89.

61. Henry Suso, *Life of the Servant*, 1.15, 1.16, 1.18; in *Henry Suso: The Exemplar with Two German Sermons*, ed. and trans. Frank Tobin (Mahwah, NJ: Paulist Press, 1989), 87–89, 97.

62. Arnold Angenendt, "Seuses Lehre vom Ablaß," in Remigius Bäumer, ed., *Reformatio ecclesiae* (Paderborn: Ferdinand Schöningh, 1980), 149–150.

63. Henry Suso, *Little Book of Eternal Wisdom*, 1.14, in *Henry Suso*, ed. and trans. Tobin, 251–252. Although Suso does not here use the word *indulgence*, his reference to

the "treasure of merit" is unmistakable. Several years after Suso wrote *Little Book of Eternal Wisdom*, Pope Clement VI declared official the treasury of merit doctrine in the bull *Unigenitus* (1343). Thus, Suso's remarks anticipated Clement's bull.

64. Ibid., 252.

65. Henry Suso, *Horologium sapientiae*, 2.7 (ed. Pius Künzle, O. P., *Heinrich Seuses Horologium Sapientiae*, Spicilegium Friburgense 23 [Freiburg: Universitätsverlag, 1977], 599): "Benedictum sit nomen domini nostri Iesu Christi Dei et gloriosae virginis Mariae matris eius in aeternum et ultra. Amen. Et de hoc exstant indulgentiae. Ratio huius orationis de hoc nomine est . . . ut inquam, hoc mellifluum nomen aliquo modo reviviscat et cordibus fidelium inculcetur ac renovetur."

66. Kieckhefer, "Sainthood," 12–13.

67. *AS* October 13:497: "In illa [peregrinatione] autem visione supernaturali intellectuali, vidit imagines et audivit voces Christi, virginis beatissimae et aliquorum sanctorum."

68. Harris, ed., *Birgitta of Sweden*, 92.

69. Harris, ed., *Birgitta of Sweden*, 94.

70. Lea, 3.47–48.

71. Harris, ed., *Birgitta of Sweden*, 168–170.

72. Cited by Vauchez, *Laity*, 127.

73. Daniel Bornstein, "The Users of the Body: The Church and the Cult of Santa Margharita da Cortona," *Church History* 62 (1993), 163–167.

74. *AS* February 3:311: "Haec lacrymosis precibus suum Patrem B. Franciscum quadam die rogavit, ut suis meritis ei dignaretur acquirere plenariam indulgentiam omnium delictorum. Qui suis suffragantibus meritis dilectae filiae Pater a Domino impetravit, ut ei vivae vocis oraculo plenissime indulgeret. Quod quidem donum Margaritae concessit Altissimus, expresse loquens in anima, dicens: Ego Jesus Christus, filius summi et aeterni Patris pro te crucifixus, ab omnibus tuis defectibus plenarie te absolvo."

75. Among the Schoolmen, St. Albert the Great entertained just such instances; see Albert, *Commentarii in IV libros sententiarum*, 4.20. etc. (*Opera omnia* [Paris: Louis Vives, 1894], 29: 847–860).

76. Lea, 3:243.

77. Bartolus of Assisi, *Tractatus de indulgentia s. Mariae de Portiuncula*, ed., Paul Sabatier (Paris: Fischbacher, 1900), 2–3.

78. Bartolus, 14: "Sanctissime pater noster, supplico ego miser et peccator quatenus facere digneris hanc gratiam generi humano, quod concedas veniam et indulgentiam omnibus et singulis venientibus ad locum istum et introeuntibus ecclesiam istam, omnium peccatorum suorum universaliter et singulariter de quibus confessionem fecerint sacerdoti et mandatum susceperint. Et supplico beatissimae Mariae matri tuae advocatae generis humani quatenus pro huiusmodi me adiuvare et apud tuam piissimam et clementissimam maiestatem intercedere dignetur."

79. Lea, 3.237.

80. The most recent examination of the abundant literature on the Portiuncula is by Pierre Pèano, "L'indulgence de la Potioncule: origine et signification," in Clementi, 47–59.

81. *Geschichte*, 2:246–247.

82. Raphael M. Huber, *The Portiuncula Indulgence*, Franciscan Studies 19 (New York: J. W. Wagner, 1938), 6–7.

83. Franz Ehrle, "Die Spiritualen, ihr Verhältnis zum Franciscanerorden und zu den Fraticellen," *Archiv für Literatur und Kirchengeschichte* 1 (1885), 544.

84. Pèano, "L'indulgence," 54.

85. *Analecta Franciscana* (Quaracchi: College of St. Bonaventure, 1897), 3:626.

86. *Analecta Franciscana* 3:627–629.

87. D. Trapp, "The Portiuncula Discussion of Cremona," *Recherches de théologie ancienne et médiévale* 22 (1955), 79–94.

88. Pierre Pèano, ed., "La '*Quaestio* fr. Petri Iohannis Olivi' sur l'indulgence de la Portioncule," *Archivum Franciscanum Historicum* 74 (1981), 73: "Vehementer valet intueri oculata fide renovacionem passionis Christi factam in mente et carne beati Francisci et experiri magnitudinem miseracionis divine manante a passionis Christi sicut homo experitur in perceptione indulgencie et in immutacione cordis ipsam concomitantis."

89. Capitani, 30.

Chapter 5

Controversy and Indulgences Prior to The Great Western Schism I

The argument over the validity of the Portiuncula pardon was but one of a number of medieval indulgence controversies. These arguments sometimes have been taken as evidence that indulgences were widely abused long before the Reformation. Just as in the sixteenth century, indulgences had heterodox critics in the high medieval period, whose views have been studied rather well. Most of these critics plainly rejected the efficacy of pardons. Figures such as Henry, a renegade monk who in 1116 managed to win control of the French town of Le Mans, preached that sinfulness rendered priests and bishops unable to bind and to loose. Henry turned the city's residents against the clergy and attacked new ecclesiastical developments such as marriage laws.[1] Similarly, the antisacerdotalism and antisacramentalism of the Waldensians, at the beginning of the thirteenth century, and Lollards, at the end of the fourteenth, meant that both sects deemed pardons a pious fraud. "[The Waldensians]," wrote the Passau Anonymous around the year 1260, "do not believe in indulgences . . . they hold the absolutions of the church as nothing. They care nothing for irregularity. They do not believe in ecclesiastical dispensations." Still, the Anonymous seems to have had some sympathy for the Waldensians' view, for he bitterly remarked that their rejection of pardons was "occasioned by the multiplication of indulgences, and because all sins can be relaxed for money."[2]

Perhaps best known are the fourteenth-century English protests against pardons. John Wyclif (c. 1330–1384), the Oxford scholar and chief authority for the English heresy of Lollardy, angrily refused to entertain the possibility that the pope could, through grants of pardon, cancel anyone's debt of sin: "Against this rude blasphemy I have . . . inveighed. Neither the pope, nor the Lord Jesus Christ, can grant dispensations or give indulgences to any man, except as the Deity has eternally determined by his just counsel."[3] Wyclif also rejected the treasury of merit and blamed the popularity of indulgences on the mendicants, who, in his words, "labor in the cause of this illusion, and of other Luciferian seductions of the church."[4] The Lollard Conclusions of 1394 thundered against the pope, "who has given himself out as treasurer of the whole Church, having in charge that worthy jewel of Christ's passion together with the merits of all the saints in heaven, whereby he grants pretended indulgence from all penalty and guilt, and is a treasurer almost devoid of charity."[5] Later heterodox opinions also surfaced, such as that of John Hus, executed for heresy by the Emperor Sigismund in 1415. According to his condemnation by the Council of Constance, Hus thought "unfaithfully, regarding the seven sacraments of the church, the keys, the duties, the censures, customs, ceremonies, and sacred affairs of the church, its veneration of relics, indulgences, and orders."[6] At the end of the Middle Ages, Wessel Gansfort argued that pardons were invalid because, as the Lollards already had pointed out, they were unsupported by Scripture; besides, a clergy as corrupt as the Catholic could not possibly mediate remission of the debt of sin.

However, as Eamon Duffy has remarked, only a small number of later medieval Englishmen were attracted to Lollardy. The great majority of English enthusiastically sought after pardons. R. N. Swanson recently estimated the number of indulgences granted for prayers for the dead in the diocese of Lincoln alone at around 1,100 for the period between 1280 and 1343.[7] The legions of men, women, and children making pilgrimages, giving alms, and participating in processions suggest similar sentiments in the Catholic countries of continental Europe. Nonetheless, those who accepted the teaching that indulgences could reduce a sincere penitent's debt of sin, like Simon of Cremona, sometimes either found certain remissions troubling or found the way in which those remissions were administered questionable, that is, *indulgences also prompted arguments between those who accepted their efficacy.* Consequently, pardons were most often and most heatedly argued about by orthodox interlocutors. In the twelfth century, for instance, the *size* of the pardons that some bishops were granting scandalized Abelard:

> And not only priests, but even the very leaders of priests, the bishops that is, are, we know, so shamelessly ablaze with this greed that when, at dedications of churches or consecrations of altars or blessings of cemeteries or at any solemnities, they have gatherings of people from which they expect a plentiful offering, they are prodigal in relaxing penances, remitting to all in common now a third, now a fourth, part of their penance under some pretext of charity, of course, but really of the highest cupidity.[8]

Like the Passau Anonymous a century and a half later, Abelard questioned the bishops' motivations and believed that many used grants of pardon to raise revenues, rather than penitential fervor. However, he did not question the efficacy of remissions as such. Abelard's was a lonely voice during the first half of the twelfth century; perhaps his radical contritionism contributed to his unique discomfort with indulgences.[9]

Around the turn of the thirteenth century, new misgivings seem to have arisen. The decree *Cum ex eo* (canon 62) of Lateran IV (1215) echoed Abelard's complaints: "Moreover, because the keys of the church are brought into contempt and satisfaction through penance loses its force through indiscriminate and excessive indulgences, which certain prelates of the churches do not fear to grant, we therefore decree that when a basilica is dedicated, the indulgence shall not be for more than one year . . . and for the anniversary of the dedication, the remission of penances is not to exceed forty days." The council declared that the Holy See itself customarily observed moderation in dispensing indulgences—arguable, given Innocent III's extension of the crusade indulgence to noncombatant contributors—and other prelates of the church should imitate its example.[10]

Indulgences served as the source for a number of other disputes between orthodox contestants in the thirteenth and fourteenth centuries. In these quarrels, no one doubted that the merit of one member of the church could be applied to another, nor did anyone naysay the church's authority to transfer the debt of one to another, nor that a debt of penalty remained after valid sacramental confession, just as the critics of the Portiuncula and Cremona indulgences did not question pardons, as such, but disputed whether they had been conceded in accord with the canons. In the thirteenth and fourteenth centuries, then, legal and procedural objections typified orthodox disputes over indulgences in the fourteenth century.

A PENA ET A CULPA?

Simon of Cremona not only raised irregularities of documentation against the Cremona indulgence but also criticized how the Franciscans preached that remission. The pardon's Franciscan advocates preached that at Cremona, like at the Portiuncula, penitents received remission *a pena et a culpa*, that is, from both penalty and guilt. Peter of John Olivi answered the same charge against the Portiuncula indulgence. On the face of it, this objection was very serious, since Simon plainly accused the Franciscans of a gross theological error, that is, that the indulgence relaxed both the guilt and the penalty of sin. Indeed, such a teaching might amount to heresy, since the church taught that sacramental confession and absolution cancelled guilt, while penances and indulgences cancelled penalty.

The sources suggest that by 1300 some indulgences had long been preached *a pena et a culpa*. The phrase itself may first be found in Huguccio's twelfth-century commentary on the *Decretum*. In this text, the great canonist described the effect of public penance, although not indulgences, as the cancellation of penalty and guilt.[11] The first pardons so preached, however, were crusade indulgences, which meant that they were plenary remissions of the debt for sin.[12] The use of the phrase to describe crusade indulgences seems to have originated with itinerant preachers of indulgence, who were often the source of medieval disputes concerning indulgences.

While the genius of Geoffrey Chaucer, not to mention the revolt of Martin Luther, has given preachers of indulgence a bad name, many famous and admired figures in the history of the medieval Church, such as Bernard of Clairvaux, who preached the Second Crusade in 1146, publicized indulgences. Some of these celebrity preachers claimed that the crusade pardon was *a pena et a culpa*. Around 1213, James of Vitry, bishop of Acre, delivered two sermons *ad crucesignatos*. In the first, he announced that "God offers many and great things to you [who take up the cross], to which you ought willingly to hasten, namely, the remission of all sins, penalty as much as guilt, and eternal life besides."[13] In the second sermon, James preached that "crusaders, who are going to the service of God truly confessed and contrite, when they die in the service of Christ, are reckoned true martyrs, freed from all venial and mortal sins, from all enjoined penance, absolved from the penalty of sin in this life and from Purgatory."[14] James's remarks here are noteworthy, in that whereas in one text he described the crusade indulgence as being *a pena et a culpa*, his teaching in the second text was perfectly in accord with traditional teachings about sin and atonement. Penitents first needed to regret and confess their sins, which would remove any eternal penalty their sins might incur. Having received absolution from the confessor, penitents needed to satisfy the debt of punishment they had incurred because of those sins. For crusaders, the taking up of the cross after contrition and confession would complete atonement. James further explained that the assumption of the cross should be an outward sign of the warrior's sincere amendment of life, so he should refrain from committing serious sin again: "They must hasten to confession and, finally, be eager to abstain from sins, lest they lose a great good."[15] The "taking of the cross" served as an outward sign of an interior conversion.

A generation later, other famous preachers also described the crusade indulgence as cancelling the entire debt of sin. Eudes of Chateauroux served as papal legate to the French king, Louis IX, who in 1245 was making preparations for his crusade. Eudes preached to the king and his warriors that fulfilling all the conditions of the crusade indulgence would liberate the crusader from all sin.[16] In the same sermon, Eudes reminded his listeners: "If you wish to take the cross profitably, you must repent your sins and abandon them." Humbert of Romans, master general (1254–1263) of the Dominicans, an order founded especially to preach, wrote in a handbook for preachers of crusade that one of the graces received by crusaders through the mediation of the church was to be freed not only from Hell but from Purgatory besides: "The first grace is plenary indulgence of all sins, through which men are freed not only from infernal penalty, but also Purgatory."[17] What Humbert called a "second grace" was really simply another explanation of the first: "The second [grace] is a relaxation of penalties. For when penances for temporal penalty are served in the present life, for which the sinner remains obligated after the cancellation of guilt, it is certain that the debt of penalty having been removed, the obligations, which because of the debts had been owed, are cancelled, and therefore men are freed from all penances through such pardons, although men ought not to be without some penance because of the doubt of uncertainty."[18]

Furthermore, Humbert placed indulgences within the traditional scheme of atonement:

> The Catholic faith holds that through mortal sin a man incurs the obligation of eternal penalty. . . . When he repents, though the guilt is removed, penalty is not remitted for him completely, unless contrition should be so great that through it he is sufficiently punished. But in this he is acted upon mercifully because the eternal penalty is commuted into temporal, which, if it is not completed in this life by penance, it shall be required that he complete it in Purgatory. . . . If, then, plenary indulgence is granted to someone, he is freed from all such temporal penalty, for which he had been obliged after the said contrition. . . . This is the faith which ought to be held and which all doctors teach. . . . This is the faith which the whole church holds.[19]

Indeed, said Humbert, the church's power to remit the debt of sin depends on the disposition of penitents: "If pardon is extended to those having confessed and in sincere contrition, the guilt is cancelled for them by the divine power and the church remits the entire owed penalty by the power of the keys."[20] Like James, Humbert offhandedly equated indulgences *a pena et a culpa* with plenary remissions. Furthermore, he used that phrase within a theologically proper explanation of efficacious indulgence.

Humbert's fellow Dominican, Thomas of Cantimpré, described the benefits of crusade indulgences in much the same terms. If a crusader confessed and repented his sin, said Thomas in his *Two books of miracles* (written c. 1258), the effect of the pardon (note—not the confession or sacramental absolution) will be to remove all remaining penalty incurred by the penitent: "Concerning indulgence, which is preached to those who take up the cross, none of the faithful is permitted to doubt that the truly penitent and confessed receive remission of all sins, and in that desire of ardent longing, through which they rejoice in death for the faith, should they reach the Holy Land, they shall be wholly absolved of penalty and guilt."[21] Thomas added that even commuted crusader vows could entirely cancel the debt of sin: "Because the route of the work may be disagreeable . . . warriors seek dispensations; Rome empowers the legates, who sanctify the soldiers for the contribution of money and render them free from sin by letters. Holy sanctification, which frees from sin—they grant holy and blessed letters, which secure and cleanse soul from all guilt and penalty."[22] Many nobles who took the crusaders' vow never fulfilled it because of age or illness or some other licit reason. Others, of course, sought a convenient excuse. Whatever their motivations, the crusader vow was binding in canon law and, thus, required a formal dispensation, for which the popes and their legates received numerous requests. Thomas believed, however, that those whose crusader vow was commuted by the proper authority could nonetheless receive the full remission, if they would instead make some other contribution to the military campaign. His ideas simply followed the logic of Innocent III's first extention of the crusade indulgence to noncombatant contributors in the decree *Ad liberandam*, the sixty-second canon of Lateran IV.

By the middle of the thirteenth century, then, the use of the phrase *a pena et a culpa* to describe the benefits of a crusade pardon circulated throughout Latin Christendom. Furthermore, those who spoke thus about crusader indulgences—some of whom, like Bernard of Clairvaux and James of Vitry, were by no means theological or canonistic illiterates—understood by that phrase a full cancellation of the *penalty* of sin, but not the *guilt*. The indulgence was efficacious if and only if the crusader had made a valid confession, in which case he regretted having sinned. The fulfillment of the crusader's vow, or as in the remarks of Thomas of Cantimpré, a commutation of a crusader's vow, cancelled whatever temporal penalty remained after a valid absolution. Consequently, the mid-thirteenth-century sources present a widely accepted and employed disconnect in *terminology*, but not *theology*, between academic theologizing and ordinary usage.

Towards the end of the thirteenth century, theologians revisited the topic of pardons *a pena et a culpa*. Franciscan apologists, such as Peter of John Olivi, explained the benefits of the Portiuncula remission in terms James of Vitry, Humbert of Romans, and Thomas of Cantimpré used to describe the crusade indulgence. In his *quaestio* on the Portiuncula, Peter addressed an objection that Simon of Cremona later raised against its sister remission, the Cremona indulgence. All questions of documentation aside, did the pope possess the power to grant an indulgence that cancelled both guilt and penalty? Peter answered affirmatively and argued that as a result his confrères preached the Portiuncula indulgence correctly: "It is truly proper that the pope's power over all, which should not be doubted, ought to be displayed through a remission of guilt and penalty in our time, at a particular place."[23] Like earlier teachers, Peter too emphasized that the pardon was only valid for those who were truly confessed and contrite: "No penance is more useful and severe, than are contrition and confession and a change of life for the good; indeed indulgence of this kind is granted only to such persons." While Francesco Bartoli's treatise of 1323 may be the most famous defense of the Portiuncula, other treatises were written upholding the pardon's validity. In his account of the remission, Theobald, the bishop of Assisi, claimed that Pope Honorius himself had described the pardon as a remission of both guilt and penalty. St. Francis, wrote Theobald, pleaded with the pope to grant a plenary remission to every visitor of the church who had confessed and been absolved by a priest. The pope agreed: "Henceforth, we grant that anyone truly confessed and contrite who shall travel and enter the said church shall be absolved from penalty and guilt."[24]

In support of the Portiuncula pardon, furthermore, Bartoli presented the example of another papal remission. The bull *Inter sanctorum solemnia*, which Pope Celestine V promulgated on September 29, 1294, granted indulgence *a pena et a culpa* to the Benedictine church of Collemagio.[25] The pardon was offered to pilgrims who visited this church on the anniversary of Celestine's coronation (August 29). Presumably, Celestine granted the indulgence because his coronation liturgy had been celebrated there. The language of the bull echoed James of Vitry and Humbert of Romans: "We absolve from guilt and penalty, all the truly penitent and confessed who shall visit the said church on the anniversary [of our coronation], from all their commissions of sin and omissions of sin since baptism."[26] The Collemagio pardon was fully documented, so the legal challenges which had been made against the Portiuncula could not be raised. Furthermore, in this case, the pope himself described a plenary indulgence as a remission *a pena et a culpa*, yet at the same time also demanded the requirements of contrition and confession.

A generation after the composition of Peter of John Olivi's *quaestio*, however, a papal decretal seems to indicate that the preaching of indulgences *a pena et a culpa* had become more controversial than in the days of Humbert of Romans. The decretal *Abusionibus* contains some material first promulgated as canon 31 of the Council of Vienne (1311–1312). Later additions were made to it when Pope John XXII (1316–1334) promulgated the Clementine collection in 1317. *Abusionibus* targeted preachers who abused their preaching privileges: "Because of abuses, which some preachers of alms proclaim in their sermons, such that they deceive the simple and extort gold from them by subtle or outrageous scheming."[27] Along with other crimes, the decree cited illegal and deceptive preaching of indulgences: "Hence, because some among the preachers in this way, just as it has been brought to our attention, grant indulgences to the people *de facto* on their own initiative, not without a great impudence of rashness and the deception of a great number of souls."[28] *Abusionibus* further said that such preachers "dispense from vows and absolve confessants from perjury, murder, and other sins . . . given some amount of money they remit a third or a fourth part of enjoined penance, they liberate three souls or more, of parents, or of their friends from Purgatory (as they falsely claim), of those who give them alms."[29] Finally, these scalawags claim to "lead to the rejoicing of Paradise for the benefactors of the places on behalf of which they were named as preachers, and some of their number grant them full remission of sins, and absolve (as we may put in their words) from guilt and penalty."[30] *Abusionibus* closed by urging the bishops in whose dioceses the transgressions were committed, or would be committed in the future, to punish offenders. The council commanded that bishops publicly announce the excommunications.

Historians have sometimes argued that *Abusionibus* proves that by the end of the thirteenth century, trafficking in indulgences harmed the church in two interrelated ways. First, many preachers falsely claimed that the indulgences they preached cancelled both guilt and penalty. Second, many persons believed that a grant of pardon excused them from sacramental confession. The erroneous teachings of wayward and ignorant preachers jeopardized the salvation of souls and threatened to undermine the authority of the church. If these claims are true, that would mean that something had gone terribly wrong since the time of James of Vitry, Humbert of Romans, and Thomas of Cantimpré. The earlier evidence gives few grounds for imagining that employment of the phrase *a pena et a culpa* constituted widespread erroneous preaching of pardons, but does *Abusionibus* suggests otherwise for a later generation? Do these texts mark the beginning of a trend many historians have identified? Had plenary indulgences degenerated by the close of the thirteenth century into a breeding ground for deception in the later medieval Church?

To begin with, *Abusionibus* addressed essentially legal, not theological, objections to the activities of certain *quaestores*. The decretal attacked not indulgences *a pena et a culpa* but those who had not been licensed to grant them. The crucial phrase "by their own words" suggests that the real offense of some *quaestores* was that they assumed some powers without the approval of either pope or bishop. The phrase was objectionable only because of the legal status of some who frequently employed it. The pardons preached by these *quaestores* did not liberate from guilt and penalty because these itinerant preachers of indulgence lacked the requisite authority.

Another question that must be confronted involves the gullibility of the audience. Does not *Abusionibus* suggest that most rustics were easy pickings for the pardoners? On the contrary, most parishioners would have been suspicious of any newcomer to their village or manor. While hospitality was prized and expected, an itinerant preacher would have had to prove himself, both to the lay leadership of the village and to the parish priest. Pardoners would have had to present themselves to the bishop of the diocese in which they desired to preach. Credentials had to be presented and examined for authenticity, and presumably some kind of interrogation also took place. If he believed the preacher legitimate, and if he sympathized with the church, monastery, or hospital on whose behalf the itinerant preached, the bishop then licensed the *quaestor* to work in the diocese, or parts of the diocese. Many licences would indeed have been granted, both for reasons of charity and episcopal self-interest. Bishops were probably inclined to grant permission to foreigners, so that their own wandering preachers would receive the same welcome. However, no bishop was obliged to order his diocesan clergy to accept even the most unobjectionable preachers. The most he could do was plead for charitable hospitality, as did Boniface VIII in *Super cathedram* (February 18, 1300):

> We strictly command, all prelates of churches, of whatever pre-eminence, status or dignity, and the parish priests, pastors and rectors, out of their reverence for God and the apostolic see, to show friendliness to these orders and their members, not being difficult, severe, or hard or austere to the friars, but rather gracious, favourable and kind, showing them a spirit of holy generosity. They should accept the friars as suitable fellow-workers in the office of preaching and explaining God's word . . . admitting them with ready kindness and affection to a share in their labours, so as to increase the reward of eternal happiness and the fruitful harvest of souls.[31]

Unless the bishop insisted, rectors could refuse to allow preachers to enter their churches. Rectors probably consulted with curates and chaplains before accepting an itinerant preacher. Given what recent scholarship has discovered about the substantial lay involvement in the late medieval liturgy, influential laypersons were likely consulted as well. Consequently, itinerant preachers of indulgence, whether they were laymen like the pardoners or professed religious like the Dominicans, had to pass muster with a formidable vetting procedure.

Of course, sermons were delivered outside the pulpit as well; indeed, preaching outside of churches and apart from the liturgy was common in the Middle Ages. Whether by native or foreign clergy, sermons sometimes were preached in the open or in a town square. Both heretical and orthodox preachers exploited such venues. News of the arrival of a famous and gifted preacher might turn out great audiences. Furthermore, many medieval sermons involved dialogue with the audience, a kind of question and answer session. Sermons given apart from the liturgy could prove embarassing for several reasons. Very able outsiders might attract larger crowds than either the bishop or diocesan clergy. In such venues, even though all preaching fell under the jurisdiction of the diocesan bishop, the discipline of the canons might be more difficult to enforce. While rectors were probably of little help in these cases, deans and archdeacons might be able to ensure that church discipline was maintained. In any event, such extra-liturgical sermonizing might compromise the authority of bishops, archdeacons, and rural deans.

Still, the canons promulgated around the turn of the fourteenth century merely referred to indulgences preached *a pena et a culpa* in much the same terms as the preachers had used in the mid-thirteenth century, in fact, almost repeated the remarks of the preachers verbatim. This observation does not mean, however, that there was no argument, but it does mean that the preaching of indulgences came to be part and parcel of the ongoing spat between mendicant and diocesan clergy. The church required the services of both, for the mendicants served mostly urban dwellers, and diocesan clergy ministered to rustics. The papacy was caught in the middle of their rivalry, as the mendicants (theoretically) answered directly to them. At the same time, bishops often entreated with the pontiffs on behalf of parish priests. The popes first favored one side, and then the other. For instance, the bull *Etsi animarum* (November 21, 1254) of Pope Innocent IV revoked the mendicants' privileges concerning preaching, hearing confessions, and burial rights, but one of the first official acts of his successor Alexander IV (1254–1261) was to restore them.[32] While Lyons II (1274) prohibited professed religious from "the office of preaching and hearing confessions and the right of burial," Dominicans and Franciscans were exempted, because "their approval bears witness to their evident advantage to the universal church."[33] In another effort to quiet the quarreling, Boniface VIII promulgated *Super cathedram*, which recognized that the lengthiness of the bickering was scandalous: "For a long time past there has existed between prelates and rectors or priests and clerics of parish churches throughout the different provinces of the world on the one hand, and the friars Preacher and Minor on the other, grave and dangerous discord . . . in matters of preaching to the faithful, hearing their confessions, enjoining their penances, and burying the dead who choose to be buried in the churches or lands of the friars."[34] The diocesan clergy had eight complaints about the mendicants, chief among which were that they encouraged the people to hear Mass in their churches, instead of parish churches; that they publicly humiliated the diocesan clergy, including the bishops; that they interfered with the writing of wills; and that they did pastoral work in parish churches without the permission of the rectors and in spite of canon law. Boniface ordered that mendicants preach, hear confessions, and celebrate burials only in their own churches. They could do so in parish churches only with the permission of the rector. *Super cathedram* also stipulated that one-quarter of mendicant burial fees should be paid to parish priests. Boniface's immediate successor Benedict XI (1303–1304) repealed *Super cathedram* with his own bull *Inter cunctas* (February 17, 1304), and the quarreling reheated. Shortly before the council of Vienne convened (1311), the provincial synod of Trier prohibited any priest from solemnizing a marriage, performing a burial or a baptism, or hearing a confession without the permission of the rector.[35] Bishops at Vienne pressured Clement V to repromulgate *Super cathedram*.

   Given their mission, the mendicants probably did in fact encourage parishioners to forgo Mass and confession in their own parish churches. Especially in the thirteenth century, however, parishioners needed little encouragement, as the training and formation of mendicant clergy surpassed that of the diocesan. Still, parish priests must have seethed with envy when their parishioners asked that a Preacher or Minor celebrate the funeral of a deceased member of the family. They also probably found mendicant requests—even if episcopal permission had been obtained—to preach in parish churches tiresome and intrusive. Diocesan priests correctly charged that the mendicants violated the ancient custom of the church, which insisted that the people hear Mass in their local church on Sundays and holy days. The seventh-century synod of Nantes, for example, had commanded priests to inquire whether anyone from a neighboring church had come to Mass either on Sunday or a holy day. If such a person was found in the church, he was to be expelled and was urged to return to his own church for worship.[36] Lateran IV upheld that traditional discipline in *Omnes utriusque sexus* (canon 21), which enjoined annual confession to the parish priest. But late antique and early medieval Church discipline and organization was less suited to the more urbanized culture of the High Middle Ages. In contrast, the mendicant orders, founded to serve an urban ministry, captured the religious imagination of the thirteenth century as well as the Cistercians had in the twelfth.

The ranks of the orders swelled, and mendicant friars were in demand as confessors and preachers, which also meant requests for burial in their churches and pious donations to those churches in wills. That also meant that mendicants received fees customarily paid to parochial clergy, with the consequent reduction of incomes. However, the pastoral gap between mendicant and diocesan clergy began to close as bishops implemented the reforms of Lateran IV and as new pastoral handbooks for priests, such as Raymond of Peñafort's *Summa de poenitentia et matrimonio,* circulated ever more widely. The education and effectiveness of diocesan clergy improved further with the promulgation of Boniface VIII's constitution, *Cum ex eo,* and the publication of John of Freiburg's *Summa confessorum* in 1298. Boniface's decree provided that rectors could take time away from their parishes for study at university, if a substitute could be found in the meantime. John of Freiburg's manual for confessors superceded Raymond of Peñafort's book, because he included the best psychology found in the thought of the Schoolmen. As a Dominican, he especially appropriated Thomas Aquinas's ideas about vices, virtues, and human acts.[37] The number of surviving copies, and of later printed editions, testifies to the influence this book had within the later medieval priesthood. The rivalry between mendicant and diocesan clergy quieted down, ultimately because the ability and education of parish priests came to resemble that of the mendicants. When Pope John promulgated the Clementines, diocesan clergy had caught up to their mendicant counterparts closely enough for him to make *Super cathedram* the final word in the tussle between diocesan and mendicants over preaching, confessions, and burials. Of course, since they were publicized through preaching and, like confession, formed part of the process of atonement, indulgences occasioned some of the conflict between friars and rectors.

Therefore, *Abusionibus* really offers no proof that numerous itinerant preachers usurped the right to preach indulgences *a pena et a culpa,* nor does it suggest that the preaching of such indulgences was widely misunderstood. The decree was intended, rather, to settle disputes between competing classes of clergy, rather than calling to attention the theologically erroneous preaching of indulgences. In keeping with an ancient custom, Clement V asked the bishops assembled at the Council of Vienne for help in devising the council's reform agenda. Consequently, the legal sources reveal what concerned the bishops, and what concerned the bishops were the stormy relations between friars and parsons in their dioceses, as well as their relative pastoral effectiveness.

The canonistic commentaries on *Abusionibus* agree with this interpretation of the canon. The most influential of the commentators explained that the phrase *a pena et a culpa* merely referred to plenary indulgences. The decretalist and diplomat Johannes Andreae (c. 1270–1348) taught canon law at both Padua and Bologna and represented the latter city as ambassador to the court of St. Peter in 1328. A prolific scholar and a layman, his glosses on the *Liber sextus* and the *Clementines* long served as the standard commentaries on those texts. Johannes understood the phrase in the very same way as James of Vitry and Humbert of Romans: "This is that fullest remission of sins which crusaders are given for aid to the Holy Land . . . which is given during the Jubilee year according to the *extravagantes* of Boniface [VIII], which only the pope concedes."[38] In the opinion of Johannes, the real danger was false preachers of indulgence: "Some preachers of alms perpetrated so many abuses such that they extorted money from the people."[39] Because of the threat from illegal preachers, he highlighted the Council of Vienne's reaffirmation of the decree of Lateran IV (canon 62), which enjoined itinerant preachers to present their credentials to the bishop before preaching in his diocese: "The Council of Vienne decreed that no preacher shall be admitted unless he present letters from the Lord Pope or the diocesan through which the authority and licence of preaching was extended to him."[40] Neither did Johannes express any concern for improper teaching in his commentary on the *Liber sextus*, promulgated by Boniface VIII in 1298. He explained that, if a penitent received an efficacious, plenary remission, his entire debt of sin was cancelled: "For if the pope remits all penalty of sin, as he does for crusade to the Holy Land, all penalty of sin is removed, so long as the crusader shall be worthily contrite, through which contrition sin is cancelled before God."[41]

Other fourteenth-century canonists largely echoed the opinions of Johannes Andreae. The influential Benedictine William of Montlaudun (d. 1343) equated indulgences *a pena et a culpa* with full remission.[42] Boniface of Amanatis argued likewise:

> Only the pope grants full pardon of all sins to the contrite heart. . . . That indulgence of all sins is only pardon of temporal penalty. . . . Therefore, the pope does not absolve from penalty and guilt, but only from temporal penalty.[43]

He too denounced not pardons *a pena et a culpa* in themselves but those preachers of indulgence without the authority to proclaim or grant them:

> Note that only the Roman Pontiff is to grant indulgence or full pardon of sins . . . and that is one abuse of these preachers who because of their temerity conceded full remission of sins to their benefactors. However, this pardon is efficacious only if there is heartfelt contrition, and then sins are remitted completely by the mercy of God, and the eternal penalty inflicted because of those sins commuted into temporal penalty.

And thus, the said indulgence is invalid for sins so remitted; it shall be efficacious, therefore, in regard to the temporal penalty, such that the indulgence amounts to a complete remission.[44]

Once again, the deception here is the preacher's claim to authority he lacked.

The chroniclers' descriptions of the Jubilee indulgence of 1300 *a pena et a culpa* agree with these canonistic commentators. Guillelmo Venturi of Asti wrote that anyone who had visited on fifteen successive days the churches of Sts. Peter and Paul in Rome would be free of all penalty and guilt: "They stated that any Christian . . . who stayed at Rome and visited on each of those days the churches of the apostles Peter and Paul would be free from all guilt and penalty incurred since the day of their baptism."[45] The Florentine Giovanni Villani recorded that, with the Jubilee, the pope extended to pilgrims arriving and praying in Rome remission of both penalty and guilt.[46] A German cleric likewise described the Jubilee indulgence, and repeated the necessity of confession and contrition for efficacious reception of the pardon.[47]

Thus, the sources nearly universally agree that the phrase *a pena et a culpa* was simply a vulgar expression for plenary indulgences. Most late medieval Catholics—whether lay or ordained—used this phrase, no matter how potentially troublesome and misleading, to describe the condition of a penitent who had received an efficacious plenary indulgence. Indeed, some theologians and canonists believed the phrase, like many developments in the history of pardons, originated among the laity. In a sermon *de sanctis*, the Franciscan theologian Francis Mayron (d. 1327) observed that no indulgence liberated *a pena et a culpa*, nor may the phrase be found in letters of pardon: "No indulgence is granted for penalty and guilt, because just as penance directly removes guilt, so indulgence adequately removes penalty. And this example is upheld, because the church never uses this expression."[48] In his commentary on the Sentences, however, Francis conceded that full remissions sometimes were preached as though they cancelled both penalty and guilt, although they should not be: "It is commonly taught that indulgence is given for penalty and guilt. . . . It ought not to be so taught, because pardon is not granted for guilt."[49] Francis's misgivings about such terminology were rare, as later learned commentators observed that commoners used the same discourse, but made no recommendations against it. The Bohemian canonist Stanislaus commented that the Jubilee of 1300 "remitted, as is said commonly (*vulgariter*), guilt and penalty."[50] Boniface of Amanatis likewise noted the discourse of the theologically imprecise:

Note that absolution from penalty and guilt is not so-called by law, but in common usage. And only the pope grants this pardon, as it is clear, to crusaders for the relief of the Holy Land . . . and for the Jubilee."[51]

This terminology lasted until the end of the Middle Ages. Commentators of the later fifteenth century largely agreed with the opinions of the earlier theologians and canonists. Ulrich Stöckel, a member of the council of Basel, wrote that unlearned priests and layfolk referred to plenary indulgences as *a pena et a culpa*, as did the theologian Anthony of Florence and the canonist John of Torquemada.[52] Literary evidence agrees with the canonistic. Even Truth "purchaced [Piers Plowman] a pardoun *a pena et a culpa*." Alastair Minnis is doubtlessly correct when he asserts that Langland would not have used a phrase he deemed suspicious. Truth could not deceive.[53]

The sources, then, uphold the opinion of John Bossy, who asserted that the comments of Johannes Andreae meant that by the turn of the fourteenth century the proper reception of indulgences had become commonly understood. Certainly, the phrase seriously troubled few theologians or canonists, who knew full well that indulgences remitted only *pena*.[54] The gap here—if that it is—between academic theology and vulgar expression parallels other seeming disconnections between "elite" and "folk" medieval religious culture, but like the others this one is more apparent than real. As Eamon Duffy has explained, little separated the charms recited by fourteenth-century rustics for good health or crops, on the one hand, and the liturgies celebrated by the pope to dispel the Black Death, on the other. The differences were even narrower for indulgences "from penalty and guilt."

INDULGENCES FOR THE DEAD

A parallel development took place with regard to indulgences for the dead. Like pardons preached *a pena et a culpa*, remissions for the dead seem to have originated with itinerant preachers of indulgences. Some historians have named such indulgences as one of the most scandalous abuses within the late medieval Church. Like pardons for penalty and guilt, the "controversy" surrounding pardons for the dead had much to do with terminology. Whereas a handful of indulgences *a pena et a culpa* can be verified in the documents after 1295, not a single proclamation of remission granted to the dead in Purgatory survives before 1343; the evidence for their earlier existence comes from chronicles and the commentaries of theologians and canonists. Medieval authors were themselves aware of this curious lack of documentation. In his commentary on the *Sentences*, Albert the Great confessed that he had never seen an authentic document proclaiming an indulgence for the dead: "It must be said that I have never seen such a form in some authentic document which came from the Curia."[55] While the learned commentators did have differing views regarding pardons for the deceased, rather more striking is the agreement on these indulgences, especially given the lack of official documentation.

The earliest references to pardons for the dead come from the late eleventh century, by which time Christians had for many centuries undertaken works of charity and piety on the behalf of departed loved ones. The origins of indulgences for the dead may be understood as an intersection between this ancient religious practice and the then new benefit granted through the authority of the church. The earliest examples seem also to have arisen from crusading fervor, for a document of 1096 relates that two brothers named Gaufred and Guigo assumed the cross for the sake of their own souls and the souls of their dead parents.[56] The sources, however, record no such pardons for the next century and a half. Remissions for the dead surface once again around the middle of the thirteenth century; once again a crusade indulgence was involved. Stephen of Bourbon wrote that a preacher had once told him of a very gallant knight who took up the cross in the Albigensian crusade. This knight tired of the adventure and wished to go home. A certain William, archdeacon of Paris, accompanied the crusaders as papal legate. William approached the knight and claimed that his legation gave him the power to extend plenary indulgence not only to crusaders but to their deceased relatives as well, provided forty days' service was completed: "The legate said to him that by the authority of God and the pope and the church he granted indulgence to his dead father, and the knight continued his toil there on the behalf of his father for another forty days."[57] After the time of service had passed, this knight had a dream in which his father appeared, and thanked him—the son's service had freed his father from Purgatory. Although containing little literal truth (for no William, archdeacon of Paris, served as legate to Innocent III, nor did that pope ever extend crusade indulgences to the dead), the story still indicates that thirteenth-century people believed that such indulgences were available, if uncommon. Albert the Great also knew of pardons for the dead; again the context was the benefits of crusade indulgences:

> The church preaches the crusade, and she proclaims [its benefits] at the choice of the crusader for himself, and for two or three or ten or however so many souls among the living as among the dead. But these souls are sometimes in hell, sometimes in Purgatory, sometimes, however, they are also among the living. Therefore, it seems that crusade indulgence may be valid for all those who are called souls.[58]

Finally, in 1249 the Spanish bishop Lucas of Tuy wrote a polemic against the Albigensians, in which he refuted the heretics' charge that indulgences for the dead were worthless. Lucas countered that indulgences that bishops grant on holy occasions benefit the dead as well as the living: "The indulgences of days [of remission], which are granted by the shepherds of the church on the feasts of the saints and for other works of charity, are profitable not only for the living but also for the dead."[59]

The preaching of pardons for the dead worried some churchmen. In a sermon preached in 1225, Caesarius of Heisterbach fulminated against preachers of crusade indulgences who proclaimed that acceptance of the cross liberated a certain number of souls from Purgatory and even Hell. Such preachers "do not consider what they preach, so that they captivate many. Such are today certain crusade preachers, because they wish to be singled out, either free all souls from Purgatory, or, because most of them are mad, liberate from Hell!" Caesarius further denounced the preaching of such indulgences as a crass purchase of the dead in Purgatory.[60] The chronicle of Conrad of Ursperg described one instance whereby the people had come to believe they could aid the dead:

> In that time (1221), the lord cardinal bishop Conrad of Portugal, in legation to the Apostolic See, was sent to Germany for the business of the Holy Land, namely, so that he might persuade crusaders to once again take up the cross, and that he might name preachers who would encourage others to go on crusade. Then, a certain man by the name of John, of the Order of Preachers, coming from the town of Strasbourg, zealously broke out into a sermon both reasonable and absurd, so that he almost violently reproached the vices and sins of men. And in order to captivate souls, he devised certain teachings until now unheard of, some of which yet might be able to be defended through reason, for they may have contained the truth. Still many ideas presented were discerned to have brought forth evils, since the listeners understood them in the wrong way, and in order to justify the most frightful acts. And shamefully inclined deeds were done, among which the lord archbishop of Cologne, Engelbert, was murdered by his relatives, and many priests were killed. For these evildoers said: "I may do evil, because I shall be pardoned, also I shall *free the souls of many dissolute persons by accepting the cross.*[61]

In the light of other evidence, Conrad's reliability here may well be questioned. Furthermore, he entertained the idea that not everything John said to the people was deceitful or illegal. He seems more uncomfortable with John's methods rather than the content of what the Dominican said. However oblique, the reference to the liberation of souls should probably be understood as meaning the deceased in Purgatory, an idea which Conrad seemed willing to hear out. Certainly that idea found favor with John's audience.

In the popular fourteenth-century story, *The Spirit of Guy* (*De spiritu Guidonis*), the dead themselves ask for indulgences on their behalf. Guy's ghost had explained to Jean of Gobi and his confrères that for sins committed against his mother he had to suffer for two years in Purgatory, unless living benefactors offered suffrages for him. The friars then asked what suffrages could alleviate his suffering. Guy's ghost enumerated the various kinds of suffrages the living can offer to spare the dead the purgatorial flame.[62] Jean of Gobi inquired whether indulgences could help:

> Brother Jean: Could indulgences acquired by me be profitable for you, if I deprived myself of them and applied them to you?
> Guy's Ghost: Yes.
> Brother Jean: Then I deprived myself, insofar as I was able, of all the indulgences I received the past year, and gave them to him.[63]

The rest of the tale is a catalogue of other medieval devotionalisms for which indulgences often were granted. The ghost emphasized three times that Mary's intercession was vital for relief, whether in prayers or Masses celebrated in her honor. The ghost's last charge to his wife was to live in chaste widowhood and endow three hundred Masses for the succor of his soul, one hundred of which should be to honor Mary.[64] The ghost likewise asked that he be remembered at eucharistic devotional rites.[65] His penalty was further reduced because he had given money to a cousin, an impoverished student.[66]

The first documented indulgence for the dead was granted a generation after John of Gobi wrote the story of Guy's ghost. Doubtlessly, the heightened concern for the welfare of the dead in the fourteenth century, along with that era's preoccupation with Purgatory, was largely responsible for this first concession, made in 1343 by an Italian bishop who granted a remission of one year and forty days "for the dead as well as for the living."[67] Clearly, indulgences for the dead must have been rare up until the mid-fourteenth century. They must also have been granted in response to pleas from those who received the pardons, and then asked grantors or preachers whether deceased loved ones could also benefit from them. In such cases, the bishops and their preachers must have been pressured into being generous.

Throughout these developments, the academic theologians and canonists confronted substantial questions of the church's power to cancel penalties for sin. How could the requirements for efficacious indulgence be satisfied by those already dead? The treasury of merit could clearly be drawn upon by those able to fulfill the requirements of a pardon. But the dead could fight no crusade nor give alms nor make pilgrimages. Did, then, indulgences for the dead have the same efficacy as for those still living? Or did they differ somehow? Furthermore, an efficacious indulgence required that a bishop grant it. To whose diocese might the dead belong? Did the church have jurisdiction over Purgatory? Consequently, two main problems preoccupied the thoughts of the learned commentators. First, should an indulgence for the dead be understood in much the same terms as a pardon for the living, and second, to what extent did the church possess authority over the souls in Purgatory? All medieval commentators agreed that pardons for the dead had some value, otherwise the universal church was in error, which was impossible. They also agreed, however, that the dead received indulgences differently from those yet alive.

The teaching of the Franciscan Bonaventure represented one authoritative opinion. He began his discussion of indulgences for the dead by remarking that a grant of indulgence required two acts—a grant from the treasury of the church, and a proper absolution, that is, a legitimate application of church authority. Only the pope, as caretaker and sovereign over the universal church, can communicate her suffrages to the dead. But, since the dead are no longer under the jurisdiction of the church, these indulgences constitute an intercession, not an exercise of jurisdiction, on behalf of the souls in Purgatory. Indulgences could not be as efficacious for the dead as for those still living:

Therefore, I say that because the goods and treasury of the church are in the power of the pope—and those who are in Purgatory, by reason of charity, are fit to receive spiritual benefits—that the pope is able to grant them the benefits of the church. However, in regard to the authority to judge, because the deceased have now left the forum of the church and of ecclesiastical judges, it seems that absolution is only possible for them in the way of intercession; and so, strictly speaking, indulgence is not granted to them. But if indulgence may be called broadly an outlay of someone's help, and a dispensation of the goods of the church, thus is indulgence granted to them, but pertains not to an act of judgment, but rather of a suppliant.[68]

Bonaventure had defined indulgence as a transformation of penalty, which is initiated in the sacrament of penance. Since this sacrament does not exist in Purgatory, neither should indulgences. However, he would defer to the authority of the pope:

Indulgence properly speaking is not only called a jurisdictional cancellation; it is also truly said to be a commutation into some penalty assumed voluntarily and with devotion, and so we see this in all indulgences. This commutation is not then able to exist for those in Purgatory because they are beyond the state in which the devout and voluntary assumption of some penance may be able to be useful to them. And therefore indulgence is not possible for them, unless perhaps through an intercession or through accident. For if someone may wish to assume the cross for his dead father, it ought not to be denied that if it is the will of the pope, indulgence is indeed possible for them.[69]

Thus, Bonaventure understood pardons for the dead as an especially powerful suffrage of the church, but unlike other indulgences, they did not represent an act of episcopal jurisdiction. Furthermore, if indulgence could be extended to the dead at all, only the pope might possess such power.

The Dominican schoolmen Albert the Great and Thomas Aquinas agreed that indulgences could be offered to the dead but, in contrast to Bonaventure, also believed that church jurisdiction extended to Purgatory. Albert discounted the worthiness of indulgences for those in Hell, but asserted that souls in Purgatory benefitted a great deal from the indulgences obtained for them by their living relatives and friends: "those existing in hell profit nothing from indulgences; but those dwelling in Purgatory profit much."[70] He argued that the church did have jurisdictional authority over the dead in Purgatory, because like the living, they were on the path to salvation. They still belonged to the Church Militant:

> For Purgatory is in one sense a path, and in another sense an end, and the demonstration is this: because they are no longer able to sin, they are at an end, but in so far as not yet having arrived at the perfection for which they are cleansed, they are still on the way and on the journey to salvation.[71]

Furthermore, their entrance into Purgatory meant that they had died truly confessed and contrite, and the church extends indulgences to all faithful in a state of grace:

> [To a proclamation] of indulgence is thus always added: "To the confessed and to those undertaking penitence, or who are confessed and have accepted penitence." All these, however, are either penitents still alive, or those completing satisfaction in Purgatory by suffering in penalty for what they have done. And therefore indulgence is very profitable for them.[72]

In a further comment, however, Albert's language approached Bonaventure's. Indulgences, he said, belong to the most powerful suffrages of the church (*indulgentiae de praecipuis suffragiis sunt ecclesiae*) and therefore enjoyed full efficacy. Although he expressed himself much as Bonaventure did later, Albert was more confident that the church could grant fully efficacious pardons of sin to the dead in Purgatory. And although his interpretation of these indulgences was rather more juridical than the Franciscan's, he still believed indulgences for the dead differed from pardons conceded to penitents yet alive.

The opinion of Thomas Aquinas resembled his teacher's, but was more consistent. He agreed that the dead in Purgatory could receive indulgences, provided the pardons had been specifically proclaimed that the deceased might receive them (the blessed did not need them and the damned could not use them), because the dead, like the living, were on the road to salvation, and all such Christians were under the jurisdiction of the church. Besides, the church granted indulgences for the dead, and the church did not err: "It is conceded by everyone that indulgences have some worth, because it would be impious to say that the church does something in vain."[73] Thomas upheld the indefectibility and authority of the church with a typically scholastic distinction between the two types of pardon:

> Indulgence is able to be profitable to someone in two ways: in the first way directly, in another way indirectly. For indulgence is directly profitable for him who accepts the indulgence, that is, he who performs the work for which the indulgence is given, such as the one who visits the tomb of some saint. Hence, since the dead are not able to do that for which indulgence is given, indulgences are not able to be valid for them directly. However, indulgences are able to be profitable secondarily and indirectly to one for whom someone performs that work which is the cause of the indulgence; this way can sometimes be legitimate, sometimes however it is not able, according to the various forms of indulgence. For if such should be the form of the indulgence—"whoever does this or that good work, he shall have so much of indulgence"—he who performs this work is not able to transfer the benefit of the indulgence to another person, because it is not his to apply to another the intention of the church, through which is dispensed the common suffrages from which indulgences receive their value, as it is said above. If however, indulgence is phrased in this form—"whoever will do this or that work, he and his father, or whomever of his other relatives detained in Purgatory, will receive so much indulgence,"—such an indulgence will be profitable not only to the living, but to the dead as well. For there is no prohibition whereby the church may be able to transfer the common merits, from which indulgences have worth, to the living yet not the dead.[74]

Thus a bull of indulgence may state that not only the receiver, but also one of his deceased relatives in Purgatory obtains the remission of the indulgence. However, unless such an intent is clear in the prelate's proclamation, the dead in no way benefit from the indulgence. Like Albert, Thomas understood pardons for the dead in essentially juridical terms. But, an indulgence for the dead, while licit in itself, was still not quite the same as a pardon granted to a living person.

The opinions of Albert and Thomas Aquinas passed into the common baggage of Dominican pastoral theology through the *Summa confessorum* of John of Freiburg, which was the most influential of the penitential *summae* of the later Middle Ages. John compiled his handbook for confessors, which he intended to be a revision of Raymond of Peñafort's *summa*, between 1280 and 1298. His opinion on indulgences for the dead was the same as his two Dominican predecessors'. He explicitly cited Albert as his source, although his presentation indicates a heavy reliance on Thomas as well. The dead, John said, can receive indulgences when the grantor of the indulgence so declares in the document of proclamation.[75] He repeated Thomas's distinction between the two ways to receive indulgence, and further agreed with Thomas that the dead in Purgatory may indirectly obtain indulgence if a living person is willing to perform a good work on their behalf and if the dispenser of the indulgence stated explicitly that the merit of the indulgence may be applied to a dead loved one.[76] That his pastoral manual was so successful can only mean that many others in the fourteenth century came to share the view of Albert and Thomas.

The canonists carried on their own discussion of indulgences for the dead. Of course, canonistic discussions of remissions for the dead concentrated on whether the church could exercise jurisdiction in Purgatory. The decretalist Hostiensis, who wrote his commentary on the Decretals of Gregory XI in the 1250s, denied the efficacy of indulgences for the dead, because he believed that while the church could offer intercessions on behalf of the departed, nothing in tradition indicated that the church had jurisdiction in the afterlife, and proper jurisdiction was a necessary condition of efficacious indulgence:

> But neither are remissions of this type profitable for the dead, although other suffrages of the church may be profitable, because only is this charity [of suffrages] efficacious in Purgatory, since fortunately, works may be offered on behalf of all the faithful . . . in the end, it seems to me that charity is such that the power of the keys does not exist in the afterlife, nor does it follow that the church looses and binds after death.[77]

These comments would seem to entirely remove any possibility of pardons for the dead. However, Hostiensis's ideas about indulgences for the dead paralleled his thinking about excommunications and absolutions that the church imposed on the dead. These impositions, he reasoned, should be understood in an equivocal sense, much like indulgences for the dead should be. Excommunication of the dead, he suggested, should be understood as a refusal of the Church Militant to pray for the repose of a soul.

Absolutions and indulgences for the dead should be understood as special forms of intercession, but not as real, that is, jurisdictional, pardon of sin or temporal penalty:

> Because there [in Purgatory] indulgence is made for the consolation of the living faithful, and a dead person is remitted, which means that it may be shown that before death that person had been absolved through contrition . . . but truthfully, for those who are already dead nothing may be done.[78]

Hostiensis, then, seems to deny any benefit that indulgences might be able to confer on the deceased. His opinion found few advocates.

In contrast, like Albert and Thomas, Pope Innocent IV asserted in his massive commentary on the Decretals that the church did indeed have jurisdiction in Purgatory. His argument invoked the array of intercessions that the church offered on behalf of the dead. He maintained that through the good work of living benefactors, the church granted indulgences for the dead. All Christendom agrees that the prayers, thanksgiving, almsgiving, and other good works that the living perform on behalf of the dead relieve the suffering of the souls in Purgatory. Indulgences proclaimed to benefit the dead are also efficacious. The pope specifically upheld papal indulgences for the dead in his gloss of *Quod autem*:

> *By his judge*, through which [phrase] it seems that indulgences are not valid for those who are in Purgatory, because now they have no earthly judge, but they are relegated to the judgement of God, [for] . . . prayers, the contribution of alms, and fasting may be valid for the dead, because such intercessions are not offered by reason of jurisdictional competence. But it is otherwise with indulgence. For here it seems nonetheless that if someone serves the church or, commanded by a bishop, makes a pilgrimage to a chosen site on behalf of the dead, that that work should be more valid for the dead than if he should do something else. If the pope so ordains, we do not deny that they are valid for the dead.[79]

Innocent thus asserted that indulgences for the dead had some sort of benefit for the souls in Purgatory, on the sole ground that the indefectible pope sometimes grants them.[80] He did not insist that they have the same efficacy as an act of jurisdiction exercised over a living member of the church, indeed, his comments suggest that they work somewhat differently.

The very narrow difference of opinion concerning pardons for the deceased continued into the fourteenth century, when the issue proved more interesting to the intellectuals of the religious orders than of the diocesan clergy.[81] The only thinkers who argued that the church exercised jurisdiction in Purgatory were Dominicans and Augustinians. These authors, however, also conceded that pardons for the dead differed from those granted to the living. The most influential intellectuals who claimed the church possessed jurisdiction in Purgatory were the Dominican, Peter Paludanus (1277–1342), and the Augustinian, Augustine of Ancona (1241–1328). Other defenders were the Dominicans, William of Cayeux, Albert of Brescia, John of Dambach, and Rainer of Pisa.[82]

Augustine had argued in *Summa de potestate ecclesiastici*, and Peter in his *Summa de potestate papae*, for the supremacy of the pope over other authorities within Christendom; indeed, Augustine had asserted that all authority—both ecclesiastical and secular—issued from the pope. His explanation of pardon for those in Purgatory resembled that of Thomas Aquinas. Whereas Thomas had said that indulgence could be received directly or indirectly, Augustine made a similar distinction, and argued that the merit won through indulgences could be amending or conditional. Amending merit could be received only directly and was, therefore, impossible for the dead. Conditional merit was received through benefactors, and since the dead in Purgatory are still *viatores*, they may receive this merit from the pope:

> For merit may be of two types. One type [is] capable of absolving, by which someone merits eternal life by his own work because of the root of charity. Concerning such merit, it is true that those who are in Purgatory are not able to gain it, because now souls in Purgatory have merited eternal life through the charity in which they perished. Moreover, such merit does not depend on the work of another, but on one's own work. Another type is conditional merit, by which someone merits either reduction or alleviation of penalty whenever some other person does for them what is stipulated by the church in order to bring about the remission of penalty. Thus, conditional merit is so understood that it depends on the work of another person. Those who are in Purgatory are able to gain such merit—and of so much of it since souls in Purgatory are not yet possessors but seekers—from the power of the pope, because they are able to be remunerated by the treasury of the church through the granting of indulgences, by which others do for them that work for which the indulgence was promulgated. [83]

Peter Paludanus addressed the validity of all indulgences for the dead. He claimed that prelates could grant indulgences to the living and the dead as they saw fit, just as a man disposes of his goods freely:

> The souls of the dead are freed by the pardons of prelates, for just as a prelate is able to dispense the treasury of the church, as though they were his own goods—thus may I grant my goods to the living and the dead as I wish—just so a prelate offers to the living the merits and payments of the saints, whilst that for which it is offered to the living it is yet given to the dead.[84]

This argument, which sounds much like that of Innocent IV, asserts that bishops and popes, as the lawfully appointed stewards of the goods of the church, may distribute those goods as they see fit, even unto the deceased. Neither Peter nor Augustine took into consideration the objection that the dead are no longer under the jurisdiction of the church. Their arguments affirmed the validity of such pardons on the basis of the indefectibility of the church.

Following their thirteenth-century predecessors, all Franciscan thinkers of the fourteenth century, such as Francis Mayron, Alexander of Alexandria, and William of Rubione, denied the church's jurisdiction in Purgatory. Alexander, who was elected minister-general of the order in 1313, agreed with Bonaventure that indulgences for the dead could only be understood as a suffrage made of charity.[85] Both Alexander and William argued that pardons for the dead should be understood as a particularly powerful suffrage of the church. Joining these prominent Franciscans were the Dominican theologian Durand of St. Pourçain (1275–1334) and the Cluniac canonist William of Montlaudun.

One fourteenth-century Franciscan denied virtually any validity to indulgences for the dead. Francis Mayron, like Hostiensis, saw no way in which pardons could alleviate the condition of souls in Purgatory:

> Note that concerning he who said that there could be indulgences for those in Purgatory, such that for the contribution of a denarius one day in Purgatory shall be remitted, and for two denarii, more, etc. But this is not true for the reason that when someone departs from the competence and forum of the church, the church is not able to give that person indulgences; remissions are only profitable when someone is in this life. Moreover, this is not the case regarding suffrages, which are granted through the means of supplication. Indulgences, however, are granted through the means of authority and jurisdiction. But the church does not have jurisdiction in Purgatory. Therefore, it is error to say that the church grants pardon, or that such indulgence was ever given.[86]

Outside of William of Montlaudun, one of the few fourteenth-century canonists to offer an opinion on the issue, Mayron's view found few sympathizers.[87] That such influential figures persuaded few others that indulgences for the dead had absolutely no value must suggest that many seekers wanted also to apply their indulgences to the dead.

A greater diversity of opinions may be found among the later Dominicans. Both Peter of Tarentaise (the first Dominican pope as Innocent V, reigned in 1276) and Durand of St. Pourçain dissented from the views of Albert and Thomas. Although Peter believed that indulgences could benefit the dead, he denied that the church had any jurisdiction in Purgatory.[88] Durand devised a combination of Bonaventure's and Hostiensis's arguments. He argued that the power of the keys gave the church authority over those *super terram;* hence, indulgences could not extend to souls who no longer dwelt on the earth. But he also accepted the Bonaventuran concept of indulgences as suffrage:

> It is clear that indulgences are not valid for those who are in Purgatory directly, although these are in charity, because they are not able to do that which the indulgence requires, and besides they are not in the forum of the church, and because the power was given to Peter to absolve and loose *on earth*, as it is written: *I shall give to you the keys of the kingdom of heaven, and whatever you shall hold bound on earth, etc.* Hence the power of the pope extends directly only over those who are among the living. Still, indulgences are able to be valid for the dead in Purgatory indirectly in the way of suffrage, such that someone who receives indulgence for doing that for which pardon is granted, with the intention, he transfers his satisfaction for another in Purgatory.[89]

Although there were real differences of opinion regarding pardons for the dead, the parameters of the argument were narrow indeed; in fact, the agreement among the intellectuals is rather more striking than the differences. All save two commentators who broached the subject conceded that indulgences could benefit those in Purgatory—the argument was over how those benefits worked. Furthermore, that the considerable authority of Hostiensis and Francis Mayron was rejected testifies to the general sentiment in favor of applying the benefits of pardons to the souls in Purgatory. Notable too is the caution with which theologians and canonists approached the subject, as indicated by the consensus that even if they could benefit the dead, pardons for Purgatory differed from pardons for the living. Still, the ancient traditions of the indefectible church taught that the living could do much good for the deceased, and the commentators themselves offer evidence that by the mid-thirteenth century, pardons had been applied to the dead, probably in informal ways at the request of the laity. Again, practice antedated learned reflection, probably by a lengthy stretch of time, and again the church found some way to embrace and approve and regulate the untidiness of medieval Christianity. Only in 1477 did the Bonaventuran view become the standard. In that year, Pope Sixtus IV, who had, in the year preceding, conceded the first documented papal indulgence for the dead, had to issue a decree explaining the benefits of that remission. The pope proclaimed that these pardons had efficacy *per modum suffragii*, and were no exercise of papal jurisdiction. Indulgences could benefit the dead in Purgatory, but only as an especially efficacious intercession.

Indulgences preached *a pena et a culpa* and for the dead further illustrate a point that, according to the Passau Anonymous, highlighted the differences between orthodox Catholics and the Waldensians: "They [i.e., the Waldensians] do not believe in indulgences." In contrast, the Catholics certainly did. Indulgences preached *a pena et a culpa*, contrary to some historians' interpretations, simply do not constitute evidence for a widespread ignorance about the reception of efficacious remission. Rather, the sources demonstrate that this phrase merely represents a colloquial way—used by trained preachers perhaps as well as by the unschooled—of referring to plenary indulgences. Nor should these indulgences be taken as evidence that deceitful itinerant preachers of remission infested Latin Christendom. The repetition of Lateran IV's decree by subsequent provincial councils and pastoral manuals—much like the repetition of imperial decrees in the later Roman Empire—means instead that that council's legislation was yet efficacious. Crooked preachers there may have been, but the protocols—the efficacy of which was reaffirmed over the generations by popes, general councils, and provincial synods—offered bishops, rectors, and their parishioners effective weapons with which to combat sleazy confidence men parading around as pardoners.

Indulgences for the dead were unique in that the sources first preserve much more speculation about them than they preserve actual bulls of indulgence. Still, the discussions of the theologians and canonists in this case are probably not simply scholastic thought-experiments. In any event, the learned speculations, on the one hand, combined with the lack of documentation, on the other, must mean, first, that remissions for the dead were scarce prior to the mid-fourteenth century and, second, that the lay desire for them was primarily responsible for the coming into being of pardons for the deceased. The first dispensation of indulgences for the souls in Purgatory in 1343 probably should be interpreted as the church hierarchy's first attempt to gain control of them. Like many other developments, indulgences for the dead germinated out of an ancient inheritance of medieval religious culture, namely, the desire and responsibility of the living to aid deceased family and friends who were yet *viatores*—those on the way to salvation.

Since pardons for the dead, as well as pardons preached *a pena et a culpa*, involved generally held issues and convictions, these two pardons attracted the attention of a number of commentators from all over Latin Christendom. However, indulgences also occasioned a number of arguments rather narrower in extent, confined to regions or short periods of time. One such argument is especially well attested in the sources, and merits careful consideration.

NOTES

1. Edward Peters, ed., *Heresy and Authority in Medieval Europe* (Philadelphia: University of Pennsylvania Press, 1980), 75–77.

2. Peters, ed., *Heresy and Authority*, 161.

3. Peters, ed., *Heresy and Authority*, 268.

4. Peters, ed., *Heresy and Authority*, 270.

5. Peters, ed., *Heresy and Authority*, 280.

6. Peters, ed., *Heresy and Authority*, 287.

7. R. N. Swanson, "Indulgences for Prayers for the Dead in the Diocese of Lincoln in the Early Fourteenth Century," *Journal of Ecclesiastical History* 52 (2001), 199.

8. Luscombe, ed. and trans., *Peter Abelard's Ethics*, 111.

9. In fact, Abelard's was a lonely voice. See Anciaux, 502.

10. Tanner and Alberigo, 1:264.

11. Huguccio, *Summa decretorum*, C. 33 q. 22 c. 12, s. v. *post absolucionem* (Munich, Staatsbibliothek Clm 10247, fol. 262vb): "Potest penitenciam publicam vel sollemnem [*sic*] que absolvit a pena et a culpa."

12. Once again, all work on this subject is indebted to Nikolaus Paulus, "Die Anfänge des sogenannten Ablasses," 67–96. This article takes the issue to the end of the fourteenth century. For indulgences *a pena et a culpa* in the fifteenth century, see 252–279. There are corresponding chapters in *Geschichte*, 2:105–113 and 3:277–296.

13. Jean Baptiste Pitra, ed., *Analecta novissima spicilegii Solesmensis* (Paris: Typis Tusculanis, 1888), 2:422: "Tanta et talia offert vobis, quod sponte currere debetis, remissionem scilicet cunctorum peccatorum, quantum ad poenam et culpam, et insuper vitam aeternam." See Powell, 55–56.

14. Pitra, 2:426: "Unde cruce signati, qui vere contriti et confessi ad Dei servitium accingantur, dum in Christi servitio moriuntur, vere martyres reputantur, liberati a peccatis venialibus et mortalibus, ab omni poenitentia sibi injuncta, absoluti a poena peccatorum in hoc saeculo, a poena purgatorii in alio."

15. Pitra, 2:429: "Ad confessionem currunt et de caetero a peccatis abstinere student, ne tantum bonum perdant."

16. Pitra, 2:328: "Fit liber et immunis ab omni peccato."

17. Humbert of Romans, *Tractatus solemnis fratris Humberti quondam magistri generalis ordinis predicatorum de predicatione sancte crucis* (cited in Paulus, "Die Anfänge des sogenannten Ablasses," 71, n. 5): "Prima (gracia) est plenaria indulgentia omnium peccatorum, per quam liberantur homines non solum a penis inferni, sed etiam purgatorii."

18. Humbert of Romans, *Tractatus* (Paulus, "Die Anfänge des sogenannten Ablasses," 72, n. 1): "Secunda est relaxatio penarum. Cum enim penitentie fiant in presenti ratione pene temporalis ad quam remanet obligatus peccator post culpe deletionem, certum est quod relaxato debito pene, relaxantur obstagia que ratione debiti debebantur, et ideo ab omnibus penitentiis . . . per talem indulgentiam omnes homines liberantur, quamvis non debeant homines esse sine aliqua penitentia propter dubium incertitudinis."

19. Humbert of Romans, *Tractatus* (Paulus, "Die Anfänge des sogenannten Ablasses," 73, n. 1): "Fides catholica tenet quod per mortale peccatum incurrit homo obligationem ad penam eternam . . . cum vero penitet, etsi dimittatur culpa, non tamen remittitur ei pena ex toto, nisi contritio esset ita magna quod per illam se sufficienter puniret. Sed in hoc agitur cum eo misericorditer, quod commutatur illa pena eterna in transitoriam, que si non sustinetur in hoc seculo in penitentiis, oportebit eam sustinere in purgatorio . . . si vero alicui plena indulgentia conferatur, liberatur plene ab omni huiusmodi pena transitoria, ad quam remanebat obligatus post contritionem predictam . . . hec est fides quam tenendam docent omnes magistri . . . hec est fides quam tota tenet ecclesia."

20. Humbert of Romans, *Tractatus* (Paulus, "Die Anfänge des sogenannten Ablasses," 73, n. 2): "Sicut fit modo in vere contritis et confessis, quibus virtute divina culpa dimittitur et virtute clavium tota pena debita ab ecclesia relaxatur."

21. Thomas of Cantimpré, *Miraculorum libri duo* (Douai: B. Bellini, 1597), 108: "De indulgentia autem, quae crucem suscipientibus praedicatur, nullus fidelium dubitare permittitur, quin integraliter vere poenitentes et confessi indulgentiam recipiant omnium peccatorum, et in ea desiderii voluntate, qua pro fide, si se obtulerit locus, mori gestiunt, totaliter a poena simul absolvantur et culpa."

22. Thomas of Cantimprè, *Miraculorum libri duo*, 109: "Cum laboris iter displicuerit . . . quaerunt dispensationes, legatos Roma multiplicat, qui eos, pecunia mediante, sanctificent liberosque a peccatis per litteras recommendent. Bona sanctificatio, quae liberat a peccatis, bonae et beatae litterae, quae securam et mundatam animam ab omni culpa et poena fecerunt."

23. Péano, "La '*Quaestio*,'" 72: "Valde decuit, quod eius [Papae] potestas super universali remissione culpae et poenae in tempore consummante notificacionis sue in alico [*sic*] sic debuit revelari, quod indubitabilis foret."

24. Paulus, "Die Anfänge des sogenannten Ablasses," 82.

25. Potthast, *Regesta*, no. 23981.

26. Francesco Bartoli, *Francisci Bartholi tractatus de indulgentia S. Mariae de Portiuncula*, 182.

27. Clem. 5.9.2 (*CIC* 2.1190): "Abusionibus, quas nonnulli eleemosynarum quaestores in suis proponunt praedicationibus, ut simplices decipiant et aurum subtili vel fallaci potius ingenio extorqueant ab eisdem."

28. Ibid.: "Ad haec cum aliqui ex huiusmodi quaestoribus, sicut ad nostram audienciam est perlatum, non sine multa temeritatis audacia et deceptione multiplici animarum indulgentias populo motu suo proprio de facto concedant."

29. Ibid.: "Super votis dispensent, a periuriis, homicidiis, et peccatis aliis sibi confitentes absolvent . . . data sibi aliqua pecuniae quantitate, remittant, tertiam aut quartam parten de poenitentiis iniunctis relaxent, animas tres vel plures parentum vel amicorum illorum, qui eleemosynas eis conferunt, de purgatorio, (ut asserunt mendaciter), extrahant."

30. Ibid.: "Et ad gaudia paradisi perducant, benefactoribus locorum, quorum quaestores exsistunt, remissionem plenariam peccatorum indulgeant, et aliqui ex ipsis eos a poena et a culpa, (ut eorum verbis utamur), absolvant."

31. Tanner and Alberigo, 1:368–369.

32. Herbert J. Schroeder, O. P., ed. and trans., *Disciplinary Decrees of the General Councils* (St. Louis: B. Herder, 1937), 386.

33. Tanner and Alberigo, 1:327.

34. Tanner and Alberigo, 1:366. Clem. 3.7.2 (*CIC* 2:1161–1164).

35. Mansi, 25:269.

36. C. 3 q. 2. c. 4 (*CIC* 1:508).

37. VI 1.6.34 (*CIC* 2:964–965). On the significance of the constitution, see L. E. Boyle, O. P., "The Constitution '*Cum ex eo*' of Boniface VIII," *MS* 24 (1962), 263–302.

38. Johannes Andreae, *Clementis quinti constitutiones in concilio Vienensi edite*, Clem. 5.9.2 (Venice: Octavianus Scotus, 1525), 96r: "Ista est illa plenissima peccatorum remissio que concedatur crucesignatus pro subsidio ultramarine . . . que datur in anno centenario in extravagantes Bonifacii *Antiquorum habet*, quam solus papa concedit."

39. J. Andreae, Clem. 5.9.2 (95r): "alique questores elemosynarum plures abusus perpetrabant ut subtraherent pecunias a populo."

40. Ibid.: "Concilium decrevit: ut nullus questor admittatur, nisi ostendat litteras domini pape vel diocesani per quas fit ei concessa facultas et licentia faciendi."

41. Johannes Andreae, *In sexto decretalium novella commentaria*, X 5.38.4, s. v. *subsunt* (Venice: Franciscum Franciscium, 1581), 5:123b: "Nam si papa remittat omnem poenam peccati, sicut facit pro subsidio terrae sanctae, omnis poena peccati deletur, dummodo utens illa fuerit bene contritus, per quam contritionem peccatum dimittitur quoad Deum."

42. William of Montlaudun, *Sacramentale*, q. 9 (Munich, Staatsbibliothek Clm 23947, fol. 178v): "Et fit talis plena remissio."

43. Bonifatius de Amanatis, *Lectura super constitutionibus Clementis pape quinti, quas Clementinas nominitant*, Clem 5.9.2 (Paulus, "Die Anfänge des sogenannten Ablasses," 92, n. 1): "Papa potest solus concedere plenariam indulgentiam omnium peccatorum corde contrito . . . ista indulgentia omnium peccatorum est indulgentia solum pene temporalis . . . non ergo papa absolvit a pena et a culpa, sed solum a pena temporali."

44. Bonifatius de Amanatis, *Lectura*, Clem. 5.9.2 (Paulus, "Die Anfänge des sogenannten Ablasses," 92–93, n. 2): "Nota quod solius romani pontificis est, indulgentiam seu plenariam remissionem peccatorum concedere . . . et iste est unus abusus horum questorum qui concedebant eorum temeritate benefactoribus ipsorum plenariam remissionem peccatorum. Hec autem indulgentia non operatur nisi corde contritis, et tunc peccata remittuntur in totum misericordia Dei, et pena eterna pro eis inflicta tunc commutatur in temporalem. Sicque dicta indulgentia nihil operatur quoad peccata iam remissa; operabitur ergo quoad penam temporalem, ut illa censeatur in totum remissa."

45. Louis Muratori, ed., *Rerum scriptores italicarum* (Milan: Societatis Palatinae in Regia Curia, 1727), 11:191–192: "Statuerunt, ordinaverunt, et decretum fecerunt, ut quisquis christianus . . . steterit Romae per dies xv visitando omni die ecclesias beatorum apostolorum Petri et Pauli, liber sit a die baptismi ab omni peccato suo tam a culpa quam a pena."

46. Giovanni Villani, *Nuova cronica*, 9.36.7–14 (ed. Guiseppe Porta [Parma: Fondazione Pietro Bembo, 1991], 2:57): "Fece somma et grande indulgenza . . . tutti fece piena et intera perdonanza di tutti gli suoi peccati, essendo confesso o si confessasse, di colpa et di pena."

47. *MGH*, Scriptores 24:487.

48. Francis Mayron, *Sermones de sanctis* (Basel: Pforzheim, 1498), 95a: "Nulla potest indulgencia data a pena et a culpa, quia sicut penitentia directe respicit culpam, ita indulgencia adequate respicit penam. Et illud documentum confirmatur, quia ecclesia nunquam utitur tali forma." A largely, although not completely, true statement, since the indulgence of Celestine V was proclaimed *a pena et a culpa*.

49. Francis Mayron, *In quattuor libris sententiarum*, 4.20 (Venice: Luceantonii de guinta Florentini, 1519), 215a: "Communiter docetur quod datur indulgentia a pena et a culpa . . . nec sic debet doceri, quia super culpam non imponitur."

50. Paulus, "Die Anfänge des sogenannten Ablasses von," 90–91.

51. Bonifatius de Amanatis, *Lectura*, Clem. 5.9.2 (Paulus, "Die Anfänge des sogenannten Ablasses," 93, n. 1): "Nota quod absolutio a pena et a culpa sic vocata est non a iure, sed a vulgo. Et illam concedit solus papa, ut patet in crucesignatis pro subsidio ultramarine . . . et in anno jubileo."

52. Paulus, "Der sogenannte Ablass von Schuld und Strafe im späteren Mittelalter," 254. Anthony of Florence, *Summa theologica* 1.10.3 (Graz: Akademische Druck- u. Verlagsanstalt, 1959), 1:603: "Sciendum, quod quamvis tales plenariae indulgentiae vulgariter nuncupentur indulgentiae de culpa et poena, locutio tamen talis proprie non est vera, quia culpae solus remissor est deus auctoritative." John of Torquemada, *Repertorium in omnes commentarios Ioannis a turrecremata super decretum* De pen. D. 1 c. 87, s. v. item in *Levitico* (Venice: Haeredem Hieronymi Scotius, 1578), 5:95b: "Sciendum quod vulgariter indulgentia plenaria nominatur indulgentia a poena et culpa."

53. Alastair Minnis, "Reclaiming the Pardoners," *The Journal of Medieval and Early Modern Studies* 33 (2003), 321.

54. John Bossy, *Christianity in the West, 1400–1700* (New York: Oxford University Press, 1985), 54. Unfortunately, Bossy offered no documentation for his opinion. The foregoing obviously supports his argument.

55. Albert the Great, *Commentarii in IV sententiarum*, 4.20.18 (*Opera omnia*, 29:855): "Dicendum quod ego numquam vidi talem formam in aliquo authentico emanare a curia."

56. M. Guérard, ed., *Cartulaire*, 1:168: "pro peccatorum nostrorum et animarum nostrarum nostrorumque parentum salute."

57. A. Lecoy de la Marche, ed., *Anecdotes historiques, légendes et apologues tirés du recueil d'Étienne de Bourbon* (Paris: Librairie Renouard, 1877), 37: "Dixit ei legatus quod auctoritate dei et pape et ecclesie concedebat patri suo defuncto indulgenciam, et ipse pro eo per aliam quadragesimam sustineret laborem ibi."

58. Albert the Great, *Commentarii in IV sententiarum*, 4.20.18 (*Opera omnia*, 29:853): "Ecclesia praedicat crucem, et facit praedicari pro se et duabus vel tribus vel quandoque decem animabus tam vivorum, quam mortuorum, ad electionem cruce signati. Sed illae animae sunt quandoque in inferno, quandoque in purgatorio, quandoque autem sunt adhuc vivorum. Ergo videtur, quod indulgentia crucis valeat omnibus illis qui dictae sunt animabus." Thomas referred to the same crusade indulgences, in almost the same language, in *Commentum in IV libros sententiarum*, 4.45.2.3.2.

59. Lucas of Tuy, *Lucae Tudensis episcopi de altera vita fideique controversiis adversus Albigensium errores libri III* (Ingolstadt: Ioannis Hertsroy, 1612), 13: "Indulgentiae dierum quae a pastoribus ecclesiae in sanctorum festivitatibus vel alias ob caritatis opera fiunt, non solum vivis, verum etiam mortuis fidelibus prosunt."

60. Caesarius of Heisterbach, *Fasciculus moralitatis* 3.46 (cited in *Geschichte*, 2:335 [chap. 20], n. 44): "Non attendunt quid predicent, dummodo multos capiant. Tales sunt hodie quidam predicatores crucis, qui signari volentibus, quotquot vel quas animas requirunt, de purgatorio vel, quod maioris vesanie est, de inferno repromittunt?"

61. *MGH Scriptores*, 23:379.

62. Schleich, ed., lvi–lvii.

63. Schleich, ed., lviii: "Frater, Si indulgentiae perme acquisitae poterant sibi proficere, si ego me eis exspoliarem et eum induerem? Respondit quod sic. Et tunc ego exspoliavi me, quantum poteram, de omnibus indulgentiis conquistis per unum annum, et dedi sibi."

64. Schleich, ed., 42, 108.

65. Schleich, ed., 70, 78.

66. Schleich, ed., 58.

67. *Geschichte*, 2:339, (chap. 20) n. 87: "Omnibus . . . unius anni et 40 dierum tam pro mortuis quam pro vivis indulgentiam concedimus."

68. Bonaventure, *Commentaria in IV libros sententiarum*, 4.20.1.5 (*Opera omnia*, 4:538): "Dico igitur, quod quia bona et thesaurus ecclesiae est summi pontificis potestate, et illi qui sunt in purgatorio, ratione caritatis idonei sunt spiritualia beneficia recipere; quod papa potest eis bona ecclesiae communicare. Quantum autem ad auctoritatem iudicandi, cum illi iam exierint forum ecclesiae et ecclesiasticum iudicium, videtur, quod eis non possit fieri absolutio nisi per modum deprecationis; et ita, proprie

loquendo, non fit eis relaxatio; sed si large dicatur relaxatio cuiuscumque auxilii impensio et bonorum ecclesiae communicatio, sic potest eis relaxatio fieri; sed hoc non tenet modum iudicii, sed potius suffragii."

69. Bonaventure, *Commentaria in IV libros sententiarum*, 4.20.1.5 (*Opera omnia*, 4:538): "relaxatio proprie dicta non tantum dicit iudiciariam absolutionem, verum etiam dicit aliquam commutationem in poenam aliquam voluntarie assumtam et cum devotione; et hoc videmus in omnibus indulgentiis; hoc autem non potest esse quantum ad eos qui sunt in purgatorio, quia sunt extra statum illum, in quo posset eis persuaderi alicuius poenae devota et voluntario assumtio: et ideo non competit eis relaxatio nisi forte per medium sive per accidens. Si quis enim vellet crucem pro mortuo patre assumere, non est aliquatenus negandum, quodsi voluntas sit summi pontificis, quin indulgentia illi possit."

70. Albert the Great, *Commentarii in IV sententiarum*, 4.20.18 (*Opera omnia*, 29:855): "Existentibus in inferno nihil prosunt indulgentiae; sed existentibus in purgatorio prosunt multum."

71. Albert the Great, *Commentarii in IV sententiarum*, 4.20.18 (*Opera omnia*, 29:855): "Purgatorium enim quodammodo via et quodammodo terminus est: quantum enim ad confirmationem, quia peccare amplius non possunt, sunt in termino: sed quantum ad non pervenisse adhuc ad emendationem qua emendantur, sunt adhuc in via et in transitu ad patriam."

72. Albert the Great, *Commentarii in IV sententiarum*, 4.20.18 (*Opera omnia*, 29:855): "Semper adjungitur: 'Confessis et poenitentiam suscipientibus, vel qui confessi sunt et poenitentiam susceperunt.' Illi autem omnes vel sunt in via adhuc poenitentes, vel in purgatorio satisfacientes luendo in poenis quod fecerunt. Et ideo tantum illis valet."

73. Thomas Aquinas, *Commentum in IV libros sententiarum*, 4.20.1.3.1 (*Opera omnia*, 7:843): "Ab omnibus conceditur indulgentias aliquid valere: quia impium esset dicere, quod ecclesia aliquid vane faceret."

74. Thomas Aquinas, *Commentum in IV libros sententiarum*, 4.45.2.3.2 (*Opera omnia*, 7:1127): "Indulgentia dupliciter alicui prodesse potest: uno modo principaliter; alio modo secundario. Principaliter quidem prodest ei qui indulgentiam accipit, scilicet qui facit hoc pro quo indulgentia datur, ut qui visitat limina alicuius sancti. Unde cum mortui non possint facere eorum pro quibus indulgentiae dantur, eis indulgentiae directe valere non possunt. Secundario autem et indirecte prosunt ei pro quo aliquis facit illud quod est indulgentiae causa, quod quandoque contingere potest, quandoque autem non potest, secundum diversam indulgentiae formam. Si enim sit talis indulgentiae forma: quicumque facit hoc vel illud, habebit tantum de indulgentia; ille qui hoc facit, non potest fructum indulgentiae in alium transferre quia eius non est applicare ad aliquid intentionem ecclesiae, per quam communicantur communia suffragia ex quibus indulgentiae valent, ut iam supra dictum est [in *Commentum in IV libros sententiarum*, 4.20.1.3.3.ad 2]. Si autem indulgentia sub hac forma fiat: quicumque fecerit hoc vel illud, ipse et pater eius, vel quicumque ei adjunctus, in purgatorio detentus, tantum de indulgentia habebit, talis indulgentia non solum vivo, sed etiam mortuo proderit. Non enim est aliqua ratio quare ecclesia possit transferre merita communia, quibus indulgentiae innituntur, in vivos, et non in mortuos."

75. *SC* 3.188.

76. *SC* 3.191.

77. Hostiensis, *Summa aurea*, 5.66 (288ra): "Sed nec mortuis prosunt remissiones huiusmodi, licet alia suffragia ecclesie prosint, quia hec charitas sola prodest in purgatorio, cum secundum prosperum fit in omnibus fidelibus operosa . . . charitas est ut mihi videtur in fine sed potestas clavium non habet ibi locum, nec obstat quod ecclesia solvit et ligat post mortem."

78. Hostiensis, *Summa aurea*, 5.66 (288ra): "Quia ibi fit absolutio ad consolationem vivorum fidelium et absolvitur mortuus, id est, antequam moreretur absolutus fuisse per contritionem monstratur . . . sed in veritate quo ad alios qui iam mortui sunt nihil operatur."

79. Innocent IV, *Commentaria*, X 5.38.4, s. v. *suo iudice* (ed. Frankfurt, 544ra): "Per hoc videtur, quod indulgentie, non valeant illis, qui sunt in purgatorio, quia iam non habent iudicem in terra, sed dei iudicio relicti sunt . . . orationes et eleemosynae sacrificia et ieiunia eis valeant, quia illa non fiunt ratione fori vel iurisdicitionis, sed secus est in indulgentia. Et hic videtur tamen quod si aliquis facit ecclesiam, vel peregrinatur pro defuncto in loco electo a praelato, quod plus valet defuncto, quam si alias faceret. Si tamen papa facit, non negemus, quin valeant in defunctis."

80. On the "indefectibility" of the pope versus his "infallibility" among thirteenth-century popes and canonists, see of course Brian Tierney, *The Origins of Papal Infallibility, 1150–1350* (Leiden: E. J. Brill, 1972), and also the important comments by Alfons Stickler, "Papal Infallibility—A Thirteenth-Century Invention?" *CHR* 60 (1974), 427–441, and David L. D'Avray, "A Letter of Pope Innocent III and the Idea of Infallibility," *CHR* 64 (1980), 417–421.

81. The secular canonists Guido of Baysio and Johannes Monachus said nothing about indulgences for the dead. The lay canonist Johannes Andreae was likewise silent, as was the late thirteenth-century secular master Henry of Ghent.

82. Peter Paludanus, *Scriptum in IV sententiarum* 4.45.1 (Venice: Bonetus Locatellus, 1493), 217; Augustine of Ancona, *Summa de potestate ecclesiastica*, q. 29, (Rome: Francisci de Cinquinis, 1479), no pagination; and John of Dambach, *De vir. indul.*, q. 3 (Heiligenkreuz MS 208, fol. 89r). See also Shaffern, "Learned Discussions," 377.

83. Augustine of Ancona, *Summa de potestate ecclesiastica*, q. 29 Rome: 1479), no pagination: "Est namque duplex meritum. Unum est emenale absolutum quo quis meritur vitam eternam propria operatione per radicem charitatis. Et de tali merito verum est quod illi qui sunt in purgatorio non sunt in statu merendi quia iam meruerunt vitam eternam per caritatem cum qua decesserunt. Tale namque meritum non dependet ab opere alterius sed ab opere proprio. Alius est meritum conditionale quo quis meretur pene etiam missionem vel accelerationem dummodo alii pro eis faciant illa que instituta sunt ab ecclesia ad pene remissionem consequendam. Talis autem merito conditionali quod dependet ab opera alterius. Illi qui sunt in purgatorio mereri possunt. Et quantum ad tale meritum cum non dum sint comprehensores adhuc sunt viatores, et de foro pape, quia possunt stipendiari thesauro ecclesie per communicationem indulgentie, ex quo alii faciunt pro eis illa propter quod indulgentie sunt ordinate."

84. Peter Paludanus, *Scriptum in IV sententiarum*, 4.45.1.3 (ed. Venice, 217): "Anime defunctorum liberantur indulgentiis prelatorum, sicut enim prelatus potest dispensare thesaurum ecclesie, sicut privatus bona propria, unde sicut bona mea possum

communicare indifferenter vivo et mortuo, sic prelatus merita sanctorum et supereroga-
tiones eorum, dum tamen illud pro quo mortuo datur fiat a vivo."

85. *Geschichte*, 2:136.

86. Francis Mayron, *In libros sententiarum*, 4.21.1 (ed. Venice, 209): "Nota de illo
qui dicebat se habere indulgentias pro illis qui sunt in purgatorio, ita quod pro uno
denario una dies eis remittebatur et pro duabus plus, etc. Sed hoc non est verum, ex quo
enim aliquis exit limites ecclesie et forum istud non potest sibi ecclesia dare indulgentias nisi pro quando sunt hoc lucrati. Non sic autem est de suffragiis que impetrantur per
modum obsecrationis. Indulgentie autem dantur per modum auctoritatis et jurisdictionis.
Non autem habet ecclesia iurisdictione in purgatorio. Ideo error esse dicere hoc dare,
nec unquam talis indulgentia fuit data."

87. William of Montlaudun, *Sacramentale, De indulgentiis*, q. 9 (Munich, Staatsbibliothek Clm 23947, fol. 177v–178r): "Nec illis qui sunt in purgatorio prosunt, quia cum
fiant et procedant ex virtute clavium, et clavis non liget nec absolvat mortuos qui relicti
sunt iudicio divino." Folios cited incorrectly in *Geschichte*, 1:424, (chap. 11) n. 35.

88. Peter of Tarentaise, *In librum sententiarum commentaria*, 4.20.3.3.2

89. Durand of St. Pourçain, *In Petri Lombardi sententias theologicas commentariorum libri IV*, 4.20.3 (Venice: Guerraea, 1571), 2:354: "Per idem patet quod indulgentiae non valent existentibus in purgatorio directe, quamvis ipsi sint in charitate: quia
ipsi non possunt facere id pro quo datur indulgentia, et iterum non sunt de foro
ecclesie. Et quia potestas data Petro est absolvere et ligare super terram, sicut dictum
est ei: *Tibi dabo claves regni celorum, et quodcunque ligaveris super terram, etc.*
Unde potestas papae per se directe extendit se solum ad statum presentis vitae: possunt
tamen in eis indirecte valere per modum suffragii, quatenus aliquis quod indulgentiam
recipit faciendo id pro quo datur indulgentia ex intentione transfert eam in satisfactionem eius quod est in purgatorio."

Chapter 6

Controversy and Indulgences Prior to The Great Western Schism II

While many fourteenth-century theologians and canonists throughout Latin Christendom debated the nature and validity of indulgences for the dead and pardons *a pena et a culpa*, other controversies, generally of smaller scope, likewise arose. In particular, one fourteenth-century quarrel, which as far as the sources indicate attracted the attention of only one prominent author, was confined to the central German Empire. Since the only source was written in the midst of the controversy, the narrative of the story may be known only imperfectly and the beginning and termination of the story only inferred. Furthermore, the source preserves only one point of view, so the viewpoint opposing its author must be reconstructed at second hand.

Nonetheless, the basic quarrel seems clear enough. Sometime in the middle of the century, certain unnamed adversaries—probably a coalition of Franciscans, diocesan clergy, influential burgers, and imperialists—claimed that in preaching the indulgences that were available at their convents, German Dominicans proclaimed greater remissions than the church canons warranted. The evidence for this controversy lies in the first independent canonistic treatise on indulgences. *De quantitate indulgenciarum* (*On the quantity of indulgences*) was the work of John of Dambach (1288–1372), also the author of *De virtute indulgenciarum*. In twelve scholastic *quaestiones*, John affirmed that in their preaching of indulgences, the German Dominicans transgressed no papal or conciliar canons and, at the same time, followed protocols commonly observed throughout the church. That John of Dambach was determined to defend the legality—not the theological correctness, which was not challenged—of the Dominicans' preaching of their indulgences is clear from the prologue to the treatise:

Since sometimes the quantity of indulgences which Dominicans grant with the permission of prelates during sermons, or proclaim or have proclaimed during their holy feast days, is opposed by certain commentators, as though the brothers are doing what they ought not or cannot in this matter, I shall therefore write a treatise, if it please, for the defense of the brothers, to be called *On the quantity of indulgences*, in which I shall proceed thus.[1]

His purpose was not to theologize about pardons but to argue that the Dominicans were legally empowered to preach indulgences as they had been doing, and for which certain opponents accused them of violations of church law.

De quantitate indulgenciarum survives in seven manuscripts. All were copied in the central Holy Roman Empire. Two of the manuscripts bear dates. The earliest copy belongs to the Basel Universitätsbibliothek and is dated 1363.[2] The excellent Heiligenkreuz manuscript is dated 1373.[3] The other five manuscripts have no date; according to Kaeppeli, one of these is a fourteenth-century copy, the others fifteenth-century.[4] Consequently, only the *terminus ad quem* of the treatise may be established with certainty. John must have written the treatise by 1363, the date of completion of Basel C V 18. Paulus conjectured that John began writing *De quantitate indulgenciarum* during his tenure as theology professor at the newly founded University of Prague (1347–1350?), as a response to disputes over the archbishop's jurisdiction.[5] While archiepiscopal jurisdiction is discussed in the treatise, that of other prelates is as well. No other known evidence supports Paulus's claim, nor does any other compiler of John's works offer a date for the treatise.[6] Probably John began writing *De quantitate indulgenciarum* sometime during the 1340s, for in that decade a number of provincial councils reaffirmed the precepts of *Cum ex eo* of Lateran IV. The copy belonging to the Austrian Cistercian monastery of Heiligenkreuz, which received grants of collective indulgence in 1327 and 1328, suggests that not only Dominicans but also other religious orders found John's treatise useful to have on hand and, perhaps, that they too faced criticism of their indulgences.[7] The dates, provenance, and possession of the manuscripts, as well as John's clear preoccupation with German Dominican convents (the only ones mentioned in the text), all suggest that the treatise was written in response to regional concerns.

That regional controversy took place within the context of the papal-imperial rivalry of 1317–1346. The imperial election of 1314 was disputed, since the Wittelsbach candidate, Ludwig of Bavaria, received five votes. Two votes were cast for Ludwig's rival, Frederick of Habsburg. Civil war broke out between the supporters of the rival candidates. Angry that he had been ignored in the dispute, Pope John XXII (1316–1334) declared the imperial throne vacant in 1317. For the next twenty years, the cities and principalities of the German Empire vacillated between the two claimants. At the command of its bishop, John of Dambach's home city of Strasbourg received Frederick in 1314, although the burgers declared themselves neutral. The bishop managed to maintain a tense peace within the city until 1320, when Ludwig invaded Alsace. Political tensions abated by 1326, when Frederick died and no other Habsburg assumed the family's claim to the imperial title.

But in 1328, the ongoing political turmoil created an even greater ecclesiastical confusion, for in that year Ludwig nominated the Spiritual Franciscan Nicholas of Corbara as anti-pope Nicholas V. Although the schism was over by 1330, Germany had been divided in two, as the rival popes attempted to win allegiance through the dispensation of church privileges, such as the right to grant indulgences and the imposition of penalties. In response to Ludwig's support of Nicholas, Pope John placed the whole empire under interdict. Many bishops, such as Bertold of Strasbourg, first honored the interdict. Support for the pope among the bishops and diocesan clergy withered, however, as the interdict wore on. Religious orders fell into schism as some members supported the pope, others the emperor. Conventual and Spiritual Franciscans sided with the pope and emperor respectively. The Dominicans, however, united in support of the pope, and the Strasbourg convent was exiled from the city in 1339, when imperial forces took control of the city. The Strasbourg Dominicans remained in exile until 1345. The election of Charles of Bohemia as emperor in 1346 improved relations between empire and papacy, but administration of the sacraments resumed in some regions of the Empire only as late as 1350.[8] Their support of the pope cost the Dominicans dearly, as imperial loyalists sought ways of damaging his allies.

De quantitate indulgenciarum, then, constitutes a defense of vested interests, and offers a glimpse into rivalries between church factions in a time of political and religious strife. The treatise also holds some clues concerning the relationship between penitential piety and bishops' jurisdictions. By the middle of the fourteenth century, pilgrims had long been travelling far and wide to receive the pardons available at churches, monasteries, and convents throughout Latin Christendom. For instance, crowds of French, English, and German pilgrims each year descended into Spain to worship at the shrine of St. James at Compostela. By the end of the twelfth century, the shrine of St. Thomas Becket attracted legions of pilgrims whose homes were far away from Canterbury. Questions, then, about the boundaries of episcopal and archiepiscopal jurisdiction arose. Since many penitents travelled far beyond the borders of their home dioceses to visit indulged holy sites, by whose authority could they be understood to have received the remissions available at those sites? Was it their own bishop, or the bishop of the diocese in which the holy site was located? How could the pilgrims' own bishops be understood to have granted an indulgence in a foreign diocese? How could the bishop of Basel or Strasbourg grant an indulgence to the subjects of another diocesan bishop? In what way could any Catholic receive an indulgence from a prelate who was not one of his "own authorities" (*proprii iudices*), by whom were meant the diocesan bishop, the metropolitan bishop, and the pope?

Furthermore, over the generations, bishops, legates, and popes had from time to time favored numerous churches and monasteries with successive grants of indulgence, which is to say that one convent could have been indulgenced by several prelates at different times or by several prelates at the same time. In just one instance, in 1280, the patriarch Guido of Grado, along with three bishops, granted the Dominican convent at Zara visitation indulgences of one year and forty days each. A few years later, the bishop of Arbe granted the same convent another indulgence of one year and forty days. Did these remissions add up, in which case would the magnitude of the pardon exceed the amounts stipulated in church legislation? Or did a visitor to such a place receive only part of the entire amount available at the site? Or only the papal indulgences granted to the site, since the universal pontiff exercised jurisdiction over all Catholics everywhere? For their part, the Zara Dominicans preached that five years and two hundred days of indulgences were available at their convent.[9]

Other Dominican convents also benefitted much from indulgences. Indeed, few convents had been given as many visitation pardons as that in Basel, a house well known to John of Dambach. The bishop of Basel had enthusiastically greeted the arrival of the Dominicans in that city in the 1230s. He welcomed their expertise in preaching and the hearing of confessions. To aid their mission in his diocese, the bishop granted an indulgence to those who funded the construction of the Dominicans' first church, cloister, and convent.[10] Thereafter, popes and bishops granted indulgences to anyone who donated money or labor either to the construction of the Dominicans' new buildings or to the maintenance of their existing structures in Basel. Pope Gregory IX (1227–1241) granted a visitation indulgence of twenty days.[11] Pope Innocent IV and Albert the Great (as bishop of Regensburg) granted visitation indulgences to aid the convent in the execution of a new, ambitious building program.[12] Indulgences helped the Dominicans establish a permanent presence in Basel and also supplemented their mission of preaching and hearing confessions. In 1307, Bishop Otto confirmed that the Dominicans could preach and hear confessions within the diocese. Otto also permitted them to grant indulgences of forty days to his subjects who heard their sermons and made their confessions to the friars.[13] Bishop Nicholas of Villach, himself a Dominican, granted another letter of indulgence to the brothers in 1350.[14]

John of Dambach, then, reported in *De quantitate indulgenciarum* that the Dominicans of Basel preached indulgences much as did their confreres in Zara:

> I maintain the opinion that, with regard to the one hundred days of indulgence given by the pope to the Dominicans in the area of Basel, and the forty days then given to them by the bishop of Basel, there ought to be no question nor doubt when the pope gives a hundred and the bishop forty—nor when the cardinal of Tusculum, the legate *a latere*, gives twenty. Indeed, it is clear from the bull of the pope and the letters of the legate and the aforesaid bishops, that it is rash to attack the brothers, or thereby to condemn them, because they grant to the subjects of the bishops who are in the area one hundred forty days of indulgence.[15]

Neither the jurisdiction of the pope nor that of the bishop impeded each other, so indeed the magnitude of the indulgences they granted to the Dominican convent in Basel *did add up*, and could be preached thus. In another example, John argued that papal authority, as mediated by the legate Hugh of St. Cher (cardinal of St. Sabina and a Dominican himself), upholds the legitimacy of the Dominicans' indulgences and, consequently, the brothers' preaching of those pardons:

> Mention has been made concerning the presence of the lord Hugh, cardinal of St. Sabina, who by that letter sealed with his seal, in the possession of the Basel convent of the Dominicans, according to which what the aforesaid pope said is thus written (among other things); moreover, indulgences of this kind are valid and they are just and reasonable, as if the pope makes a prophetic announcement, and these indulgences possess in themselves the strength of durability when bishops grant them with the consent of the diocesan.[16]

At least as far as concerned papal remissions, the magnitude of such indulgences can certainly be calculated in terms of their face values. The brothers committed no deception if they added together all the papal indulgences granted to the Basel convent, because all those indulgences were fully valid in perpetuity.

Furthermore, John's comment reveals a concern with the documentation of the pardons that Dominicans had been empowered to grant and preach. The Friars Preachers had long been especially attentive to maintaining careful records of their indulgences. Indeed, shortly after they were formally established as a religious order, general chapters issued guidelines for the friars to observe with regard to pardons. The Dominican general chapter of 1235 prohibited any Dominican from preaching indulgences without the permission of his prior.[17] The 1249 chapter repeated the prohibition.[18] The general chapter of 1243 issued a series of instructions for preaching indulgences. The friars, who often travelled in pairs, should be careful not to sound as if they were preaching two indulgences, if in fact they had been commissioned to preach only one.[19] From 1272 on, a number of general chapters deemed it especially important to keep good records. Pardons were to be recorded in sealed episcopal or papal documents:

> We enjoin all conventual priors that they in every way keep and obtain bulls belonging to the community that record all indulgences and privileges, or at least transcripts sealed with the authentic seals of the bishops and popes, or confirmations with signatures.[20]

The general chapters of Pamplona in 1355 and of Verdun in 1356 issued the same order, but with the addition that management of Dominican indulgences be more centralized. Copies of indulgences and privileges should be sent to the master-general, the prior of Paris, or the procurator of the order, as well as the general chapter itself.[21] The Dominican general chapter of 1355 once again recommended that the Preachers keep careful records of the indulgences they had been empowered to grant.[22] A century of legislation by the general chapters, then, prepared John of Dambach to defend the indulgences preached by Dominicans of the German province.

THE JURISDICTION OF BISHOPS

But John had a canonistic, as well as documentary, case to make. The twelve scholastic *quaestiones* of *De quantitate indulgenciarum* consist of an exposition of various church authorities to grant pardons. These *quaestiones* fall into four parts, of which *quaestiones* one through three consider a bishop's power to grant pardon. In the first *quaestio*, John argued that bishops possess the ordinary right to grant the privilege of dispensing indulgences to others, that is, bishops need no permission either to grant a partial indulgence or to give the privilege of granting partial indulgences to some religious institution or site. "The first question is whether any bishop who is not a legate is able in his own right to grant pardon of forty days."[23] The first *quaestio*, then, essentially served as a commentary on the decree *Accedentibus* of Lateran IV (canon 60), which declared that abbots had not the same powers as bishops:

> We have come to know of serious and great excesses of certain abbots who, not content with the boundaries of their own authority, stretch out their hand to things belonging to

the episcopal dignity: hearing matrimonial cases, enjoining public penances, even granting letters of indulgence and like presumptions It sometimes happens from this that episcopal authority is cheapened in the eyes of many. Wishing therefore to provide for both the dignity of bishops and the well-being of abbots in these matters, we strictly forbid by this present decree any abbot to reach out for such things . . . unless by chance any of them can defend himself by a special concession or some other legitimate reason in respect of such things.[24]

Innocent III needed to clarify jurisdictions within the church several times during his pontificate.[25] Many bishops, owing to church business, political conflict, or negligence, were long absent from their dioceses, and of course the spiritual needs of the people did not thereby vanish. Furthermore, in some dioceses the popularity and power of an abbot—who was a prelate of the church—was greater than that of the bishop, either for reasons of personal holiness or wealth, or because of the important immunities from episcopal jurisdiction that many monasteries had accumulated over the years. Although the abbots' motivations may well have been benevolent, as the decree notes, their assumption of episcopal power could erode the authority of the bishop in the eyes of the people. With *Accendentibus*, Lateran IV clarified the jurisdictional competence of authorities within the church.

By the mid-fourteenth century, bishops had been granting partial indulgences of forty days for two centuries. Consequently, in this *quaestio*, John made no effort to raise a dustcloud of controversy. He merely revisited what every orthodox believer accepted as right teaching about the authority to grant indulgences. John's restatement of bishops' rights over partial remissions was for the most part borrowed from the influential canonist Hostiensis, who was well-known for his strong advocacy of episcopal authority and status. John correctly paraphrased Hostiensis, who had been a bishop, an archbishop, and the cardinal-bishop of Ostia, by saying that nothing impedes bishops from granting partial indulgences to persons or religious institutions: "In his *summa*, Hostiensis says that bishops, throughout the whole of their province, that is, the whole of their dioceses, in so far as bishops are able to grant general pardons, which through letters are granted for sermons, and for the building or repair of hospitals, churches, bridges, or for other pious sites and reasons."[26] John continued that such indulgences are valid, unless they were supernumerary and granted after the proclamation of *Cum ex eo* at Lateran IV, "by which—unless at the dedication of a church, where they may grant up to a year—bishops are limited to forty days in all other cases, through which restrictive prohibition is it clear enough that before Lateran IV bishops were able to grant greater indulgences, and some by abusing their power gave indiscrete pardons."[27]

Likewise, John relied on the arguments of the French Dominican Peter Paludanus, the influential Dominican theologian, apologist, and papal court theologian, who in his commentary on the *Sentences* of Peter Lombard (written between 1310 and 1315) also upheld the ordinary right of bishops to dispense indulgences. Peter's argument appealed to common church practices. By their ordinary power, bishops delegate to Dominicans and other religious orders the right to grant indulgences, yet "something delegated by the prince in those things which belong to the faith are not able to be subdelegated. But bishops empower preachers to grant indulgences. Therefore the bishop is ordinary in the dispensation of indulgences. Moreover, the law gives ordinary jurisdiction, yet it is by law that a bishop grants forty days of pardon."[28] Bishops, then, granted remissions by the authority that inhered in their status as bishops, rather than by a special privilege from the pope, and have full power to grant others the privilege of conceding indulgences. The pardons, then, which the bishops gave to Dominican convents were fully legitimate.

Still, the pope was head of the universal Church, and had proclaimed legislation that limited episcopal dispensations of remission. By what canonistic argument could such canons be understood? John noted that bishops receive ecclesiastical powers from the pope in two ways:

> Something can be received from the pope in two ways, namely, either through merit or privilege, or by an appropriation in canon law which is given through the pope. The bishops cannot possess the first way by ordinary authority because they receive it from the pope as an extraordinary power. Yet they are well able [to exercise] by ordinary authority what they receive in the second way. And in this second way bishops receive from the pope the power to grant indulgences or letters of indulgence.[29]

The authority to grant indulgences comes not from a privilege, which by its nature is extraordinary, but from papal appointment to an episcopal see. John's reasoning resulted from the canonists' suggestion that a bishop's authority had two distinct elements, the first of which, in the case of a vacancy, devolved to inferiors (the chapter), and the second of which passed to a superior (the pope), namely, whatever powers consecration conferred.[30] In discussing the relationship between bishops and the pope, canonists generally described both as having the fullness of power (*plena potestatis* or *plenitudo potestatis*), with the important distinction that the pope exercises his authority over the universal Church, but a bishop only in his own diocese. Consequently, bishops could grant indulgences in their dioceses; the pope anywhere in the Christian world. Nonetheless, the comparison was crucial, since it implied that the bishop was like unto the pope within the borders of his diocese.

The first *quaestio* of *De quantitate indulgenciarum*, then, repeated commonly accepted ideas about the basic unit of church government—the diocese presided over by the bishop. At the same time, however, this *quaestio* also served as the foundation upon which John constructed the rest of the arguments in his treatise. The succeeding eleven *quaestiones* addressed practical concerns with regard to the concession of indulgences, as well as ongoing debates over ancient and recent church laws regulating the dispensation of pardons. In *quaestio* two, for instance, he confronted the issue of whether a bishop could "grant indulgences to his subjects who were outside of the diocese,"[31] and in *quaestio* three, he considered "whether a bishop is able to give indulgences not only to his own subjects, but also to others, that is, to the subjects of other bishops, with at least the consent and approval of those bishops."[32] Behind these *quaestiones* were the making of pilgrimages to distant dioceses. Could a bishop grant indulgences to his subjects for visiting a shrine outside his diocese? What about the subjects of other bishops who came to his diocese on pilgrimage? Church authorities addressed these questions with a practical simplicity. To be sure, the council of Aquileia (1339) criticized bishops for granting indulgences to those who did not belong to their jurisdictions: "And they grant indulgences not only in the churches of their own jurisdiction, but also in foreign churches, not only to penitents in their presence, but others besides."[33] The council, however, called not for an end to such grants, only that they be approved by other bishops:

> Moreover, we proclaim that no patriarch or archbishop presume to grant any indulgence outside his diocese, unless one of his subjects shall go to a foreign church, and the diocesan or metropolitan of that diocese grant permission [to receive it in that foreign diocese]. If some prelate should transgress the remission aforesaid, or shall grant any place indulgence outside his jurisdiction, we deprive him of the authority of granting indulgences for one month.[34]

The council, echoing Lateran IV, added that unless moderation were observed in the granting of indulgences, ordinary believers might come to hold them in contempt.[35]

As for John of Dambach, he agreed that bishops could exercise jurisdiction over their subjects in foreign dioceses. His argument compared a diocese with a town (*civitas*). As the canonist Johannes Monachus (1250–1313), a cardinal and advocate of the authority of the College of Cardinals, had already remarked, the decretal *Si civitas* of Boniface VIII made clear that an interdict imposed on a town included the town's suburbs and surrounding countryside. Thus, by a town is understood an association of persons, "since a town is a unity of citizens."[36] While in Strasbourg, for instance, a citizen of Basel remains a citizen of Basel. In the same way, no matter where one of his subjects may happen to be, a bishop may exercise jurisdiction over that subject, since "no polity by the name of towns or of a diocese is understood to be the walls or a plot of ground, but are most commonly able and ought to be understood as associations or as the persons of the towns and diocese."[37] Persons, not walls or plots, were subject to the authority of bishops, and so, for instance, no matter where Strassburgers might go, the authority of the bishop of Strasbourg went with them.

John also argued that a bishop could grant pardon to the subjects of other bishops, since in three cases bishops customarily exercised jurisdiction over the subjects of other prelates. First, canon law already recognized that "in matters of disputed jurisdictions, one is able to be judged by someone other than his bishop, with the permission of his own bishop."[38] Consequently, a citizen of Basel should be able to receive an indulgence from the bishop of Strasbourg, if the bishop of Basel consented. Second, since many bishops were absent from their dioceses for long periods of time—like those who accompanied crusaders— "a foreign bishop is able to consecrate a church in the diocese of another bishop with the consent of the same. Therefore, a foreign bishop is able to grant remission to the subjects of another bishop with the consent of that bishop."[39] Finally, with the permission of their rector, a priest may absolve the subjects of another priest; so also may bishops, with the proper permission, grant pardon to the subjects of another bishop.[40] These three cases—to which no serious objections had ever been raised— prove that bishops licitly exercise jurisdiction over Catholics not ordinarily subject to them. A bishop therefore may licitly grant remissions to the subjects of another bishop, if the said bishop consents.

THE MAGNITUDE OF INDULGENCES

With *quaestiones* four through six, John proceeded to the consideration of another set of issues, canons, and jurists. While no one would have disputed a bishop's authority to grant indulgences to his own subjects, or, with their permission, to the subjects of other bishops, still canon law limited the magnitude of the partial indulgences that bishops could grant. The concession of collective indulgences, such as those granted to the Austrian Cistercian house of Heiligenkreuz in 1327 and 1328, however, seemed to violate the canons that limited episcopal remissions. In a collective indulgence, a number of prelates granted remission all at the same time. Pardons also added up as over the generations prelates granted indulgence to the same convent again and again. The case of the Basel Dominicans, among others, illustrates that many churches, monasteries, and convents had by the mid-fourteenth century petitioned for and received a number of indulgences. But the decree of Lateran IV, *Cum ex eo*, declared that

> because the keys of the church are brought into contempt, and satisfaction through penance loses its force through indiscriminate and excessive indulgences, which certain prelates of churches do not fear to grant, we therefore decree that when a basilica is dedicated, the indulgence shall not be for more than one year, whether it is dedicated by one bishop or by more than one, and, for the anniversary of the dedication, the remission of penances is not to exceed forty days.[41]

Thirteenth-century provincial councils, such as Narbonne (1227), Mainz (1233), and Tarragona (1239), among others, reaffirmed *Cum ex eo*, as did the decree *Indulgentiae* of Boniface VIII.[42] *Cum ex eo* retained its authority well into the fourteenth century. A provincial council that met in Aquileia in 1339 chastised bishops for granting remissions greater than the canons allowed: "For those bishops, amply exceeding the rule established by the sacred canons, bestow indulgences lavishly on them to whom concession is made."[43] A provincial synod that met in Padua the following year repeated that any pardons which violated *Cum ex eo* were *ipso facto* null and void.[44] Clearly, the issue of supernumerary indulgences needed to be addressed.

As Dominican apologist, then, John's task was to demonstrate whether *Cum ex eo* invalidated any indulgences given to the Friars Preachers. In the fourth *quaestio* of *De quantitate indulgenciarum*, he considered whether "pardons which were granted either by one bishop alone or by a number acting together—with the permission of the diocesan bishop, in whose diocese the indulgences were to be available—either for the dedication of a church or for its anniversary or for other pious reasons, are valid in part or completely, if they exceed the statute of Lateran IV, but were given before the meeting of that council."[45] John replied that any such pardons, all of which would have been granted before 1215, were entirely valid, "so long as at the same time they be not notably excessive. The reason is that the statute of the council does not apply to those things which antedate the council, before which the bishops were able to grant great pardons, as the council stated." John may here be thought to be pondering a purely academic question, because the vast majority of Dominican indulgences postdated the council, the order itself having been formally sanctioned by Pope Honorius III in 1216. However, the repetition of *Cum ex eo* by numerous provincial councils, and the commentaries on the canon by the decretalists, attest to its efficacy and could be used to argue against the validity of many indulgences conferred *after*

Lateran IV. In this *quaestio*, in contrast, John resorted to an old principle of both Roman and canon law, which was that the law could neither prohibit nor punish actions taken *before* the promulgation of that law.[46]

More problematic for John was the legality of the many collective indulgences granted since Lateran IV, in particular those granted towards the close of the thirteenth century, an issue that concerned the interests not only of Dominicans but also other religious orders, as well as diocesan churches and clergy. For example, the formidable Pope Boniface VIII proclaimed the first Jubilee in response to the eschatological expectations as the year 1300 approached. As millenial expectations intensified penitential piety, cardinals and titular prelates flooded Western Christendom with new collective indulgences.[47]

The efficacy of the numerous remissions dispensed over the course of the thirteenth century was a topic John of Dambach had to address. In *quaestio* five of *De quantitate indulgenciarum*, he considered "whether pardons, granted after Lateran IV but before the promulgation of the *Liber sextus*, which exceeded the intention and statute of the council were yet entirely valid."[48] Once again, John answered affirmatively, unless such remissions were notably immoderate (*notabiliter immoderate*). Rather than explain that vague phrase, John observed that *Cum ex eo*, like so much law in the Roman and canon law traditions, invalidated only the grossest infractions because the decretal contained no procedures for any cancellations of indulgences: "The reason [*Cum ex eo* does not cancel them] is if they were no longer valid, this would be because of a prohibition of the council. But the decree contains no prohibition of the council."[49] The decree of the council imposed guidelines on the bishops, but contained no protocol for the nullification of supernumerary remissions.

Whether the papal decree *Indulgentiae* nullified any pardons granted since its promulgation in 1298 was another question. The sixth *quaestio* of *De quantitate indulgenciarum* explored "whether indulgences granted for a church dedication, or any other pious reason, not only after Lateran IV but also after the promulgation of the *Liber sextus*, contrary to the intention of the council, are valid at least in part."[50] This *quaestio* essentially repeated the argument of the fifth *quaestio*, but at the same time allowed that an indulgence might be cancelled only in part, for its language hinted that *Indulgentiae* cancelled only the supernumerary part of a pardon, for instance, if an indulgence was for sixty days, only twenty would be removed from that pardon. John observed that while the canonist Johannes Monachus believed that any excessive pardon was completely invalid, two other commentators on the *Liber sextus* had a different view.[51] Guido de Baysio (c. 1250–1313), known as "the "Archdeacon," whose commentary on the *Liber sextus* enjoyed great popularity, and Johannes Andreae, differed with Johannes Monachus. Guido "believed true the more generous opinion," namely, that such pardons were valid "at least in that part or number of days which bishops have long been able to grant legitimately," which, of course, meant forty days of pardon.[52] Johannes Andreae likewise argued that *Indulgentiae* invalidated only that part of any remission which exceeded the intention of Lateran IV. As John of Dambach wrote: "according to Johannes Andreae, for whom an excessive pardon granted contrary to the intention of the council has its days or parts, each one separable, the valid able to be separated from the invalid, and so the useful, by the power of the council, and moreso by the name of the law, that is, by the decretal *Indulgentiae*."[53] Such arguments had ancient precedents in Roman law, where the jurists attempted to sort out whether water supplies, herds, and fields could or should be separated. For instance, if a shepherd who could by law graze twenty sheep in a meadow grazed twenty-five, should he lose the rights to graze all twenty-five, or just for the five he was not licensed to graze? The answer was generally that violators should not lose all their rights but should be restricted to their legal access to water, herds, and fields.[54]

OVERLAPPING JURISDICTIONS?

In the next set of *quaestiones* (seven through nine) in *De quantitate indulgenciarum*, John of Dambach discussed the magnitude of indulgences granted collectively by various ranks in the church hierarchy to the same site: "The seventh question is whether—if to the same convent a diocesan bishop grants forty days of pardon, and an archbishop another forty days, and on one and the same day—it is read in a letter of such indulgence at one and the same place, the penitent giving alms may in this case receive eighty days."[55] The canons and the arithmetic piety characteristic of era suggested this *quaestio*. In his answer, John observed that visitation indulgences rarely demanded almsgiving, although piety often persuaded the pilgrims to contribute money. Instead, the pardons only required that prayers be offered, and therefore visitation indulgences gave penitents an incalculable benefit, namely, the removal of the debt of sin. Such an indulgence, therefore, belonged more properly to the visitors than to the Dominicans' church:

> Suppose that in Dominicans' shrines that although such a place may be visited, or a visitor gives money to it because of the indulgence, still, that indulgence is not acquired by the convent, but by the subjects of the grantor or grantors. Consequently, the bishop of Basel is able to give forty days to his subjects for going to the convent and contributing to the Dominicans' church, just as for going to town to the cathedral church.[56]

The magnitude of remissions, then, could be used to measure and compare their efficacy. The greater the remission, the more powerful and profitable the pardon. Pilgrims had to decide which churches, monasteries, and convents were worth their while, and they must have weighed such factors as distance, safety, and the power of the indulgence, that is, pardons *competed with each other.*

Grantors, then, were tempted to augment their indulgences' magnitudes and make them more attractive than other pardons, yet abide by such church decrees as *Cum ex eo.* One way obviously was for different ranks in the hierarchy to cooperate in the proclamation of a collective indulgence, as, for instance, *quaestio* seven suggests. If a bishop and archbishop both grant indulgence of forty days to a Dominican convent, how should the magnitude of that remission be calculated? Neither of the prelates contributed more than forty days, the standard partial remission as laid down by Lateran IV. Numerous proclamations clearly show that virtually all of the prelates who participated in collective indulgences honored the dictates of *Cum ex eo.*[57] In such indulgences, each prelate contributed but forty days' remission. However, as the example of the Zara and Basel Dominicans, among others, illustrates, the preachers of these indulgences ordinarily announced the *sum* of the pardons to pilgrims who visited their convents. That total would then amount to much more than forty days of remission.

Did that preaching of indulgences violate canon law? Not at all, argued John, for according to Hostiensis, a penitent could receive eighty days of remission, "if the grant is made with the provision that the pardons of neither the bishop nor the archbishop exceeded [the statute of Lateran IV]."[58] John added that "just like a bishop in his diocese, so an archbishop is able to grant pardon of forty days throughout his province by ordinary authority."[59] Indeed, the decree of Pope Honorius III, *Nostro postulasti,* confirmed that archbishops had the right to dispense pardons throughout their provinces: "you are freely able to grant letters of indulgence throughout your province, so long as you do not exceed the statute of the general council."[60] Since penitents were subject to a number of hierarchs, they could licitly receive indulgences from each one.

John continued further that Johannes Andreae's comments on the decretal *Romana ecclesia* likewise upheld the archbishop's authority to grant pardons throughout his province. Pope Innocent IV had promulgated that decree in response to a lengthy argument between the archbishop of Rheims and his suffragans. In the 1220s, the archbishop hired itinerant preachers (*quaestores*) to announce an indulgence for the building of a church. When those preachers entered the dioceses of his suffragan bishops, they had compelled the people to hear their sermons. The suffragans complained to Pope Honorius (1216–1227) that the actions of these preachers amounted to a violation of episcopal power. The case dragged on until Innocent IV ruled on it in the bull *Romana ecclesia* (March 17, 1245). Innocent declared that while the *quaestores* of the archbishop certainly could preach in the dioceses of his suffragans, and while they could grant pardon to the subjects of the suffragans, the preachers could not compel those subjects to attend their sermons. *Romana ecclesia* also reaffirmed that archbishops must abide the limitations on indulgences laid down by Lateran IV.[61] Johannes Andreae commented that *Romana ecclesia* "was a case in which the archbishop wielded jurisdiction over the subjects of his suffragans."[62] Finally, John added that *Cum ex eo* only limited the size of archiepiscopal indulgences, not the archbishop's jurisdiction over the subjects of his suffragans:

> Besides, the council limited diocesan bishops, of whom it alone speaks, who are not empowered outside their dioceses to grant indulgence to the subjects of another diocesan without the licence of that diocesan. But it does not follow, nor is it true, that the council limited archbishops, whom it does not mention, and who *without the licence of the diocesan* are able to grant remissions as much as diocesan bishops, although they too are limited because they cannot exceed the statute of Lateran IV, because they do not when archbishops themselves do not grant more than a year for the dedication of a church, and forty days for its anniversary, and other feasts.[63]

John employed the same principle in *quaestio* eight of *De quantitate indulgenciarum*, where he examined the magnitude of pardons proclaimed collectively by legates and bishops: "The eighth question is whether if a diocesan bishop in his diocese grants a pardon of forty days to some convent for a certain reason, and a legate *a latere*, whose legation extends to that diocese, grants [pardons to] the same convent, for the same reason, that legate is able to add another forty days of indulgences."[64] John here applied the decree of Pope Gregory IX, *Nemini dubium*, which proclaimed that "the statutes and edicts of the legates of the Apostolic See shall stand in the provinces committed to them as if they were perpetual, although the same legates have likewise afterwards departed [their legatine mission]."[65] So, whatever a legate had granted to a convent was perpetually valid because of the papal authority invested in that legate, regardless of what the benefit happened to be: "[those remissions] are valid forever, just like a statute, for although administration is temporal, whatever is enacted by a legate is perpetual."[66] Furthermore, noted John of Dambach, legates possess a jurisdiction similar to archbishops, who like legates preside over provinces: "this legate *a latere* is able [to grant indulgences] in the province committed to him like an archbishop in his province."[67] Unlike archbishops, however, the authority legates wield comes from the universal authority of the Apostolic See.

Besides, continued John, none of the canons which regulate the dispensation of indulgences are relevant to the jurisdiction of the legate:

> Since none of these canons contains any mention of the restriction of legates, then a legate *a latere*, excepting something reserved to the pope, is as if another pope, and he represents the person of the pope, of the vicar of Christ in the province commissioned to him. Consequently, understand that diocesan bishops or even archbishops may be limited in this way or that by the council in the granting of pardons, but it may not be said, nor is it true, that the council intended that legates *a latere* should be limited as much as diocesan bishops, just as it did not limit the pope.[68]

In no way, then, could the jurisdiction of the bishop and the legate impede one another. When bishop and legate granted to a convent forty days of indulgence—like the actual example of Hugh of St. Cher and the bishop of Basel—eighty days were in fact available. These pardons could not be considered supernumerary; nor could they be *ipso facto* cancelled.

The ninth *quaestio* of *De quantitate indulgenciarum* touched on a thornier canonistic problem: "The ninth question is whether more than one bishop, even if they amount to one hundred or one thousand, either at the same time or successively, may grant pardons to be sought after to the same place and for the same reason, such that each of them grants forty days of pardons to be sought after there."[69] Unlike the previous cases, which dealt with different ranks in the ecclesiastical hierarchy, all these grantors of indulgence belonged to the same rank. Since each bishop could by his ordinary authority grant forty days of pardon, each of his subjects who might visit the so-favored convent received that much remission: "As there may be one hundred bishops and each grants a pardon of forty days to be sought at the convent of the Dominicans in Basel for the feast of St. Dominic, each subject of whichever of those bishops, by visiting the church of the Dominicans in that city on the day of that feast, receives a remission of forty days . . . as follows from what was said in the first and second questions."[70] John continued that all these bishops, whether at the same time, as in the case of a collective indulgence, or over the course of the generations, as had taken place at Basel, could contribute forty days of pardon,

> because it is not the intention of [*Cum ex eo*] that all indulgences able to be given together at the same time by bishops for visiting such a place on such a feast, or for some similar reason, do not exceed the number expressed in *Cum ex eo*, but that they do not exceed the number for each grantor, for then those pardons are not excessive or unnecessary or indiscrete . . . to each subject of those bishops, for visiting such a convent on such a feast only receives so much pardon as his bishop gave to the place, that

is, only so much as the forty days contributed by his own bishop, which number does not exceed the number expressed by Lateran IV.[71]

In this case, then, the logic of the canons, not to mention his own argument, compelled John to admit that penitents could receive remission only from their *proprii iudices*, which as he had shown in *quaestiones* seven through nine of *De quantitate indulgenciarum*, meant their own diocesan bishop, the archbishop of their province, and the papal legate assigned to their province, and whomever else might have received license to do so.

THE EFFICACY OF THE CANONS AND "ARITHMETIC PIETY"

The last three *quaestiones* of *De quantitate indulgenciarum* offer further proof of the continuing efficacy of the canons that regulated the dispensation of indulgences. The tenth *quaestio* served as a commentary on two decrees:

> The tenth question is whether indulgences, given in accord with the intention of the council [Lateran IV] or the statute *Cum ex eo*, by several bishops to the same place and for the same reason, are profitable for all those for whom their lawful judges indulged them spiritually, so that these indulgences would profit them, whether the lawful judges belong to the number of grantors of such indulgences or not.[72]

This *quaestio* not only invoked *Cum ex eo* once again but also revisited an older decree, *Quod autem*, of Pope Alexander III (1159–1181). *Quod autem* was Alexander's response to an inquiry from the archbishop of Canterbury. The pope informed the archbishop that penitents could receive indulgence not only from their ecclesiastical superiors but also from those whom their ecclesiastical superiors had licensed:

> Because you have asked whether remissions, which are granted for the building of churches, or to contributors to the building of bridges, are of benefit to those who are other than the subjects of the grantors, we firmly declare that Your Fraternity hold that, since no one may be validly bound or absolved except by the one in authority over him, we judge the previously mentioned remissions to be profitable only to those for whom the proper judges have specially indulged to be profitable.[73]

Alexander thus allowed that bishops might permit their subjects to receive an indulgence dispensed by another bishop. By proclaiming that subjects receive the permission of their ordinary before obtaining indulgences proclaimed by other bishops, Alexander gave his approved pardon extended to those who contributed to the building of churches and bridges, but whose own bishops had not conceded the indulgence, and at the same time reaffirmed episcopal authority over the reception of these remissions. For the sake of right order in the church, bishops had to have supervision over piety.

Clearly, sensitive pastoral issues were at stake here, not to mention the credibility of the church. As John wrote, "it would be a great deception if [the indulgences] were only profitable to those who are subject to the grantors, since the subjects of many different bishops seek the indulgences."[74] As with the first proclamation of indulgence for the dead in 1343, church authorities were probably trying to catch up with piety. The legions of pilgrims who availed themselves of pilgrimage indulgences must have arrived from many different dioceses ruled by bishops who had had no hand in the proclamation of the pardon, but like the formal dispensors, most of them probably wanted the benefits of the indulgence offered to as many as possible. Pilgrims' requests for permission to benefit from indulgences their diocesans had no hand in granting must lurk behind John's arguments as well, for the prelates and the pilgrims held the same ideas about the power of indulgences to prepare confessed and contrite Catholics for the afterlife.

John of Dambach argued, then, that a bishop could permit his subjects to receive an indulgence even though his name did not appear on the document proclaiming the indulgence—a "spiritual" pardon, in the language of John's *quaestio* and of *Quod autem*. John argued that since the law did not explicitly prevent bishops from allowing their subjects to receive indulgences that they had not formally granted, the law could not be interpreted as preventing the bishops from doing so:

> I say that they are [able to spiritually indulge their subjects], because where the law does not distinguish, neither ought we to distinguish, as is clear from the laws. If the law vaguely says that these remissions, which are granted to pilgrims for the dedications of churches, or to the contributors to the building of a bridge, are profitable for pilgrims and benefactors such that the lawful judges indulge them spiritually, as it says in . . . *Quod autem*, and it is the same reason for those indulgences, which according to the intention of the council, are given for other pious reasons as well. Therefore, indulgences are profitable to all indistinctly for whom the lawful judges have indulged spiritually, such that the indulgences may be beneficial.[75]

The observation that no distinctions should be made where the law made no distinctions (in this case between the remissions granted by the prelates who contributed to the collective indulgence) may be taken as an invocation of an important principle of the Roman law, which had long since been adopted into canon law, namely, that interpretations of law could be certain only where the legislation was certain. Where the law was mute or vague, the text could be construed quite reasonably in a number of different ways. Thus, John took a generous view of it, also in accord with canonical rules of interpretation, for in a passing reference to *A nobis*, a decree of Pope Clement III (1187) on the sentence of excommunication, John argued that that canon "speaks of the sentence of excommunication, which belongs to the number of ecclesiastical penalties, which are quite vexatious and ought to be restrained. It is otherwise with indulgences, which are agreeable, and so should be augmented."[76] At the same time, indulgences granted in this way were, as he stated, "indistinct" and therefore conferred spiritual benefits upon the pilgrims differently than a grant of pardon given to them by their own diocesan bishop.

Not only could bishops indulge the subjects of other diocesans "spiritually," but each of the bishops participating in a collective remission contributed the fully permissible amount of pardon, that is, forty days:

> The eleventh question is whether several bishops are able to grant indulgences to the same place and for the same reason with the licence and approval of the diocesan bishop, so that each of them gives by himself forty days distinct from any other forty days granted by another bishop. I say that they are, so long as all those indulgences are at the same time not excessive.[77]

Since *Quod autem* permitted that a bishop could allow his subjects to be indulgenced by a prelate other than himself, "he is able to consent, licence, and approve that other bishops may grant to [his own subjects] indulgences which are not contrary to the intention of the council, by which licence and approval the remissions are in this way an available benefit."[78] John thus reasoned that preachers who pointed out entire sums of remissions available at indulgenced convents were acting legally, so long as each bishop granted only forty days: "But that there are several bishops, of whom each himself gives forty days of pardon—distinct from any other forty days given by his collaborators—to the same place and for the same reason, does not transgress the intention of the council, but is wholly in accord with the intention."[79] The last phrase here is noteworthy. Not only is the remission granted by each bishop separate from all the remissions granted by other bishops, but to think of the pardons in this way was more in agreement with the intent of Lateran IV than to think otherwise!

De quantitate indulgenciarum closes with its twelfth *quaestio*. In it, John of Dambach concluded his treatise by considering whether all indulgences granted in accordance with *Cum ex eo* could be received "spiritually" by those pilgrims whose diocesan bishops had not given indulgence to the church or convent they visited:

> The twelfth question is whether several bishops are able to grant indulgences either at the same time or successively, to the same place for the same reason, so that each of them gives by himself one year for the dedication of a church, or forty days for other pious places and reasons; all those indulgences may be profitable so that the indulgences may be profitable for those whom the lawful judges have indulged spiritually.[80]

Of course, he answered in the affirmative: "I say that they are, whether those judges had been among the grantors of the pardon or not, so long as the remission of years or of days is not excessive."[81]

John's explanation of that answer owed everything to the arithmetic piety of his day. A negative answer to the *quaestio*, for instance, would have meant that many, perhaps most pilgrims, were wasting their time. Since John allowed that the remissions would only have been invalid if "excessive," an important subsidiary issue involved the definition of an excessive indulgence. Was it excessive to add up the remissions available at a given pilgrimage destination? If so, did a bishop's power to grant pardon become eviscerated in some way when he chose to participate in a grant of collective remission, that is, in order to remain under the limitation of forty days, were these bishops prevented from contributing forty days of pardon? John argued that that could not be the case:

> When it is said if each of the number of bishops is each able to give forty days, and so on, then indulgences given by more than one bishop, in an instance in which more than one bishop participates, they exceed several years, [and are therefore supernumerary]; I say that in this case it is not necessarily so, because the present question does not ask about a precise, especially very great plurality of bishops. Whence it is enough by way of answer to the question that it is able to be examined with regard to a plurality of three bishops or of two, because according to the rule of law, *two is enough to call a plurality*, and if each of this plurality gives forty days they are nothing other than eighty, or if of three bishops each gives forty, they are nothing other than one hundred [*sic*], and neither of these numbers exceeds several years, nor even one year, even if there are eight bishops.[82]

John continued that if the remission of a collective indulgence due to any recipient cannot be the sum of the individual contributions, then the remission is no more profitable than that granted by one bishop. If the total remission available in any one collective indulgence may be no more than forty days, the power of the indulgence was dissipated and therefore unprofitable to penitents:

> It seems inconvenient spiritually in Hostiensis's argument that they can divide up the pardon as the bishops see fit, because if out of one year of pardon each bishop gives his own portion to a number of days of remission, then no one bishop gives forty days. Therefore, the subjects of none of the bishops are able to receive the stipulated forty days of pardon except the subjects of the diocesan, who permits another bishop to grant the indulgence [in his diocese] and his own subjects to receive it . . . [if the pardon is so divided] a bishop only gives one day if the bishops number forty, or two days if they are twenty, or four days if they are ten, and so on in proportional terms. But that such a subject of the participating bishops does not receive forty days, but only as much as one or two or four, is mistaken.[83]

John, the writer of a treatise on the *power* of indulgences (*De virtute indulgenciarum*), could not accept that the efficacy of such a beneficial ministration of the church could or should be diluted. He contended that such an assertion must plainly be false, otherwise collective indulgences

> are given in error because they are given without spiritual usefulness . . . and thus the plurality of the grantors is not profitable to the pilgrims such that the indulgences are profitable to those whom their own authority has indulged spiritually. But this is plainly against the intention of the decretal *Quod autem*.[84]

The logic of the metaphor of the treasury of merit concurred that a pardon granted by more than one bishop should be more powerful than one granted by a bishop acting alone: "but further it is contrary to reason that indulgences given by a plurality, all other things being equal, should not be more profitable than indulgences granted by one alone."[85] John's thinking here could well be attributable to a habitual reliance on the ancient traditions of the church, which taught that the efficacy of the ministrations and petitions of the whole Church—as in the Mass, where the Church Militant and the Church Triumphant were joined in praise of the Holy Trinity—exceeded the power of other intercessions. A collective indulgence should have more power, more efficacy, than an indulgence conceded by a bishop acting alone.

Considerations other than the authority of bishops and the credibility of the Church Militant also had to be weighed here. John noted the gravity of human sinfulness as well. Even if he was right about the calculation of collective pardons, they could not be deemed scandalously supernumerary, much less excessive and contradictory to the canons, relative to the weighty consequences of human sin:

> Now should it be thought a great deed if six bishops participate (of whom each having given one year, the pardons should not be excessive), for on account of which the keys of the church are brought into contempt and penitential satisfaction compromised? Contempt and compromise of such a kind is *more* prominent in pardons given by several popes, of whom one is said to remit a seventh part of penance, another a third, perhaps another a half—in seeking several such indulgences one may be able to be liberated from all his sins![86]

The magnitude of the papal pardons dwarfs those of the collective indulgences, but no one has denounced them! For good reason, as even remissions vastly greater than what John was considering fell far short of cancelling the entire debt of sin: "Nor should it be thought [excessive] if six or seven bishops grant one year, because such a pardon does not remove the debt of sin resulting from *one* mortal sin, since for each mortal sin one is responsible for at least *seven* years of penance; according to the laws, five of such sins committed by one man constitutes an infinite debt of sin."[87] The spiritual accounts were generally far in the red.

Finally, John continued, the canonists differ concerning the accounting of collective indulgences. Johannes Monachus, Bernard of Bottone, and Guido de Baysio all contradict one another. Besides, the fame and reputation of these doctors do not compel assent:

> Howsoever great a doctor argues something, his opinion ought not to be troubled over, unless he proves it through the canons or scriptural authority. But that this one's opinion, or that of Bernard, or of whatever other doctors who agree with him on this matter, are correct, and those opposed wrong, is in this way not able to be convincing concerning the canons of Lateran IV with which these doctors are preoccupied, the text of which is able to be rationally explained by a different argument.[88]

Since the leading juristic authorities reasonably subjected the canons to a variety of interpretations, John of Dambach could argue that his own view fell within the frontiers of accepted thinking.

How the controversy ended—that first prompted John of Dambach to write *De quantitate indulgenciarum* and, for that matter, possibly also compelled him to write its theological counterpart, *De virtute indulgenciarum*— cannot be known with certainty, although a probable reconstruction may be imagined. *De quantitate indulgenciarum* was written in the midst of great turmoil within the German Church. The dispute over the imperial succession, and Pope John XXII's intervention in it, exacerbated tensions between mendicant and secular clergy that had existed prior to the conflict. By the latter half of the thirteenth century, the mendicants had worn out their welcome in many German cities. In 1283, the Strasbourg *Rat*, angered by the Dominicans' acquisition of real estate in the city, limited the amount of land the friars could either purchase or receive as a pious donation. While the Franciscans accepted the decision of the *Rat*, the Dominicans refused, and violence broke out between the townsmen and the friars in 1286. That encounter led the papal legate John of Tusculum to impose an interdict on the city, and the Dominicans voluntarily went into exile. This dispute only ended in 1290, when the bishop of the city, Conrad, intervened and mediated an agreeable settlement between the *Rat* and the Dominicans.[89]

Ill will towards the Friars Preachers nonetheless persisted. The German Dominicans were collectively assailed again in the later 1320s when their great mystical theologian Meister Eckhart came under suspicion for heresy. John of Dambach both witnessed and participated in Eckhart's trial, for he signed the *Rechtsfertigungschrift* (document of vindication), presented to the investigating tribunal on Eckhart's behalf.[90] In this document, Eckhart denied that he had taught anything heretical but acknowledged that he may have unwittingly proposed "erroneous" ideas, which he would freely submit to the discipline of the church. The *Rechtsfertigungschrift* seems to have been at least partly effective, since the tribunal acquitted Eckhart. The judges nonetheless commanded that he recant those of his teachings which the tribunal judged erroneous. The chief lesson John may have learned from Eckhart's trial was that a well-crafted, brief apology might be a very effective defense of fellow Dominicans, their mission, and their interests. Indeed, over the next several decades, John of Dambach wrote a number of short treatises, which included *De quantitate indulgenciarum*, dedicated to the defense of his order.[91] That John's canonistic discussion of indulgences came in the form of the first independent treatise on the subject highlights its polemical, rather than academic, purposes. *De quantitate indulgenciarum*, like John's other short treatises, was then the product of a narrow time and space. The death of Pope John XXII in 1334, the deposition of Ludwig of Bavaria in 1346, and the accession of the Luxembourg Emperor Charles IV (1346–1378) that same year, signaled the beginning of reconciliation between the antagonists in the German Church. The old irritation that the papal-imperial rivalry intensified perhaps lingered a bit longer.

John of Dambach and his adversaries probably never appeared in a court to present arguments before Church authorities; indeed, according to John, the accusations came not from bishops or legates but from private persons learned in the law (*iurisperiti*). A plaintiff's "activation" of the law was a revered tradition of Roman law.[92] Lawbreakers were indicted not by a grand jury but by private citizens who brought violators to the attention of the authorities. Each side was then granted the time and opportunity to make a case. Many medieval legal disputes went on for years and came before several different courts and authorities. Many cases simply faded away as plaintiffs and defendants lost money or interest. The case involving John of Dambach and his brother Dominicans was most likely just such an instance. He was probably right in depicting the accusations of illegal preaching of indulgences as a settling of scores on the part of the Dominicans' enemies within the divided German Church of the days of Ludwig and Pope John.

The arguments of both John of Dambach and his opponents were entirely self-serving. The south German Dominicans on whose behalf John wrote benefitted much from the numerous indulgences granted their convents. The *iurisperiti* would have handicapped the mission of the Friars Preachers by reducing those benefits. They seem to have had little motivation other than harming the interests of Dominicans, for they raised no concerns about indulgences being a threat to penitential fervor, as they well could have done, since the text of *Cum ex eo* certainly did. Nor did they suggest that the numerous penitents who visited churches and monasteries to gain the indulgences available at those sites were ignorant of the proper protocol for the efficacious reception of indulgences. No other contemporary sources mention irregularities with Dominican preaching of indulgences, whether in south Germany or elsewhere; indeed, the provenance of the manuscripts suggests that the geographic extent of the argument encompassed only a fraction of the German province, namely, the region of the upper Rhine valley, with Strasbourg as the northern frontier and Basel the southern. The *iurisperiti* directed their complaints not at the pardons but at the friars. Such bickering, akin to the antagonisms between mendicant and secular, Franciscan and Dominican, Schoolmen and humanists, plagued the late medieval church and was as scandalous then as it appears today.

At the same time, self-serving statements and arguments need not necessarily be false, unpopular, or damaging to the common good. Both John of Dambach and his opponents presented arguments that, considered sympathetically, also made sense within the world of the medieval religious imagination. John favored a liberal distribution of the treasury of merit, and he warned that spiritual accounts were bound to have far more debits than credits. The pilgrims who visited the Dominicans' shrines, and the bishops who bestowed indulgences upon them, shared John's desires. Likewise, the jurisdictional difficulties which John's opponents noted in the dispensation of collective indulgences were valid, but they did not prove persuasive. The winners, if such they were, in this dispute would have to be John of Dambach, the Dominicans, and the pilgrims to their convents, who, in the absence of authoritative judgments to the contrary, continued to preach and receive the pardons as they had been doing all along.

NOTES

1. John of Dambach, *De quantitate indulgenciarum*, introduction (Basel, Universitätsbibliothek MS C V 18, fol. 57ra): "Quoniam nonnunquam in quantitate indulgenciarum, quas ex concessione prelatorum fratres dant in predicacionibus et pronuncciant seu pronuncciari faciunt in suis festivitatibus, a quibusdam hoc minus favorabiliter interpretantibus inpingitur quasi fratres in hac parte faciant, quod non debent vel non possunt, idcirco pro excusacione fratrum intendo scribere tractatulum unum, si placet, de quantitate indulgenciarum nominandum, in quo sic procedam."

2. Basel, Universitätsbibliothek, C V 18, fols. 57–64v. This copy will be used for the subsequent discussion because of its date and clarity.

3. Heiligenkreuz MS 208, fol. 83v.

4. Heiligenkreuz, Stiftsbibliothek MS 216, fols. 19–32 is a fourteenth-century copy. Basel, Universitätsbibliothek MS A IV 22, fols. 309–320v, Krakow, Bibliothek Jagiell.

MS 1614, fols. 581–590v, Munich, Staatsbibliothek Clm 22373, fols. 69–80, and Nuremberg, Stadtbibliothek MS Cento I 80, fols. 81–87v are fifteenth-century manuscripts.

5. *Geschichte*, 1:257

6. No dates may be found in Kaeppeli, 2:403, in Iacobus Quetif and Iacobus Échard, eds., *Scriptores ordinis praedicatorum*, (Paris: J. B. C. Ballard, 1719), 1:667–670 or in Albert Auer, *Johannes von Dambach und die Trostbücher vom 11. bis zum 16. Jahrhundert*, Beiträge zur Geschichte der Philosophie und Theologie des Mittelalters 27 (Münster: Aschendorffsche Verlagsbuchhandlung, 1928), 31.

7. Delehaye, 333.

8. Luzian Pfleger, *Kirchengeschichte der Stadt Straßburg im Mittelalter* (Colmar: Alsatian Verlag, 1941), 111–114.

9. *Geschichte*, 2:53.

10. *UB Basel* 1:98, no. 141.

11. *UB Basel* 1:99, no. 143.

12. Innocent's indulgences may be found in *UB Basel* 1:172, no. 235. Albert's are contained in *UB Basel* 1:312, no. 425, and 2:15, no. 26.

13. G. Boner, "Das Predigerkloster in Basel von der Gründung bis zur Klosterreform, 1233–1429," *Basler Zeitschrift für Geschichte und Altertumskunde* 33 (1934), 296.

14. Boner, "Das Predigerkloster," 34 (1935), 182.

15. John of Dambach, *De quan. indul.*, q. 8 (Basel, Univ. C V 18, fols. 61ra–61rb): "Infero correlarium quod . . . de centum diebus indulgenciarum pro predicacione in area fratrum predicatorum in Basilea per papam, et de xl diebus pro eodem per episcopum Basiliensis dudum concessis, non debet esse questio, nec dubium, quando papa centum et episcopus xl poterunt concedere, nec de xx diebus concessis per dominum Tusculanum cardinalem legatum a latere. Prout hoc patet per bullam pape et litteras legati et episcopi predictorum, temerarium est in fratres inpingere, vel eos de hoc iudicare, quod inferioribus qui fiunt in area dant centum lx dies indulgenciarum."

16. John of Dambach, *De quan. indul.*, q. 12 (Basel, Univ. C V 18, fol. 64vb): "Facta fuit mencio presente Domino Hugone quondam tituli sancte sabine presbytero cardinali, qui cardinalis de eisdem indulgenciis in littera sigillo suo sigillata, que eciam habetur in conventu predicatorum in Basilea, iuxta ea que audivit a predicto papa, sic scribit inter alia: valent tamen huiusmodi indulgencie et iuste et racionabiles existunt, 'sicut idem summus pontifex vive vocis respondit oraculo,' et robur in se continent firmitatis quando de consensu dyocesani episcopi conceduntur."

17. *MOPH* 3:5 (Bologna, 1235): "Nullus frater per quamcumque potestatem sibi traditam faciat indulgenciam nisi secundum moderamen sui prioris provincialis."

18. *MOPH*, 3:47 (Trier, 1249).

19. *MOPH* 3:26 (Paris, 1243): "Fratres qui habent ab episcopis indulgencias in suis sermonibus faciendis in eodem die et in eodem loco non dent nisi semel indulgenciam si tamen duo praedicaverint: non det indulgenciam nisi unum."

20. *MOPH* 3:165 (Florence, 1249): "Iniungimus autem omnibus prioribus conventualibus ut modis omnibus provideant et procurent habere omnes indulgencias et privilegia bullata ad ordinem pertinencia in communi, vel saltem eorum transcripta sigillis authenticis sigillata, vel per manum publicam roborata."

21. *MOPH*, 4:368 (Pamplona, 1355), and *MOPH*, 4:373 (Verdun, 1356).

22. *MOPH*, 4:368 (Pamplona, 1355).

23. John of Dambach, *De quan. indul.*, q. 1 (Basel, Univ. C V 18, fol. 57ra): "Prima questio est utrum quilibet episcopus non ligatus possit dare de iure indulgencias xl dierum."

24. X 5.31.12 (*CIC* 2:840–841): "Accedentibus ad nos de diversis mundi partibus episcoporum querelis, intelleximus graves et grandes quorundam abbatum excessus, qui, suis finibus non contenti, manus ad ea, quae sunt episcopalis dignitatis, extendunt, de causis matrimonialibus cognoscendo, iniungendo publicas poenitentias, concedendo etiam indulgentiarum literas."

25. See Brian Tierney, *The Crisis of Church and State, 1050–1300* (Toronto: University of Toronto Press, 1988), 127–138.

26. John of Dambach, *De quan. indul.*, q. 1 (Basel, Univ. C V 18, fol. 57ra): "Hostiensis in *summa* . . . dicit quod episcopi per totam suam provinciam, id est, per total suam dyocesim, quantum ad simplices episcopos, '*generales* remissiones, que . . . *fiunt in predicacionibus, et per litteras pro edificandis vel reedificandis hospitalibus, ecclesiis, pontibus, vel aliis locis et causis, facere possunt [Summa 5, de remissionibus, Quis possit facere remissiones].*'"

27. John of Dambach, *De quan. indul.*, q. 1 (Basel, Univ. C V 18, fol. 57rb): "in quo prohibentur episcopi, ne in dedicacione ecclesie, dent ultra annum, et in aliis casibus ultra xl dies. Per quam prohibicionem restrictivam satis patet quod episcopi ante hoc statutum poterant dare indulgencias ampliores, et nonnumquam dederunt indiscretas sua potestate abutentes."

28. John of Dambach, *De quan. indul.*, q. 1 (Basel, Univ. C V 18, fol. 57rb): " '*Item delegatus a principe in his que sunt fidei non potest subdelegare. Sed episcopus committit predicatoribus dare indulgencias. Ergo etiam est ordinarius in hoc. Item, lex dat ordinariam jurisdictionem, sed a iure est quod episcopus dat xl dies*'." John here quotes Peter Paludanus, *Scriptum in IV sententiarum*, 4.20.4.2 (ed. Venice, 1493, 111vb).

29. John of Dambach, *De quan. indul.*, q. 1 (Basel, Univ. C V 18, fols. 57vb–58ra): "Aliquid potest haberi a papa dupliciter, videlicet, vel per merum privilegium vel mediante iure communi quod per papam est editum. Modo dato quod hec episcopi non possint auctoritate ordinaria quod primo modo habent a papa. Tamen quod habent a papa secundo modo bene possunt hec auctoritate ordinaria. Et hoc secundo modo habent episcopi a papa quod possunt indulgencias seu indulgenciarum litteras dare."

30. Brian Tierney, *Foundations of the Conciliar Theory: The Contributions of the Medieval Canonists from Gratian to the Great Schism* (Cambridge: Cambridge University Press, 1955), 128–129.

31. John of Dambach, *De quan. indul.*, q. 2 (Basel Univ. C V 18, fol. 58r): "Secunda questio est utrum episcopus possit dare indulgencias propriis subditis extra dyocesim suam."

32. John of Dambach, *De quan. indul.*, q. 3 (Basel, Univ. C V 18, fol. 58v): "Tercia questio est utrum episcopus possit dare indulgencias non solum suis propriis subditis, sed eciam alienis, id est, subditis aliorum episcoporum saltem de licencia consensu et approbacione ipsorum."

33. Mansi, 25:1119: "Et in haec non solum in suae jurisdictionis ecclesiis, sed etiam in alienis, non solum praesentes, sed etiam absentes attendant."

34. Mansi, 25:1119–1120: "Prohibemus autem, ut nullus patriarcha, vel archiepiscopus extra suam dioecesim quamlibet indulgentiam dare presumat, nisi praesens in aliena
ecclesia fuerit, et diocesani episcopi seu metropolitani consensus accedat. Si quis vero
praelatus supradictum numerum praefatas indulgentias concedendo transcenderit, aut
extra territorium suum indulgentiam quamlibet in absentia dederit, eum per unum mensem
concedendi indulgentias potestate privamus."

35. Mansi, 25:1119: "Hinc etiam fit, ut indulgentie dispensatorum prudentium
provida moderatione concessae in contemptu veniant ignoranti vulgo."

36. John of Dambach, *De quan. indul.*, q. 2 (Basel, Univ. C V 18, fol. 58rb): "Nam
extra *De sentencia excommunicacione, Si civitas*, libro vi, ubi dicitur: *si civitas castrum
aut villa subicitur ecclesiastico interdicto* [VI 5.11.17], ibi notat Johannes Monachus
quod civitas personas respicit, unde civitas civium unitas."

37. John of Dambach, *De quan. indul.*, q. 2 (Basel, Univ. C V 18, fol. 58va): "Nomine
igitur civitatum vel dyocesum nulla civitas est intelligere muros vel loca, sed commo-
dissime possunt et debent intelligeri universitates vel persone civitatum et dyocesum."

38. John of Dambach, *De quan. indul.*, q. 3 (Basel, Univ. C V 18, fol. 58vb): "quis in
foro contencioso iudicare possit a non suo iudice de consensu proprii iudicis." The
canon upon which this statement was based is X 2.2.18, *Significasti nobis* (*CIC* 2:255).

39. John of Dambach, *De quan. indul.*, q. 3 (Basel, Univ. C V 18, fol. 58vb): "Episcopus extraneus potest consecrare ecclesiam in dyocesi alterius episcopi de licencia ipsius.
Igitur episcopus extraneus potest dare indulgencias subditis alterius episcopi de licencia
ipsius."

40. John of Dambach, *De quan. indul.*, q. 3 (Basel, Univ. C V 18, fol. 58vb): "Alienus
sacerdos iure suo absolvit subditos proprii sacerdotis de licencia ipsius, eo quod in hac
causa data est ei materia per proprium sacerdotem. Ergo a simili alienus episcopus de
licencia proprii episcopi potest subditis illius dare iure seu nomine suo indulgencias."

41. Tanner and Alberigo, 1:264.

42. Mansi, 23:26, 23:1085, 23:513, and VI 5.10.3 (*CIC* 2:1093). Paulus has a much
more complete list of the councils that reaffirmed *Cum ex eo* in *Geschichte* 2:269–270.

43. Mansi, 25:1119: "Nam praefixam sibi a sacris canonibus regulam excedentes
largiores, quam eis concessum est, indulgentias largiuntur."

44. Mansi, 26:228.

45. John of Dambach, *De quan. indul.*, q. 4 (Basel, Univ. C V 18, fol. 59ra): "Quarta
questio est utrum indulgencie, sive ab uno solo sive a pluribus episcopis, de consensu
diocesani, in dedicacione ecclesie vel eius anniversario sive pro aliis piis causis, date
ante concilium generale excedentes statutum concilii . . . adhuc in totum vel in parte."

46. Cod. 1.14.7 and X 1.2.2. James Brundage, *Medieval Canon Law* (New York:
Longman, 1995), 162.

47. See the series of articles in *Analecta Bollandiana* by Hippolyte Delehaye.

48. John of Dambach, *De quan. indul.*, q. 5 (Basel, Univ. C V 18, fol. 59rb): "Quinta
questio est utrum indulgencie post concilium generale sed ante promulgacionem sexti
decretalium date contra mentem concilii sive statutum concilii excedentes adhuc totum
valeant."

49. John of Dambach, *De quan. indul.*, q. 5 (Basel, Univ. C V 18, fol. 59rb): "Racio
est quia si non valerent, hoc esset propter prohibicionem concilii. Sed prohibicio

concilii non obstet." See also the outstanding discussion of law and punishment in late antiquity by Jill Harries, *The Law and Empire in Late Antiquity* (Cambridge: Cambridge University Press, 1999), 81.

50. John of Dambach, *De quan. indul.*, q. 6 (Basel, Univ. C V 18, fol. 59vb): "Utrum indulgencie non solum post concilium generale sed eciam post promulgacionem sexti decretalium in dedicacione vel in quocumque alio casu date contra mentem concilii valeant saltem pro parte."

51. Johannes Monachus, *Summa aurea super VI libros decretalium*, VI 5.10.3 (Paris: Ioannem Paruum, 1535), fol. 396. John of Dambach cited this text in *De quan. indul.*, q. 6 (Basel, Univ. C V 18, fol. 59vb).

52. John of Dambach, *De quan. indul.*, q. 6 (Basel, Univ. C V 18, fol. 59vb): "Dico secundum Archidiaconum et Johannes Andree quod sic. Nam ubi decretali *Indulgencie* sepius allegata dicit quod *indulgencie que ab uno vel a pluribus episcopis in quibuscumque casibus conceduntur, vires non optinent, si statutum excesserint concilii generalis*, ibi Archidiaconus in glosa sua, super verbis, *non optinent*, dicit se hanc sentenciam benigniorem credere veriorem, quod scilicet valeant saltem in ea parte sive dierum numero que a principio episcopi legittime concedere poterunt." See Guido de Baysio, *Archidiaconus super sexto decretalium*, VI 5.10.3, s.v. *non optinent* (Lyon: Iacobi Guintae, 1547), fol. 118v.

53. John of Dambach, *De quan. indul.*, q. 6 (Basel, Univ. C V 18, fol. 60r): "Dico secundum Johannes Andrea, ex quo indulgencia excessiva contra mentem concilii habet dies sive partes, ab invicem separabiles, potest separari utile ab inutile, et sic inutile virtute concilii et magis per nominem ius, scilicet, per decretalem *Indulgencie*."

54. John cites such an instance from Ulpian, (Dig. 43.20.1.18). *De quan. indul.*, q. 6 (Basel, Univ. C V 18, fol. 60r).

55. John of Dambach, *De quan. indul.*, q. 7 (Basel, Univ. C V 18, fol. 60va): "Septima questio est utrum si eidem domui concessit dyocesanus xl dies indulgenciarum et metropolitanus alios xl dies et una et eadem die legantur littere huiusmodi, in uno et eodem loco dans eleemosinam habeat in hoc casu lxxx dies."

56. John of Dambach, *De quan. indul.*, q. 9 (Basel, Univ. C V 18, fol. 61rb): "Puta in loco predictorum fratrum quia licet locus talis visitetur vel ei cedat emolumentum ex indulgencia proveniens, tamen ipsa indulgencia non acquiritur loco, sed subditis concedentis seu concendentium. Unde ita potest episcopus Basiliensis dare xl dies subditis suis pro eundo ad heremitas et ecclesiam ibi relinquendo, sicut pro eundo super castrum ad maiorem ecclesiam."

57. Once again, the articles in *Analecta Bollandiana* by Delehaye ought to be consulted.

58. Hostiensis, *Summa aurea*, 5.67 (ed. Iacobus Guinta, 288b): "Sic si fiat obtentu indulgentie utriusque quia neuter excidit."

59. John of Dambach, *De quan. indul.*, q. 7 (Basel, Univ. C V 18, fol. 60vb): "Sicut episcopus in sua dyocesi, ita archiepiscopus per totam suam provinciam habet dare indulgenciam xl dierum ordinaria auctoritate."

60. X 5.38.15 (*CIC* 2:889): "Per provinciam tuam libere huiusmodi potes concedere litteras ita quod statutum generali concilii non excedas."

61. VI 5.10.1 (*CIC* 2:1093). The story of this case may be found in *Geschichte*, 2:210–211.

62. John of Dambach, *De quan. indul.*, q. 7 (Basel, Univ. C V 18, fol. 60vb): "Dicit quod est casus in quo archiepiscopus iurisdictionem habet in subditos suorum suffraganorum."

63. John of Dambach, *De quan. indul.*, q. 7 (Basel, Univ. C V 18, fol. 60vb): "Concilium amplius limitaverit simplices episcopos, de quibus solis loquitur, qui extra suas dyoceses non habent quod subditis dyocesani cuiuscumque possint dare indulgencias sine eius licencia. Tamen non sequitur, nec est verisimile, quod concilium archiepiscopos, quos non exprimit, et qui per se sine licencia dyocesani possunt dare indulgencias, tantum quantum simplices episcopos limitaverit, quamvis et ipsi eciam sint limitati quod non excedant statutum concilii quod nec faciunt, quando per se non dant nisi annum in dedicacione, et xl dies in anniversario dedicacionis vel in alio festo."

64. John of Dambach, *De quan. indul.*, q. 8 (Basel, Univ. C V 18, fol. 60vb): "Octava questio est utrum si dyocesanus in sua dyocesi alicui domui pro certa causa concessit xl dierum indulgencias; legatus a latere, cuius legacio ad eandem dyocesim, se extendit eidem domui pro eadem causa, possit superaddere alios xl dies indulgenciarum."

65. X 1.30.10 (*CIC* 2:186): "Quin legatorum sedis apostolicae statuta edita in provincia, sibi commissa durent tanquam perpetua, licet eandem postmodum sint egressi."

66. John of Dambach, *De quan. indul.*, q. 8 (Basel, Univ. C V 18, fol. 61ra): "Valent perpetuo sicut statuta, licet enim amministracio sit temporalis, illud quod factum est per eum perpetuum est."

67. John of Dambach, *De quan. indul.*, q. 8 (Basel, Univ. C V 18, fol. 61ra): "Potest hoc legatus a latere in provincia sibi commissa quam archiepiscopus in tota sua provincia."

68. John of Dambach, *De quan. indul.*, q. 8 (Basel, Univ. C V 18, fol. 61ra): "Cum nullum istorum capitulorum ullam mencionem faciate de restrictione legati, immo legatus a latere exceptis aliquibus pape reservatis est quasi alter papa, et presentat persona pape Christi vicarii in provincia sibi commissa. Unde esto quod simplices episcopi vel eciam archiepiscopi in dando indulgencias essent per concilium sic vel sic limitati, tamen non reperitur, nec est verisimile, quod concilium intenderit quod legati a latere tantum quantum simplices episcopi sint limitati, sicut nec papam limitavit."

69. John of Dambach, *De quan. indul.*, q. 9 (Basel, Univ. C V 18, fol. 61rb): "Nona questio est utrum plures episcopi, simul vel successive, esto quod sint centum vel mille, possint dare indulgencias in eodem loco et pro eadem causa querendas, ita quod quilibet eorum det xl dies indulgenciarum ibi querendarum."

70. John of Dambach, *De quan. indul.*, q. 9 (Basel, Univ. C V 18, fol. 61rb): "Sint centum episcopi et quilibet det indulgenciam xl dierum querendam in loco fratrum predicatorum in Basilea in festo beati Dominici, quilibet subditus cuiuslibet episcoporum illorum, visitando ecclesiam dictorum fratrum in dicto festo, consequitur indulgenciam xl dierum . . . probo quia secundam primam et secundam questiones precedentes."

71. John of Dambach, *De quan. indul.*, q. 9 (Basel, Univ. C V 18, fol. 61rb–61va): "Non est intencio illius concilii, quod indulgencie omnes simul accepte possibiles dari per episcopos pro tali loco visitando in tali festo, vel pro causa consimili non excedant numerum expressum in dicto capitulo, sed quod non excedant numerum pro eisdem personis, quia aliter non sunt excessive seu superflue, vel indiscrete . . . nam quilibet subditis illorum episcoporum visitando talem locum in tali festo non consequeretur, nisi tantum indulgenciam quantum suus episcopus ibi dedisset, id est, tantum xl dies datas a suo episcopo, qui numerus non excedat numerum expressum per concilium."

72. John of Dambach, *De quan. indul.*, q. 10 (Basel, Univ. C V 18, fol. 61va): "Decima questio est utrum indulgencie, per plures episcopos ad eundem locum et pro eadem causa date, non contra mentem concilii sive statuti *Cum ex eo*, prosint omnibus quibus ut prodessent proprii iudices spiritualiter indulserunt, sive illi iudices sint de numero dantium tales indulgencias, sive non."

73. X 5.38.4 (*CIC* 2:886): "Quod autem consuluisti, utrum remissiones, quae fiunt in dedicationibus ecclesiarum, aut conferentibus ad aedificationem pontium, aliis prosint, quam his, qui remittentibus subsunt, hoc volumus tuam fraternitatem [firmiter] tenere, quod, quum a non suo iudice ligari nullus valeat vel absolvi, remissiones praedictas prodesse illis tantummodo arbitramur, quibus, ut prosint, proprii iudices specialiter indulserunt."

74. John of Dambach, *De quan. indul.*, q. 10 (Basel, Univ. C V 18, fol. 61va): "Confirmo hoc quia esset magna decepcio si solum illis prodessent qui subsunt remittentibus cum indifferenter subditi cuiuscumque episcopi querant illas."

75. John of Dambach, *De quan. indul.*, q. 10 (Basel, Univ. C V 18, fol. 61va): "Responsio. Dico quod sic, quia ubi ius non distinguit, ibi nec nos debemus distinguere, ut per iura patet. Si ius dicit indistincte quod remissiones he que in dedicacionibus ecclesiarum aut conferentibus ad edificacionem pontium fiunt illis prosunt quibus ut prosint proprii iudices spiritualiter indulserunt, extra *De penitenciis et remissionibus*, capitulo *Quod autem*, et est eadem racio de illis indulgenciis que secundum mentem concilii dantur eciam pro aliis piis causis. Ergo prosunt omnibus indistincte quibus ut prodessent proprii iudices spiritualiter indulserunt."

76. John of Dambach, *De quan. indul.*, q. 11 (Basel, Univ. C V 18, fol. 62ra): "Loquitur de sentencia ecommunicacionis que est de numero penarum que tamquam odiose sunt restringende. Nec sequitur quod sit sic de indulgenciis que sunt favorabiles et ideo ampliande." Cf. VI 5.12.15 (*CIC* 2:1122): "Odia restringi, et favores convenit ampliari." The decretal *A nobis* may be found at X 5.39.28 (*CIC* 2:899–900).

77. John of Dambach, *De quan. indul.*, q. 11 (Basel, Univ. C V 18, fol. 61vb): "Undecima questio est utrum plures episcopi, ad eundem locum et pro eadem causa, de licencia et approbacione dyocesani episcopi, dare possint indulgencias, ita quod quilibet eorum det per se xl dies distinctos a quibuslibet aliis xl diebus ab aliis datis. Dico quod sic, dummodo indulgencie ille omnes simul non sint immoderate." By "excessive," of course, John meant a grant by an *individual* bishop of more than forty days. Surviving grants of indulgence indicate that such "supernumerary" grants of indulgence were rare, if they even existed at all.

78. John of Dambach, *De quan. indul.*, q. 11 (Basel, Univ. C V 18, fol. 61vb): "Potest consentire, licenciare, et approbare quod alii episcopi dent eis indulgencias que non sunt contra mentem concilii, per quam licenciam et approbacione prestant materiam huiusmodi."

79. John of Dambach, *De quan. indul.*, q. 11 (Basel, Univ. C V 18, fol. 61vb): "Sed quod plures sint episcopi, quorum quilibet ad eundem locum et pro eadem causa det per se xl dies indulgenciarum distinctos a quibuslibet xl diebus per alios datis, non est contra mentem concilii, sed magis secundum mentem."

80. John of Dambach, *De quan. indul.*, q. 12 (Basel, Univ. C V 18, fol. 62va): "Duodecima questio est utrum plures episcopi, ad eundem locum et pro eadem causa, possint dare

indulgencias, simul vel successive, ita quod quilibet eorum per se dante in dedicacione ecclesie unum annum, et in aliis piis locis et causis xl dies, omnes ille indulgencie prosint quibus, ut prosint proprii iudices spiritualiter indulserunt."

81. John of Dambach, *De quan. indul.*, q. 12 (Basel, Univ. C V 18, fol. 62va): "Dico quod sic, sive illi iudices de numero dancium sive non, dummodo omnes ille indulgencie annorum vel dierum non sint immoderate."

82. John of Dambach, *De quan. indul.*, q. 12 (Basel, Univ. C V 18, fol. 63va): "Quando dicitur si quilibet episcoporum plurium posset per se dare xl dies etc., tunc indulgencie date a pluribus in causa quo plures episcopi dedicacioni interessent excederent plures annos. Dico quod hoc non oporteret quia questio presens non querit de determinata episcoporum pluralitate presertim nimis magna. Unde satisfit questioni per responsionem que potest verificari de pluralitate trium episcoporum vel duorum, quia secundum regulam iuris, *pluralis locucio duorum numero contentam est* [VI 5.12.40], et si quilibet horum plurium daret xl dies non essent nisi lxxx, vel si trium episcoporum quilibet dare xl non essent nisi centum, et neutra horum numerorum excederet plures annos, immo nec unum annum, eciam si episcopi essent viiij."

83. John of Dambach, *De quan. indul.*, q. 12 (Basel, Univ. C V 18, fol. 63vb): "Satis videtur inconveniens spiritualiter per hoc quod [Hostiensis] dicit *dividant sicut placet*, quia si unius anni diebus diversis quilibet dat partem suam, tunc nullus dat xl. Ergo nullius subditi possunt consequi xl dies circumscripta indulgencia proprii iudicis preter subditos dyocesani licenciantis alios ad dandum et suos subditos . . . sed non dedit nisi partem xl dierum puta unum diem si episcopi sint xl, vel duos dies si sint xx, vel iiij dies si sint x, et sic ulterius proporcionaliter loquendo. Sed quod nullius talis episcopi subditus consequitur xl dies, sed tantum unum dierum, vel duos, vel iiij, a suo episcopo est inconveniens sentire." The quote from Hostiensis comes from *Summa aurea*, 5.67 (288rb).

84. John of Dambach, *De quan. indul.*, q. 12 (Basel, Univ. C V 18, fol. 62vb): "A pluribus darentur frustra quia sine utilitate spirituali . . . et per consequens ille indulgencie in quam a pluribus dantur non prosunt illis quibus ut prosint proprii iudices spiritualiter indulserunt. Sed hoc plane videtur contra mentem decretalis *Quod autem*."

85. John of Dambach, *De quan. indul.*, q. 12 (Basel, Univ. C V 18, fol. 62vb): "Sed eciam contra racionem est quod indulgencie a pluribus date ceteris paribus non plus prosint quam indulgencia data ab uno solo."

86. John of Dambach, *De quan. indul.*, q. 12 (Basel, Univ. C V 18, fol. 64rb): "Nam magnum factum reputaretur si sex episcopi interessent quorum quolibet dante annum, non essent indulgencie immoderate, utpote propter quas possent claves ecclesie contempni vel penitencialis satisfaccio enervari? Cuiusmodi contemptus et enervacio magis haberent locum in indulgenciis datis per plures summos pontifices quorum unus relaxare dicitur septimam partem peccaminum, alius terciam partem, alius forte medietatem, quas indulgencias quis plures querendo posset liberari de omnibus peccatis suis."

87. John of Dambach, *De quan. indul.*, q. 12 (Basel, Univ. C V 18, fol. 64rb): "Si sex vel septem episcoporum quilibet dat annum quia talis indulgencia forte non tolleret penam debitam uni peccato mortali, cum cuilibet mortali respondeat ad minum septennis penitencia; secundum iura quorum peccatorum quinque in uno homine est numerus infinitus."

88. John of Dambach, *De quan. indul.*, q. 12 (Basel, Univ. C V 18, fol. 64ra): "Hoc dicit talis vel talis doctor quia ut dicit non est curandum quantumcumque magnus doctor aliquid dixerit, nisi probet per canonem seu authenticas scripturas. Sed quod opinio sua, et Berhardi, vel cuiuscumque eciam alterius doctoris in hac materia secum sentientis sit vera, et opponitum falsum, hoc nullo modo potest convinci per canonem sepedicti concilii cui soli innituntur, cuius canonis littera secundum alium intellectum commode potest exponi."

89. Freed, 39–43.

90. M. H. Laurent, "Autour du procès de Maître Eckhart," *Divus Thomas* (Piacenza) 39 (1936), 344. On the contents and arguments of the *Rechtsfertigungschrift*, see Bernard McGinn, "Eckhart's Condemnation Reconsidered," *The Thomist* 44 (1980), 400–403.

91. For the context of one of these short treatises (*De proprietate mendicancium*), see Gabriel Löhr, "Die Mendicantenarmut in Dominikanerorder in 14. Jahrhundert," *Divus Thomas* (Freiburg) Series 3, 18 (1940), 385–427.

92. Harries, 81.

Conclusion

Unde Indulgentiae?

While much historical work remains to be done, indulgences in the Middle Ages can simply no longer be thought about according to the paradigms of traditional scholarship, regardless of where that scholarship may lie on the polemical-confessional divide. To be sure, Catholic and Protestant polemical historians ought to be credited with learning much about the history of indulgences; however, confessional historiography also generated its own shortcomings, namely, anachronisms that impeded, rather than enhanced, historians' understanding of indulgences in high medieval Latin Christianity. That no pardons were granted before the eleventh century, as Protestants have generally argued, cannot be doubted. High medieval developments, such as the rise of documentation and accounting, the piety of the *imitatio Christi* movements, and the reformers' reorganization of ecclesiastical discipline through canon law, all figured into the origins of indulgences. At the same time, as Catholic polemicists have noted, without the inheritance of the Roman, Irish, Carolingian, and Ottonian penitential regimes, pardons, if they had ever emerged at all, would have taken on a rather different form. Consequently, indulgences represent an intersection of new and old elements in eleventh-century Christian civilization.

The study of indulgences in the Middle Ages also discredits the historiographical theory that medieval Christianity consisted of an "elite" religiosity, on the one hand, and a "popular" expression, on the other. Like many other, more celebrated events in medieval Christendom, the fervor of the laity generated most indulgences. Just as the monastery of Cluny, which served as the spiritual capital of Latin Christendom for two hundred years, was founded by the pious lay magnate, William of Aquitaine, so did most pardons originate as petitions from devout laity requesting that a bishop or pope grant a desired remission. Indulgences thus resembled the wide array of liturgies and religious drama, wherein the laity often decided the feasts to be celebrated, the petitions to be offered, the prayers to be recited, and the plays to be performed. The laity requested indulgences of all sorts—for pious construction enterprises, for pilgrimages, for the recitation of powerful prayers, for members of confraternities, for taking up the sword against the enemies of Christendom both at home and abroad. These grants of pardon amounted to the prelates' endorsement of these pious enterprises, which renders erroneous any serious distinction between "lay" or "folk" or "popular" piety, over against "clerical" or "elite" religion.

The array of works for which indulgences were granted in the twelfth through fourteenth centuries multiplied. Crusade indulgences were available initially to warriors, but beginning with the reign of Innocent III, anyone willing to make some contribution to the success of the wars against Christendom's traditional enemy, Islam, might also receive a plenary remission. Legions of pilgrims made journeys that were sometimes long and perilous, although more often short and safe, to venerate numerous saints. Craftsmen could ply their trades and gain pardons while they built churches, convents, roads, dams, and bridges. The sick and dying in hospital depended on pardons for their comfort and consolation. Students studied and made satisfaction for their sins. Participants in innumerable devotionalisms received indulgences for prayers recited and liturgies attended. Confraternity members benefitted from remissions. By the end of the Middle Ages, members of archery clubs received pardons, since the bow could be used to defend Christendom from her enemies. Virtually any endeavor that could be put to the service of church and neighbor was indulgenced.

The indulgences were to be applied to Purgatory, which summoned a wide range of pictures in the imaginations of medieval Catholics. Dante's view of a strenuous climb up a mountain, where the shades of the deceased embrace each other and rejoice in their burdens, contrasts completely with Bridget of Sweden's diabolical torture chamber. Medieval Christians saw Purgatory in its best and most awful possibilities; neither became "official" in any way. Pardons would reduce the need to purify the soul in either image.

Instead of fostering "superstition," the image of treasury, by which believers pictured the benefits of indulgences, betrays just how deeply Christianity had penetrated the religious imagination by the twelfth century. The Old and the New Testaments described human salvation as a payment of the ransom from the slavery of sin. With this imagery, Christians deemed indulgences very powerful—as in John of Dambach's treatise *On the power of indulgences*—for in a treasury was deposited a great hoard of silver, copper, and gold coins, precious gems, documents, even relics—not only the ruler's wealth, but also the source of his might. Similarly, the treasury of the church was a great, dazzling repository of efficacious spiritual benefits. Penitents—well—*treasured* pardons. Indeed, the reception of an indulgence mirrored the passing by of a great lord, whose servants customarily threw money to the villagers out of a great, open treasure chest. Just as dependents and retainers expected liberality of their earthly lord, the Lord of Heaven would be generous with his subjects, friends, sons, and daughters.

One important reservation, however, must also be kept in mind. The sources show that the analogy between earthly and church authority captured imperfectly the meaning of the treasury of merit (hence the Schoolmen's presentation of several parallel analogies to illustrate their ideas). Secular governments rely on coercion and grisly punishments to maintain order; they cannot assume good will between the ruler and the ruled. In contrast, the application of church authority as expressed in a grant of pardon demanded a bond of charity tying together the bishop, the penitent, and God himself. Like Jesus in the Gospels, the church exercised power to manifest charity, not dominion. Without charity, the church's authority to apply the treasury of merits to a sinner's debts was rendered powerless.

Social and economic developments reinforced the imagery of the treasury. By the mid-twelfth century, not only merchants but many peasants as well had acquired a practical literacy, which included elementary arithmetic and the keeping of accounts. Even rustics who had not learned these skills would either rely on or deal with those who had. A variety of medieval jobs involved a pre-occupation with the calculation and payment of debts, for which accounts were an indispensable tool. As the Dominican Giordano da Pisa had observed, the buying and selling of crops and cloth encouraged the mental habits of arith-metic. Together with the scriptural imagery, the demands of making a living encouraged medieval Christians to think of satisfaction for sin as the payment of a debt which could be expressed in numbers.

The image of the treasury, moreover, illustrates the corporate nature of medieval Catholicism, for the treasury was the common possession of the universal Church. The pope and bishops were its stewards, not owners, and while the authority to grant full pardons was reserved to the pope, bishops nonetheless had broad powers of dispensation, for while canon law limited, in most instances, the magnitude of an episcopal indulgence to forty days, no restrictions were placed on the number of indulgences they could concede. Moreover, the genesis of most pardons indicates that lay Catholics thought about the treasury—held in common by the church—in much the same way they thought about common rights to pasture, meadow, and forest. Nobles may have enjoyed lordship over such lands, but within the law, any dependent of the manor could exploit their usefulness.

Contrary to the claims of some historians, the commentaries of the learned theologians and canonists suggests that most medieval Catholics were fully conversant with the basic protocol for receiving valid indulgences. After all, every effort "to explain or to justify what one believes are undertaken as much for oneself as for others. If the questions are genuine, if they go to heart of the matter and are not simply rhetorical flourishes to score points in a debate, over time they will be asked even in the absence of the other."[1] To be sure, dissident groups such as the Waldensians flatly rejected the validity of indulgences, just as they scorned other ministrations of the Catholic Church. Heretics, however, made up a small band of rebels who generally scorned intellectual pretensions; the Schoolmen wrote for no such readership. Rather, orthodox theologians and church lawyers defended the efficacy of an indulgence, or the church's authority to grant them, to those who sincerely believed in the power of pardons to make satisfaction for the debt of sin. They explained *why* the church claimed the authority she did, and the *grounds* for a valid concession of pardon. Indeed, given that William of Auvergne, Bonaventure, Thomas Aquinas, and Hostiensis, among others—along with later figures like John of Freiburg and William of Pagula, who pot-boiled the Schoolmen's work into the various pastoral manuals—wrote for professional religious like themselves, their arguments should be understood as illustrations of their tasks as preachers, confessors, and counselors. Like the Franciscan friar James of Porta, ordinary folk approached them for their advice in coping with sick children, dying spouses, and personal demons. As ministers of the church, they shared the religion of their lay neighbors. Unlike Kant in his tower at the University of Königsberg, the Schoolmen, whether secular or mendicant, celebrated the liturgy with their confrères and the multitudes of lay men and women whose religious aspirations Sts. Francis and Dominic captured, and to which the swelling ranks of tertiaries testify. That common liturgical experience imprinted the same religious imagination on all whom it touched. Hence the similarity encountered between the thoughts of the great Schoolmen, on the one hand, and the sentiments of St. Bridget, Margery Kempe, and Jane Mary of Maillé, among countless other devout mothers, daughters, sons, fathers, and husbands, on the other.

In sum, the traditional interpretation, which depicted pardons as spiritually stultifying, ought now be laid to rest. To be sure, indulgences rarely encouraged great conversion experiences; at the same time, neither did they generally reduce the Christian religion to a sterile series of robotically performed works. The view that on the one hand assumed a radical disconnection between the parts of the human soul, and on the other hand assumed another such distinction between body and soul, lay at the heart of the Reformation's rebellion against medieval ideas about the human person.

Medieval Catholics were more inclined to emphasize the unity of body and soul. The patristic tradition, inherited by the medieval church, had held that an agent's mind or soul determined the actions of that agent—the exterior act could be explained and understood as a reflection of the interior disposition, as there was an ordering of the two, although they constituted a unity. From Maximus Confessor (c. AD 650), for whom the "work is proof of a disposition," to Thomas Aquinas, for whom the soul tyrannically ruled the body, the tradition affirmed from the seventh to the fifteenth century that exterior displays of goodness necessarily originated in interior goodness. Exterior actor and interior disposition were contained in the same person, a multiplicity *and* a unity. Even allowing for the temptations and minor offenses to which all children of Eve are subject, the idea that a corrupt soul could do anything good, or that a good soul could do anything heinously wicked, made little sense to the great majority of both learned and unschooled medieval Catholics. By infused and cooperating grace, seekers of indulgences could do the good. The exterior man gave alms because the interior man had been moved to sorrow for sin and love of God and neighbor; the exterior woman recited a particular set of prayers because the interior woman was moved to greater service of God. As in the case of Henry Suso, indulgences could contribute to a program of great spiritual awareness and growth, but in the great majority of cases, pardons formed part of a penitential regime that encouraged a modest amendment of life rather more within the spiritual capabilities of most ordinary Christians, and characteristic of what Eamon Duffy has characterized as the medieval, "broad" church. That church maintained a place for those who may not be characterized as fervent or zealous (no paradigmatic conversion experiences), but who nonetheless desired to live on good terms with God and neighbor.[2]

For the past several generations, historians have been revisiting the meaning of abuse and reform in the medieval Church. Indulgences have long been studied under the rubric of especially stubborn abuses, virtually impervious to reform and alteration. This historiographical school has mostly rested on evidence from literature and canon law. However, a fresh examination of these sources rejects this view. For instance, Chaucer's pardoner would not be nearly as charming in his naughty way if the licit preaching of authentic indulgences were unknown to most medieval Englishmen. True, even medieval academic commentators entertained the objection that indulgences perverted true piety and penance, and some historians have argued that these objections, like the canonistic sources, prove that the trafficking in pardons corrupted penitential fervor. But since in expressing these misgivings the theological and canonistic commentators quote verbatim canons like *Cum ex eo*, whether their thoughts should be taken as descriptions of what actually happened or as reaffirmations of the validity of the canon (as in Boniface VIII's decree *Indulgentiae*, which simply stated that pardons that violated the decree of Lateran IV had no efficacy). Furthermore, the consistent insistence on prior contrition and confession in the *summae*, pastoral manuals, and proclamations of indulgences themselves suggest that, contrary to the view held by many modern scholars, the canonistic protocols were understood and followed generally, although perhaps not perfectly.

Several controversies involving indulgences illustrate this theme quite well. On the basis of a series of conciliar decrees and papal decretals, many historians have concluded that bishops granted time and again indulgences of such vast magnitudes as to be scandalous. In fact, the sources support a rather different interpretation. That certain legal limitations were repeated over the decades (such as that forbidding bishops to grant partial indulgences of more than forty days) almost certainly does not mean that bishops had been flouting the law of the church. Rather, the repetitions mean instead that successive generations of bishops accepted the efficacy of those prohibitions, and that the bishops took what measures they could to implement them. Other sources, most crucially proclamations of indulgences, indicate that even before Lateran IV, bishops rarely granted partial indulgences of more than forty days.

Another abuse generally characterized as endemic is the erroneous and illegal itinerant preaching of remissions. Most itinerants, however, carried out their mission within the law and with general approbation. Still, canonical protocols governed the preaching of indulgences, and the popularity of the pastoral manuals, which contained virtually all these canonical materials, indicate that bishops, priests, and devout laity understood the proper protocols for wandering preachers of indulgence. Itinerants first were required to submit their credentials to the diocesan bishop. They also had to receive the permission of rectors before they could preach in church. If these protocols were violated, the preachers could be denied permission to speak in parish churches, and, even if they were granted that permission, they could not force their listeners to give them alms. Considering that strangers would be greeted with healthy scepticism, only the most skillful forgers and liars could have duped the generally wary peasantry and town dwellers. Medieval Christians, then, relied on a number of safeguards in canon law and moral theology to preserve their money and their souls. Undoubtedly, confidence men occasionally got the better of them, but they were hardly at the mercy of these charlatans. The hucksters, who might cheapen the treasury of the church, had to contend with the formidable constabulary of bishop, priest, and parishioners.

Nonetheless, that church authorities continually reaffirmed the canons regulating indulgences does mean that they recognized actual and possible abuses, and episodic controversies did flare up. As the treatise of Simon of Cremona and Peter of John Olivi show, from time to time the Portiuncula attracted the attention of critics, owing to its lack of documentation. Indulgences might also get swept up in other arguments, as in the fourteenth-century case of the German Dominicans and their rivals. As numerous as the examples may be, though, they in no way prove that indulgences were a blight on the medieval Church. The church's governing structures and protocols ordinarily handled the proper administration of indulgences rather well. The distribution of indulgences may well be considered to have been reformed in the thirteenth and fourteenth centuries, not of course on the model of Luther's reformation, but within the context of church councils such as Lateran IV and Vienne. The implementation of the decrees promulgated by these councils subjected the preaching of indulgences to fairly rigorous protocols.

On the eve of the Great Schism, then, the sources suggest a fairly consistent picture of the regulation of indulgences over the high medieval centuries. Church authorities recognized that pardons must be preached properly, which is different from saying that indulgences were widely preached illegally. The sources indicate, instead, that at most of the stops on their itinerary, wandering preachers of indulgence needed to prove—with sealed documents, the validity of which could even be evaluated by the unlettered—that they were licitly empowered to preach specific indulgences. The sources likewise show that indulgences neither necessarily encouraged a mechanistically formal practice of religion, nor did they generally contribute to paradigmatic conversion experiences, although some examples of just such phenomena do survive. In the main, however, pardons formed part of a penitential regime that had, since antiquity, been eminently adaptable to a wide array of personal dispositions, and an equally broad range of abilities and preferences (prayer, fasting, building, not to mention drawing the sword); for some penitents, perhaps the vast majority, remissions served as modest encouragements to good work and interior reflection, and for what was probably a small minority, they could indeed fit into a profound reorientation to saintliness. Indulgences could require the completion of relatively simple tasks such as the recitation of a number of *Aves* or *Pater nosters* in the comfort of the home, or reading a catechetical text to an illiterate friend or neighbor, as well as lengthy, dangerous journeys to faraway places. The contrition that they required for efficacious reception might come from the fear, rather than the love, of God. They were still believed valid, because the merits of Christ, as mediated through the authority of bishops and popes, sufficed where human weakness fell short. No wonder that indulgences appealed to so many medieval Catholics, for whom pardon served not as an occasion for scrupulous self-torment but as a reminder of God's generosity and of the help of "fellow evencristens." Within their confidence in the power of indulgences resided the assurance of salvation, after purgation and satisfaction had satisfied the justice of God.

NOTES
   1. Robert Louis Wilken, *The Spirit of Early Christian Thought* (New Haven, CT: Yale University Press, 2003), 2.
   2. Duffy, 298.

Bibliography

Primary Sources

MANUSCRIPTS

Admont (Austria), Stiftsbibliothek 7.

Basel, Universitätsbibliothek C V 18.

Bruges, Staatsbibliothek, Cod. lat. 220.

Erlangen, Universitätsbibliothek, Cod. lat. 260.

Heiligenkreuz (Austria), Stiftsbibliothek 208.

Munich, Staatsbibliothek: Clm9546; Clm10247; Clm22233; Clm22283; Clm23947.

Oxford, Bodleian Library: Bodl. 487; Lyell 30; Rawlinson G 23; Tanner 407.

Paris, Bibliothéque Nationale: Cod. lat. 14886.

Salzburg (Austria), St. Peter Stiftsbibliothek a X 19.

Todi, Biblioteca communale 71.

PRINTED SOURCES

Acta Sanctorum. Ed. Jean Bolland, et al. 68 vols. Paris: Palmé, 1863–.

Albert the Great, St. *Opera omnia*. 38 vols. Paris: Louis Vives, 1890–1899.

Alexander of Hales. *Summa theologica*. 4 vols. Quarrachi: Ex typographia Collegii S. Bonaventurae, 1924–1948.

Allen, William. *A Treatise Made in Defense of the Lawful Power and Authorite of Priesthod to Remitte Sinnes*. Louvain: Apud Ioannem Foulerum, 1567.

Analecta Franciscana. Quaracchi: College of St. Bonaventure, 1897.

Anthony of Florence. *Summa theologica*. 4 vols. Graz: Akademische Druck- u. Verlagsanstalt, 1959.

Augustine of Ancona. *Summa de potestate ecclesiastica*. Rome: n.p., 1479

Bartolus of Assisi. *Tractatus de indulgentia s. Mariae de Portiuncula*. Ed. Paul Sabatier. Paris: Fischbacher, 1900.

Baysio, Guido de. *Archidiaconus super sexto decretalium*, VI 5.10.3, s.v. *Non optinent*. Lyon: Iacobi Guintae, 1547.

Bellarmine, Robert. *Roberti Bellarmini politiani opera omnia.* 12 vols. Paris: Louis Vivès, 1870–1874.

Berthold von Regensburg. *Seiner Predigten.* Ed. Franz Pfeiffer. 2 vols. Vienna: Wilhelm Braumüller, 1862.

Bevington, David, ed. *Medieval Drama.* Boston: Houghton Mifflin, 1975.

Bonaventure, St. *Opera omnia.* 10 vols. Quaracchi: College of St. Bonaventure, 1882–1902.

Boniface VIII, Pope. *Les registres de Boniface VIII.* 4 vols. Paris: Thorin & Sons, 1906.

Cameron, Louis, ed. *The Commonplace Book of Robert Reynes of Acle: An Edition of Tanner MS 407.* New York: Garland, 1980.

Catherine of Genoa. *Purgation and Purgatory: The Spiritual Dialogue.* Trans. Serge Hughes. New York: Paulist Press, 1979.

Chemnitz, Martin. *Examination of the Council of Trent.* Trans. Fred Kramer. 4 vols. St. Louis: Concordia Publishing House, 1971–1986.

Dante. *Inferno.* Trans. John Ciardi. New York: New American Library, 1954.

Delisle, Léopold, ed. *Recueil des historiens des Gaules et de la France.* 24 vols. Paris: Palmé, 1869–1904.

Denifle, Heinrich, ed. *Chartularium universitatis Parisiensis.* 2 vols. Paris: Delalain, 1891.

Dickinson, Francis Henry, ed. *Missale ad usum insignis et praeclare ecclesiae sarum.* Oxford: J. Parker and Soc., 1861–1883.

Durand of St. Pourçain. *In Petri Lombardi sententias theologicas commentariorum libri IV.* 2 vols. Venice: Guerraea, 1571.

Eco, Umberto. *The Name of the Rose.* trans. William Weaver. New York: Warner Books, 1984.

Ellis, R., ed. *The Liber Celestis of Bridget of Sweden.* EETS 291. Oxford: Oxford University Press, 1987.

Francis Mayron. *In quattuor libris sententiarum.* Venice: Luceantonii de guinta Florentini, 1519.

_____. *Sermones de sanctis.* Basel: Pforzheim, 1498.

Friedberg, Aemilius. *Corpus iuris canonici.* 2 vols. Leipzig: B. Tauchnitz, 1879–1881.

Giovanni Villani. *Nuova cronica.* Ed. Guiseppe Porta. Parma: Fondazione Pietro Bembo, 1991.

Gousset. Th., ed. *Les actes de la province ecclésiastique de Reims.* 2 vols. Reims: L. Jacquet, 1843.

Guérard, B. E. C., ed. *Cartulaire de l'abbaye de Saint-Père de Chartres*. 2 vols. Paris: Imprimerie de Crapelet, 1840.

Guérard, M., ed. *Cartulaire de l'abbaye de Saint-Victor de Marseille*. Paris: Typographie de C. Lahure, 1857.

Guibert of Nogent. *Self and Society in Medieval France*. Trans. John F. Benton. Toronto: University of Toronto Press, 1984.

Guido de Baysio. *Archidiaconus super sexto decretalium*. Lyon: Iacobi Guintae, 1547.

Harris, Marguerite Tjaden, ed. and trans. *Birgitta of Sweden: Life and Selected Revelations*. Mahwah, NJ: Paulist Press, 1990.

Hostiensis. *Summa aurea*. Lyons: Iacobus Guinta, 1537.

Innocent IV, Pope. *Commentaria Innocenti quarti Pont. Maximi super libros quinque decretalium*. Frankfurt: Sigismundus Feyrabendus, 1570.

_____. *Les registres d'Innocent IV*. 4 vols. Paris: Ernest Thorin, 1884–1921.

Johannes Andreae. *Clementis quinti constitutiones in concilio Vienensi edite*. Venice: Octavianus Scotus, 1525.

_____. *In sexto decretalium novella commentaria*. 6 vols. Venice: Franciscum Franciscium, 1581.

Johannes Monachus. *Summa aurea super VI libros decretalium*. Paris: Johannem Paruum, 1535.

John of Freiburg. *Summa confessorum*. Augsburg: Günther Zainer, 1476.

John of Torquemada. *Repertorium in omnes commentarios Ioannis a turrecremata super decretum*. 5 vols. Venice: Haeredem Hieronymi Scotus, 1578.

Kehr, J., ed. *Regesta romanorum pontificum*. 3 vols. Berlin: Weidmann, 1908.

Kennedy, V. L. "Robert Courson on Penance," *MS* 7 (1945), 291–336.

Langlois, Ernest, ed. *Les registres de Nicolas IV*. 2 vols. Paris: E. Thorin, 1886–1905.

Lecoy de la Marche, A., ed. *Anecdotes historiques, légendes et apologues tirés du recueil d'Étienne de Bourbon*. Paris: Librairie Renouard, 1877.

Loewenfeld, S. ed. *Epistolae pontificium romanorum ineditae*. Leipzig: Veit, 1885.

Lucas of Tuy. *Lucae Tudensis episcopi de altera vita fideique controversiis adversus Albigensium errores libri III*. Ingolstadt: Ioannis Hertsroy, 1612.

Luscombe, D. E., ed. and trans. *Peter Abelard's Ethics*. Oxford: Clarendon Press, 1971.

Luther, Martin. *Luther's Works*. Ed. Jaroslav Pelikam. 55 vols. St. Louis, MO: Concordia Publishing House, 1955–1986.

Mabillon, Jean, ed. *Annales ordinis S. Benedicti*. 6 vols. Lucca: L. Venturini, 1739–1745.

Magnum bullarium romanum a beato Leone mango usque ad s. d. n. Benedictum XIII. 19 vols. Luxembourg: Andreae Chevalier, 1727–1758.

Mansi, Giovan Domenico. *Sacrorum conciliorum nova et amplissima collectio.* 54 vols. Graz: Academische Druck-u. Verlagsanstalt, 1960 (repr. of 1758–1798 original).

Matthias Flacius Illyricus. *Historia ecclesiastica.* 13 vols. Basel: I. Oporinum, 1560–1574.

McNeill, John T., and Helena M. Gamer, eds. and trans. *Medieval Handbooks of Penance.* New York: Columbia University Press, 1990 (repr. of 1938).

Meech, Sanford Brown, ed. *The Book of Margery Kempe.* EETS 212. Oxford: Oxford University Press, 1940.

Migne, J.-P., ed. *Patrologia cursus completus: Series Latina.* 221 vols. Paris: Garnier, 1844–1891.

Mollat, Guillaume, ed. *Lettres communes de Jean XXII.* 16 vols. Paris: E. de Boccard, 1904–1947.

Muratori, Louis, ed. *Rerum scriptores italicarum.* 25 vols. Milan: Societatis Palatinae in Regia Curia 1727. Repr. 1977.

Noffke, Suzanne, O. P., ed. and trans. *The Letters of St. Catherine of Siena.* 2 vols. New York: Center for Medieval and Renaissance Studies, State University of New York at Binghamton, 1988–.

Palmer, Paul F., S. J., ed. and trans. *Sacraments and Forgiveness.* Westminster, Maryland: Newman Press, 1959.

Passuti, Peter, ed. *Regesta Honorii papae III.* 2 vols. Rome: Ex Typographia Vaticana, 1895.

Péano, Pierre. "La '*Quaestio* fr. Petri Iohannis Olivi' sur l'indulgence de la Portioncule," *Archivum Franciscanum Historicum* 74 (1981), 33–76.

Peter of Tarentaise (Innocent V). *In IV librum sententiarum commentaria.* 4 vols. Toulouse: Arnald Clomerium, 1672.

Peter Paludanus. *Scriptum in IV sententiarum.* Venice: Bonetus Locatellus, 1493.

Peters, Edward, ed. and trans. *The First Crusade: The Chronicle of Fulcher of Chartres and Other Source Materials.* Philadelphia: University of Pennsylvania Press, 1971.

_____. *Heresy and Authority in Medieval Europe.* Philadelphia: University of Pennsylvania Press, 1980.

Philippi, Rudolf, ed. *Preussisches Urkundenbuch.* 2 vols. Königsberg: Hartungsche Verlagsdruckerei, 1882.

Pitra, Jean Baptiste, ed. *Analecta novissima spicilegii Solesmensis.* 2 vols. Paris: Typis Tusculanis, 1888.

Potthast, August, ed. *Regesta pontificum romanorum*. 2 vols. Berlin: Rudolf Decker, 1874–1875.

Pressel, Friedrich, ed. *Ulmisches Urkundenbuch*. 2 vols. Stuttgart: Karl Aue, 1873.

Raymond of Capua. *Life of St. Catherine*. Trans. Conleth Kearns. Wilmington, DE: Glazier, 1980.

Raymond of Peñafort. *Summa de poenitentiis et matrimonio*. Rome: John Tallini, 1603.

Recueil des historiens des croisades: Historiens occidenteaux. 5 vols. Paris: Académie des Inscriptions et Belle Lettres, 1844–1895.

Riley-Smith, Louise, and Riley-Smith, Jonathan, eds. and trans. *The Crusades: Idea and Reality, 1095–1274*. London: E. Arnold, 1981.

Robert of Flamborough. *Liber poenitentialis*, ed. Firth, C. S. B., J. J. Francis. Studies and Texts 18. Toronto: Pontifical Institute of Mediaeval Studies, 1971.

Schleich, Gustav, ed. "The *Gast of Gy*," *Palaestra* 1 (1898), lv–lix.

Schroeder, Herbert J., O. P., ed. and trans. *Disciplinary Decrees of the General Councils*. St. Louis: B. Herder, 1937.

Simmons, Thomas Frederick, and Henry Edward Nolloth, eds. *The Lay Folks' Catechism*. EETS 118. London: K. Paul, Trench, Trubner & Co., 1901.

Suso, Henry. *Henry Suso: The Exemplar with Two German Sermons*. Ed. and trans. Frank Tobin. Mahwah, NJ: Paulist Press, 1989.

_____. *Heinrich Seuses Horologium Sapientiae*. Ed. Pius Künzle, O. P. Spicilegium Friburgense 23. Freiburg: Universitätsverlag, 1977.

Tanner, Norman, and Giuseppe Alberigo, eds. and trans. *Decrees of the Ecumenical Councils*. 2 vols. Washington, D.C.: Sheed & Ward, 1990.

Thomas Aquinas. *Opera omnia*. 24 vols. Parma: Petri Fiaccadori, 1852–1869.

_____. *Summa theologiae*. 5 vols. Ottawa: Studia Generalis O. Pr., 1945.

Thomas of Cantimpré. *Miraculorum libri duo*. Douai: B. Bellini, 1597.

Thomas of Strasbourg. *Commentaria in IV libros sententiarum*. Venice: J. Ziletti, 1564.

Trapp, D. "The Portiuncula Discussion of Cremona," *Recherches de théologie ancienne et médiévale* 22 (1955), 79–94.

Villanueva, Jaime, ed. *Viage literario a las iglesias de España*. 22 vols. Madrid: Imprenta real, 1803–1852.

Wackenagel, R. and R. Thommen, eds. *Urkundenbuch der Stadt Basel*. 2 vols. Basel: C. Detloffs Buchhandlung, 1890–1893.

Wiegand, Wilhelm, ed. *Urkundenbuch der Stadt Strassburg*. 2 vols. Strasbourg: J. H. Ed. Heitz, 1879.

William of Auvergne. *Opera omnia*. 2 vols. Paris: Andrea Pralard, 1674.

William of Auxerre. *Summa aurea*. 4 vols. Paris: Éditions du Centre national de la recherché scientifique, 1980–1985.

Wilson, H. A., ed. *Liber sacramentorum romanae ecclesiae*. Oxford: Clarendon Press, 1894.

Young, Karl, ed. *Drama of the Medieval Church*. 2 vols. Oxford: Clarendon Press, 1933.

SECONDARY SOURCES

Anciaux, Paul. *Le théologie du sacrément de pénitence au XIIe siècle*. Louvain: E. Nauwelaerts, 1949.

Auer, Albert. *Johannes von Dambach und die Trostbücher vom 11. bis zum 16. Jahrhundert*. Beiträge zur Geschichte der Philosophie und Theologie des Mittelalters 27. Münster: Aschendorffsche Verlagsbuchhandlung, 1928.

Bäumer, Remigius, ed. *Reformatio ecclesiae*. Paderborn: Ferdinand Schöningh, 1980.

Blumenfeld-Kosinski, Renate and Timea Szell, eds. *Images of Sainthood in Medieval Europe*. Ithaca, NY: Cornell University Press, 1991.

Boner, G. "Das Predigerkloster in Basel von der Gründung bis zur Klosterreform, 1233–1429," *Basler Zeitschrift für Geschichte und Altertumskunde* 33 (1934), 195–303, 34 (1935), 105–259.

Boockman, Hartmut. "Ablaßfälschungen im 15. Jahrhundert." In *Fälschungen im Mittelalter. Internationaler Kongreß der Monumenta Germaniae Historiae, Münschen 16.19. September 1986*. MGH Schriften 33. Hannover: Hahnsche Buchhandlung, 1998, 5:659–668.

_____. "Über Ablaß-'Medien,'" *Geschichte in Wissenschaft und Unterricht* 34 (1983), 709–721.

Bornstein, Daniel. "The Users of the Body: The Church and the Cult of Santa Margharita da Cortona," *Church History* 62 (1993), 163–177.

Bossy, John. *Christianity in the West, 1400–1700*. Oxford: Oxford University Press, 1985.

Boudinhon, A. "Sur l'histoire des indulgences," *Revue d'histoire et de litterature religieuses* 3 (1898), 434–455.

Bouwsma, W.J. "Anxiety and the Formation of Early Modern Culture." In B. Malament, *After the Reformation*. Philadelphia: University of Pennsylvania Press, 1980.

Boyle, Leonard E. "The Constitution 'Cum ex eo' of Boniface VIII," *MS* 24 (1962), 262–302.

_____. "Summae confessorum," in *Les genres littéraires dans les sources théologiques et philosophiques médiévales: Definitions, critiques, et exploitations*. Louvain-la-neuve: Institut d'Etudes Médiévales, 1982, 227–237.

Bratke, Eduard. *Luthers 95 Thesen und ihre dogmenhistorischen Voraussetzungen*. Göttingen: Vandenhoeck & Rupprecht, 1884.

Brodrick, James. *Robert Bellarmine*. London: Burns & Oates, 1961.

Brundage, James A. *Medieval Canon Law*. New York: Longman, 1995.

_____. *Medieval Canon Law and the Crusader*. Madison: University of Wisconsin Press, 1969.

Bull, Marcus. *Knightly Piety and the Lay Response to the First Crusade*. Oxford: Clarendon Press, 1993.

Capitani, Ovidio. "L'indulgenza come espressione teologica della '*communio sanctorum*' e nella formazione della dottrina canonistica." In Alessandro Clementi, ed., *Indulgenza nel medioevo e Perdonanza di Papa Celestino V*. Aquila: Centro celestiano, Sezione storica, 1987, 17–32.

Chénu, M. D. *Nature, Man, and Society in the Twelfth Century*. Trans. J. Taylor and L. K. Little. Chicago: University of Chicago Press, 1968.

Clanchy, M. T. *From Memory to Written Record: England 1066–1307*. 2nd ed. Oxford: Blackwell, 1993.

Cochrane, Eric. *Historians and Historiography in the Italian Renaissance*. Chicago: University of Chicago Press, 1981.

Colish, Marcia L. *Medieval Foundations of the Western Intellectual Tradition, 400–1400*. New Haven, CT: Yale University Press, 1997.

Courtney, Francis. "New Explanations of Indulgences," *Clergy Review* 44 (1959), 464–479.

D'Avray, David L. "A Letter of Pope Innocent III and the Idea of Infallibility," *CHR* 64 (1980), 417–421.

_____. *The Preaching of the Friars: Sermons Diffused from Paris before 1300*. Oxford: Clarendon Press, 1985.

_____. "Papal Authority and Religious Sentiment in the Late Middle Ages." In Diana Wood, ed., *The Church and Sovereignty, c. 950–1918*. Studies in Church History Subsidia 9. Oxford: B. Blackwell, 1991.

De Jongh, H. "Les grandes lignes des indulgences," *La vie diocésaine* 16 (1912), 69–80.

Delaruelle, Étienne. *L'église au temps du grand schisme et de la crise conciliare*. Histoire de l'église 14. Paris: Bloud & Gay, 1962.

Delehaye, Hippolyte. "Les lettres d'indulgences collectives," *Analecta Bollandiana* 44 (1926), 342–379; 45 (1927), 97–123, 323–344; 46 (1928), 149–157, 287–343.

Delumeau, Jean. *La peur en occident (XIVe–XVLLLe siècles)*. Paris: Hachette Littératures, 1978.

_____. *Sin and Fear: The Emergence of a Western Guilt Culture, 13th–18th Centuries.* trans. Eric Nicholson. New York: St. Martin's Press, 1990.

Dieckhoff, A. Wilh. *Der Ablaßstreit: Dogmengechichtliche dargestellt.* Gotha: F. A. Perthes, 1886.

Dietterle, Johannes. "Die *Summae confessorum*," *Zeitschrift für Kirchengeschichte* 24 (1903), 353–374, 520–548; 25 (1904), 248–272; 26 (1905), 59–81, 350–362; 27 (1906), 70–83, 296–310.

Dohar, William J. *The Black Death and Pastoral Leadership: The Diocese of Hereford in the Fourteenth Century.* Philadelphia: University of Pennsylvania Press, 1995.

Duby, Georges. *Rural Economy and Country Life in the Medieval West.* Trans. Cynthia Postan. Columbia, SC: University of South Carolina Press, 1968.

Duffy, Eamon. *The Stripping of the Altars: Traditional Religion in England, 1400–1580.* New Haven, CT: Yale University Press, 1992.

Ehrle, Franz. "Die Spiritualen, ihr Verhältnis zum Franciskanerorden und zu den Fraticellen," *Archiv für Literatur und Kirchengeschichte* 1 (1885), 509–569.

Foreville, Raymonde. "L'idée de jubilé chez les théologians et les canonistes (XII–XIIIe s) avant l'institution du jubilé romain (1300)," *Revue d'histoire ecclésiastique* 56 (1961), 401–426.

Frankl, Karlheinz. "Papstschisma und Frömmigkeit: Die 'ad instar' Ablässe," *Römische Quartalschrift* 72 (1977), 57–124, 184–247.

Freed, John. *The Friars and German Society in the Thirteenth Century.* Cambridge, MA: Medieval Academy of America, 1977.

Goodich, Michael. *Violence and Miracle in the Fourteenth Century.* Chicago: University of Chicago Press, 1995.

Gottlob, Adolf. *Kreuzablass und Almosenablass: Eine Studie über die Frühzeit des Ablasswesens.* Stuttgart: Ferdinand Enke, 1906.

Guillemain, Bernard. "Les papes d'Avignon, les indulgences, et les pèlerinages," in *Les pèlerinages.* Toulouse: E. Privat, 1980.

Harries, Jill. *The Law and Empire in Late Antiquity.* Cambridge: Cambridge University Press, 1999.

Hehl, Ernst-Dieter, ed. *Deus qui mutat tempora: Menschen und Institutionen im Wandel des Mittelalters.* Sigmarigen: Jan Thorbecke Verlag, 1987.

Hödl, Ludwig. *Die Geschichte der Scholastischen Literatur und der Theologie der Schlüsselgewalt.* Beiträge zur Geschichte der Philosophie und Theologie des Mittelalters 38. Münster: Aschendorffsche Verlagsbuchhandlung, 1960.

Huber, Raphael M. *The Portiuncula Indulgence*. Franciscan Studies 19. New York: J. W. Wagner, 1938.

Huizinga, Johann. *The Autumn of the Middle Ages*. Trans. Rodney J. Payton. Chicago: University of Chicago Press, 1996.

Jungmann, Joseph, S. J. *The Mass of the Roman Rite: Its Origins and Development*. Trans. Francis A. Brunner. 2 vols. New York: Benziger, 1953.

Jussen, Bernhard, and Pamela Selwyn, eds. and trans. *Ordering Medieval Society: Perspectives on Intellectual and Practical Modes of Shaping Social Relations*. Philadelphia: University of Pennsylvania Press, 2001.

Kaeppeli, Thomas, O. P., ed. *Scriptores ordinis praedicatorum medii aevi*. 3 vols. Rome: Polyglottis Vaticanis, 1975.

Kieckhefer, Richard. *Unquiet Souls: Fourteenth-Century Saints and Their Religious Milieu*. Chicago: University of Chicago Press, 1984.

_____. "Holiness and the Culture of Devotion: Remarks on Some Late Medieval Male Saints" In Renate Blumenfeld-Kosinski and Timea Szell, eds., *Images of Sainthood in Medieval Europe*. Ithaca, NY: Cornell University Press, 1991.

Knowles, David, and R. N. Hadcock. *Medieval Religious Houses: England and Wales*. New York: St. Martin's Press, 1972.

Laurent, M. H. "Autour du procès de Maître Eckhard," Divus Thomas (Piacenza), 39 (1936), 331–348.

Lea, Henry C. *A History of Auricular Confession and Indulgences in the Latin Church*. 3 vols. Philadelphia: Lea Brothers, 1896.

Lebvre, Lucien. "The Origins of the French Reformation: A Badly-Put Question?" In P. Burke, ed. and trans. *A New Kind of History* . New York: Harper & Row, 1973, 44–107.

Le Goff, Jacques. *The Birth of Purgatory*. Trans. Arthur Goldhammer. Chicago: University of Chicago Press, 1984.

Lentes, Thomas. "Counting Piety in the Late Middle Ages." In Bernhard Jussen and Pamela Selwyn, eds. and trans. *Ordering Medieval Society: Perspectives on Intellectual and Practical Modes of Shaping Social Relations*. Philadelphia: University of Pennsylvania Press, 2001.

Lepicier, A. H. M. *Les indulgences*. 2 vols. Paris: P. Lethielleuz, 1903.

Lerner, Robert E. *The Age of Adversity: The Fourteenth Century*. Ithaca, NY: Cornell University Press, 1968.

Löhr, Gabriel. "Die Mendikantinarmut in Dominikanerorden in 14. Jahrhundert," *Divus Thomas* (Freiberg) Series 3, 18 (1940), 385–427.

Malament, Barbara C., ed. *After the Reformation*. Philadelphia: University of Pennsylvania Press, 1980.

Mansfield, Mary. *The Humiliation of Sinners: Public Penance in Thirteenth-Century France*. Ithaca, NY: Cornell University Press, 1995.

Martin, H. *Le métier de predicateur en France septentrionale à la fin du môyen âge, 1350–1520*. Paris: Éditions du Cerf, 1988.

McGinn, Bernard. "Eckhart's Condemnation Reconsidered," *The Thomist* 44 (1980), 390–414.

Minnis, Alastair. "Reclaiming the Pardoners," *The Journal of Medieval and Early Modern Studies* 33 (2001), 311–334.

Moeller, Bernd. "Piety in Germany around 1500." Trans. Joyce Irwin, in Steven Ozment, ed., *The Reformation in Medieval Perspective*. Chicago: Quadrangle Books, 1971, 50–75.

_____. "Religious Life in Germany on the Eve of the Reformation," in Strauss, Gerald, ed., *Pre-Reformation Germany*. London: Macmillan, 1972.

Murray, Alexander. *Reason and Society in the Middle Ages*. Oxford: Clarendon Press, 1978.

_____. "Religion among the Poor in Thirteenth-Century France," *Traditio* 30 (1974), 287–324.

Naphy, William G., and Penny Roberts, eds. *Fear in Early Modern Society*. New York: St. Martin's Press, 1997.

Neuhausen, Christiane. *Das Ablaswesen in der Stadt Köln vom 13. bis zum 16. Jahrhundert*. Cologne: Janus, 1994.

Oakley, Francis. *The Western Church in the Later Middle Ages*. Ithaca, NY: Cornell University Press, 1979.

Oberman, Heiko. *Forerunners of the Reformation*. New York: Holt, Rinehart, & Winston, 1966.

O'Callaghan, Joseph F. *Reconquest and Crusade in Medieval Spain*. Philadelphia: University of Pennsylvania Press, 2003.

O'Connell, Marvin R. *The Counter-Reformation, 1559–1610*. New York: Harper & Row, 1974.

Owst, G. R. *Preaching in Medieval England*. Cambridge: Cambridge University Press, 1926.

Ozment, Steven. *The Age of Reform, 1250–1550*. New Haven, CT: Yale University Press, 1980.

Pantin, W. A. *The English Church in the Fourteenth Century*. Cambridge: Cambridge University Press, 1955.

Pascoe, Louis B. "Jean Gerson: The *ecclesia primitiva* and Reform," *Traditio* 30 (1974), 379–409.

_____. *Jean Gerson: Principle of Church Reform*. Leiden: E. J. Brill, 1973.

Paulus, Nikolaus. "Die Abläss der römischen Kirche vor Innocent III," *Historisches Jahrbuch* 28 (1907), 1–8.

_____. "Die ältesten Ablässe für Almosen und Kirchenbesuch," *ZKT* 33 (1909), 1–40.

_____. "Die Ablaßlehre der Frühscholastik," *ZKT* 34 (1910), 433–472.

_____. "Die Anfänge des sogennanten Ablässes von Schuld und Strafe," *ZKT* 36 (1912), 67–96, 252–279.

_____. "Der sogenannte Ablass von Schukd und Strafe im späteren Mittelalter," *ZKT* 36 (1912), 252–279.

_____. "Die Einführung des Kirchenschatzes in die Ablaßtheorie," *Theologie und Glaube* 6 (1914), 284–298.

_____. "Die Anfänge des Ablässes," *ZKT* 39 (1915), 193–230.

_____. "Die Bedeutung der älteren Ablässe," *Historische-politische Blätter für das katholische Deutschland* 167 (1921), 15–25.

_____. *Indulgences as a Social Factor in the Middle Ages.* Trans. J. Elliot Ross. New York: Devin-Adair, 1922.

_____. *Geschichte des Ablasses im Mittelalter.* 3 vols. Darmstadt: Primus, 2000 (repr. of 1922–1923).

Payer, Pierre. " The Humanism of the Penitentials and the Continuity of the Penitential Tradition," *MS* 46 (1984), 340–352.

Petersohn, Jürgen. "Jubiläumsfrömmigkeit vor dem Jubelablaß: Jubeljahr, Reliquien-translation und '*remissio*' in Bamberg (1189) und Canterbury (1220)," *Deutsches Archiv für Erforschung des Mittelalters* 45 (1989), 31–53.

Pfleger, Luzian. *Kirchengeschichte der Stadt Straßburg im Mittelalter.* Colmar: Alsatian Verlag, 1941.

Poschmann, Bernhard. *Der Ablaß im Licht der Bußgeschichte.* Bonn: Peter Hanstein, 1948.

_____. *Penance and the Anointing of the Sick.* Trans. Francis Courtney. New York: Herder & Herder, 1951.

Powell, James. *Anatomy of a Crusade, 1213–1221.* Philadelphia: University of Pennsylvania Press, 1986.

Principe, Walter H. "The School Theologians' Views of the Papacy, 1150–1250." In Christopher Ryan, ed., *The Religious Roles of the Papacy.* Vol. 8 of *Papers in Mediaeval Studies.* Toronto: Pontifical Institute of Mediaeval Studies, 1989.

Prinz, Joseph. "Vom mittelalterlichen Ablaßwesen in Westfalen. Ein Beitrag zur Geschichte des Volksfrömmigkeit," *Westfälische Forschungen* 23 (1971), 101–171.

Purcell, Maureen. *Papal Crusading Policy, 1244–1291.* Leiden: E. J. Brill, 1975.

Quetif, Iacobus, and Iacobus Échard, eds. *Scriptores ordinis praedicatorum*. 2 vols. Paris: J. B. C. Ballard et N. Simart, 1719–1723.

Rapp, Francis. "Les pèlerinages dans la vie religieuse de l'occident médiéval aux XIVe et XV siècles," in Freddy Raphaël, ed., *Les pèlerinages de l'antiquité biblique et classique à occident médiévale, Études d'histoire des religions 1*. Paris: P. Guenthner, 1973.

Rawcliffe, Carol. "The Hospitals of Later Medieval London," *Medical History* 28 (1984), 1–21.

_____. *Medicine for the Soul: The Life, Death, and Resurrection of an English Medieval Hospital, St. Giles, Norwich, c. 1249–1550*. Stroud, England: Sutton Publishing, 1999.

Riley-Smith, Jonathan. "Crusading as an Act of Love," *History* 65 (1980), 177–192.

_____. *The First Crusade and the Idea of Crusading*. Philadelphia: University of Pennsylvania Press, 1986.

Rubin, Miri. *Corpus Christi: The Eucharist in Late Medieval Culture*. Cambridge: Cambridge University Press, 1991.

Schimmelpfennig, Bernhard. "Römische Ablaßfalschungen aus der Mitte der 14. Jahrhunderts." In *Fälschungen im Mittelalter. Internationaler Kongre ß der Monumenta Germaniae Historiae München 16–19. September 1986*. MGH Schriflen 33. Hannover: Hansche Buchhandlung, 1998, 5:637–658.

Schmitz, H. J. *Die Bußbücher und die Bußdisciplin der Kirche*. Mainz: Kirchheim, 1883.

Shaffern, Robert W. "Images, Jurisdiction, and the Treasury of Merit," *Journal of Medieval History* 22 (1996), 237–247.

_____. "Indulgences and Saintly Devotionalisms in the Middle Ages," *CHR* 84 (1998), 643–661.

_____. "Learned Discussions of Indulgences for the Dead in the Middle Ages," *Church History* 61 (1992), 367–381.

_____. "*Mater et magistra*: Gendered Images and Church Authority in the Thought of Pope Innocent III," *Logos* 4 (2001), 65–88.

_____. "A New Canonistic Text on Indulgences: *De quantitate indulgenciarum* of John of Dambach, O. P. (1288–1372)," *Bulletin of Medieval Canon Law* 22 (1991), 25–45.

_____. "The Pardoner's Promises: Preaching and Policing Indulgences in the Fourteenth-Century English Church," *The Historian* 68 (2006), 49–65.

Sommerlechner, Andrea, ed. *Innocenzo III: Urbs et Orbis*. Rome: Instituto storico italiano per il medieo evo, 2003.

Southern, Richard. *The Western Church and Society in the Middle Ages*. New York: Penguin Press, 1970.

_____. *The Making of the Middle* Ages. New Haven, CT: Yale University Press, 1953.

Stickler, Alfons. "Papal Infallibility—A Thirteenth-Century Invention?" *CHR* 60 (1974), 427–441.

Sumption, Jonathan. *Pilgrimage*. Totowa, NJ: Rowman & Littlefield, 1975.

Swanson, R. N. "Contributions from Parishes in the Archdeaconry of Norfolk to the Shrine of St. Thomas Cantilupe at Hereford, ca. 1320," *MS* 62 (2000), 189–218.

_____. "Indulgences for Prayers for the Dead in the Diocese of Lincoln in the Early Fourteenth Century," *Journal of Ecclesiastical History* 52 (2001), 197–219.

Tentler, Thomas, N. *Sin and Confession on the Eve of the Reformation*. Princeton, NJ: Princeton University Press, 1977.

Thurston, Herbert, S. J. *The Holy Year of Jubilee: An Account of the History and Ceremonial of the Roman Jubilee*. Westminster, MD: Newman Press, 1949.

_____. and Donald Attwater, eds. *Butler's Lives of the Saints*. 4 vols. New York: Kenedy, 1956.

Tierney, Brian. *The Crisis of Church and State, 1050–1300*. Toronto: University of Toronto Press, 1988.

_____. *Foundations of the Conciliar Theory: The Contributions of the Medieval Canonists from Gratian to the Great Schism*. Cambridge: Cambridge University Press, 1955.

_____. *The Origins of Papal Infallibility, 1150–1350*. Leiden: E. J. Brill, 1972.

Tillman, Helena. *Pope Innocent III*. Trans. Walter Sax. New York: North-Holland, 1980.

Van Engen, John H. "The Christian Middle Ages as an Historiographical Problem," *American Historical Review* 91 (1986), 519–552.

Vauchez, André. "Influences franciscaines et réseaux aristocratiques dans la val de Loire: Autour de la bienhereuse Jeanne-Marie de Maillé (1331–1414)," *Revue d'histoire de l'église de France* 70 (1984), 97–105.

_____. *The Laity in the Middle Ages*. Trans. Margery J. Schneider. Notre Dame, IN: University of Notre Dame Press, 1993.

Wasserschleben. "Zur Geschichte der Gottesfrieden," *Zeitschrift der Savigny-Stiftung für Rechtsgeschichte* 12 (1891), 112–117.

Wilken, Robert Louis. *The Spirit of Early Christian Thought*. New Haven, CT: Yale University Press, 2003.

_____. *Clement VI: The Pontificate and Ideas of an Avignon Pope*. Cambridge: Cambridge University Press, 1989.

Index